OTHER TITLES BY THE AUTHOR

Fire It Up: Building Restaurant Brands That Blaze
(2011 / Out of Print)

*Stop Blasting My Mama: Make Email Marketing Work for Your
Restaurant* (2014 / Out of Print)

*The Bullhearted Brand: Building Bullish Restaurant Brands That Charge
Ahead of the Herd* (2021)

Mass Behaving
Unlock the Power of Branding with Archetypes

Joseph Szala

Published by

BULLHEARTED PRESS

Mass Behaving
Unlock the Power of Branding with Archetypes
A Szalapalooza, LLC Publication

Published by Bullhearted Press
10420 Santa Fe Trail
Huntersville, NC 28078
(717) 968-4846
www.bullhearted.co

First Edition February 2024

ISBN 978-0-9906155-6-9

To my wife, Elisa, my wonderful kids, Evelyn and Gabriel, and little Elsa, best pupper in the world!

Contents

Introduction

Brands are not built on aesthetics. They are not built on slogans, campaigns, or clever copy. They are not built on personality or charisma. Brands are built on behavior: the one thing most organizations forget to examine, design, and evolve. Behavior is what shapes trust. Behavior is what shapes meaning. Behavior is what creates loyalty, repels it, or quietly sabotages it from the inside.

If there is one truth this book returns to over and over again, it is this: brands behave long before they speak. And that behavior always follows a pattern.

Many companies feel this pattern long before they can articulate it. They sense the tension between what they say and what they do. They feel the drift between stated values and lived values. They notice how teams make decisions that contradict the brand's supposed identity. They feel the friction of internal misalignment. They see people respond to things they didn't predict and ignore things they thought were brilliant. They chase insights. They chase trends. They chase clarity. But the pattern, the actual psychological pattern shaping all this behavior, remains invisible.

Archetypes make those patterns visible.

Not the watered-down archetypes you see on Pinterest boards or shallow brand workshops. Not the personality-flavored archetypes the creative industry has distorted into vibes and moods. True archetypes are the universal psychological structures that sit beneath human behavior. They are the patterns of motivation, desire, tension, and identity that appear in every culture, across every era, without instruction.

They are not creative constructs. They are human constants. And if you understand them fully, behavior stops feeling chaotic and starts to become predictable.

But archetypes don't just guide brand behavior. They guide brand meaning. Behavior is the delivery mechanism. Ideals are the product.

People don't choose brands solely because of what brands do. They choose them because what those brands do align an ideal. The ideal of what those brands help them become.

Every archetype embodies a psychological ideal humans are already moving toward. It may be the promise of capability and growth, or delivering stability and structure to a chaotic time. Brands can deliver a sense of intimacy and connection, or a thumbing of the nose at the system in the name of freedom and autonomy. These aren't brand traits. They are human aspirations. They are the ideals people carry silently within themselves, the ones they express through the brands they adopt and abandon.

This is why brand loyalty is never as stable as executives believe. It shifts the moment a person sees another brand delivering their ideal more consistently, more clearly, or more honestly. A legacy brand can lose ten years of loyalty in a week when its behavior stops reinforcing the ideal a person holds for themselves. A challenger brand can win the same loyalty in minutes when its identity mirrors that person's internal story and idealistic aspirations.

Human beings follow ideals long before they follow logos.

And this is the missing link in modern branding.

Most organizations obsess over behavior as performance, boiling it down to tone, visuals, service, messaging. But they overlook the key mechanisms of shifting behavior. Archetypes reveal this deeper truth: the brand's role is not simply to act in a certain way, but to embody the emotional transformation people desire.

Get the ideal right, and behavior becomes magnetic.

Get the behavior right, and loyalty becomes resilient.

Get both right, and the brand becomes irreplaceable.

That's the enduring heart of Mass Behaving. I want to show how human behavior shapes every brand interaction, and how brands succeed or collapse depending on whether they align with the psychological truth of the people they serve. The first edition of this book cracked that doorway, but after hundreds of conversations with readers, leaders, strategists, psychologists, and clients, one thing became clear: people didn't just want theory. They wanted proof. They wanted research. They wanted deeper psychological validation. They wanted to understand why archetypes work, not just how. So this update delivers it.

You will find more depth and clarity here. It's a far richer exploration of the psychological roots of archetypes, the behavioral mechanics behind them, the internal dynamics that shape identity, and the motivations that drive people to choose one brand over another. You will find the lineage from Jung to Campbell to modern behavioral science, explained without diluting the complexity. You will find a dismantling of the industry's most harmful misunderstandings: the personality trap, the multiple-archetype myth, the creative-vibe distortion. And you will find an architecture for using archetypes not as themes or story tropes, but as behavioral and motivational frameworks that guide decisions across the entire brand ecosystem.

This book is not only a catalog of archetypes. It is a guide to meaning. Meaning as created, perceived, interpreted, and reinforced by human behavior.

Because archetypes are not about what a brand is. They are about the psychological role the brand plays in the lives of people. That's you, me, your family, everyone.

Identity is not decoration. Identity is commitment. And archetypes give brands the clarity, discipline, and emotional truth required to make that commitment consistently.

The work ahead is clear:

Understand people.

Understand the ideals that guide them.

Understand the patterns that shape those ideals.

Align your brand to the one ideal you can deliver better than anyone else.

Then behave like it relentlessly.

This book will show you how. The rest is up to you.

Get the Card Deck!

Identifying archetypes should be an interactive process as I outline later in this book. To help you and your teams identify the right archetype for your brand, or client's brands, I created a custom card deck with instructions for activities. You can get the deck, and other tools, at www.bullhearted.co!

A note on AI Use

We live in an era where leaders, authors, journalists, and beyond are using AI more and more. I've noticed a steep uptick in raw AI generated writing being passed off as thought leadership. Therefore, I feel compelled to make clear how AI was used and not used in the writing of this book.

In the first publication of this book, I used AI way too much. It's embarrassing on some levels, but I didn't trust myself to capture the weight of the psychology involved with archetypal thinking. That distrust led to me using AI for building the case, then becoming enamored with how it could help me unify the tone of voice. What happened was a book that was chock full of information, but muddied by a veneer of overly poetic phrasing. I was not happy with it, so I put pen to paper on this update with a better view on how AI can be useful to my needs.

Yes. I have used AI to help with this book. I used multiple AI engines to excavate research and help create correlative connections between my theories and the data that proves, or disproves them. The result was abandoning some of my initial thoughts as the data didn't actually support it. I found richer research and data that would have taken me months, if not years, to find, absorb, and use.

AI was also used to quickly compile the bibliography because who really wants to do that? Not me. Sorry to my high school teacher who demanded we learn it.

Finally, when writing a book one reaches levels of writing fatigue. Things start to blend together and repetitive pacing and cadences can emerge. I am human, after all. In order to fix this, I used AI as a sort of editor to help me rethink what I wrote in order for the cadence to flow better and smoother.

Here's where I did NOT use AI. I didn't use AI to write this book. The words are my own. The thoughts, my own. And yeah, I did actually use em-dash punctuation – everywhere you see it – because sometimes em-dashes are a powerful mechanism to drive home a point with added context. So, all those em-dashes were typed with my human fingers because my human brain told me it was the right use.

Thanks for reading this, and more importantly, I hope you get a ton of value, right your mindset, and put archetypes to work for your, your agency or brand, and beyond.

PART

I

Foundations of Human Behavior & Brand Meaning

CHAPTER 01

Introduction to Archetypes

Every brand tells a story, whether it realizes it or not. Some stories are intentional and cohesive. Others are accidental and chaotic. But underneath every brand story lies a deeper structure, a pattern older than advertising, older than business, and older than culture as we know it. These patterns guide how people interpret meaning, assign value, and build emotional relationships with the world around them. We call them archetypes. They are not creative themes or clever positioning tools. They are psychological blueprints that shape how people perceive themselves and everything they encounter.

Archetypes exist because human behavior is not random. Carl Jung introduced the idea that people draw from shared mental models, universal story forms that appear across cultures and eras. Whether in ancient mythology, modern film, or cultural narratives, these patterns repeat with remarkable consistency. Heroes rise. Rebels revolt. Sages guide. Lovers connect. These patterns feel familiar because they represent fundamental human motivations. They are not invented by marketers. They are discovered through centuries of cultural expression.

The reason archetypes matter in branding is simple. Brands are human creations, built by humans for humans. People understand the world through story, and archetypes are the deepest layer of that storytelling. When a brand aligns to an archetype, it becomes easier for people to understand what the brand stands for and what role it plays in their lives. When a brand fails to align, it becomes noise. People do not know how to interpret it, and as a result, they do not know why it matters.

But archetypes are not personalities. This is one of the most damaging misunderstandings in modern branding. Too many agencies treat archetypes as character traits, mood boards, or aesthetic directions. They use them as playful exercises rather than strategic foundations. They reduce them to cute labels, simple mood statements, or creative shortcuts. This dilutes their power. Archetypes are not adjectives. They are motivations. They explain why a brand behaves the way it does, not how it decorates itself.

To understand archetypes, we first have to understand that people choose brands for reasons far deeper than functionality. A brand is not just a product or a service. It is a behavioral relationship. Patrons make choices based on emotional resonance, psychological needs, and identity signals. Archetypes provide the structure that translates those internal motivations into external brand behavior. They become the lens through which a Patron recognizes, "This brand gets me. This brand fits me. This brand helps me become who I want to be."

The universality of archetypes has been demonstrated in every corner of human history. Joseph Campbell's work in "The Hero with a Thousand Faces" revealed that stories across the world follow shared narrative arcs regardless of geography or culture. Academic research in narrative identity, particularly Dan McAdams' work, shows that people understand themselves through these same story patterns. Brands that embrace archetypes are not participating in a creative exercise. They are participating in a psychological one. Archetypes work because they reflect how humans naturally process meaning.

Archetypes also create clarity. In a landscape where brands chase trends, attempt to be everything to everyone, or shapeshift with every new platform, archetypes anchor identity. They simplify decision making by providing a clear behavioral focus that guides messaging, design, product development, organizational culture, and customer experience. When a brand knows its archetype, it knows its role in the person's life. It knows how to show up and what to avoid. Archetypes eliminate guesswork.

There is a reason the most enduring brands in the world align tightly to a single archetype. Brands succeed when their behavior, message, and experience center on one archetypal motivation. Brands fail when they scatter themselves across many.

This book exists because modern branding has lost sight of this discipline. Archetypes have been over simplified, misused, and misrepresented. They have been treated as shortcuts rather than commitments. The goal of this book is to restore archetypes to their rightful place as tools for understanding human motivation and shaping brand behavior. You cannot use archetypes well until you understand people well. And you cannot understand people well unless you learn to see the layers beneath the surface.

Archetypes are more than patterns. They are promises. They tell a person how the brand will behave, how it will make them feel, and what it will help them accomplish or become. When chosen and executed properly, an archetype gives a brand cohesion that endures beyond trends, platforms, or campaigns. When chosen poorly, it becomes a costume that never fits.

To date, there has been confusion as to where and how archetypes fit the brand strategy equation. Because they are drivers of behavior, they belong at the very heart of a company's brand strategy: Purpose. Archetypes serve as inspiration for Purpose statements that immediately connect to the audience on visceral levels. They are that powerful.

The rest of this book will take you deeper into these patterns. You will learn how people think, choose, shift, and behave across different life contexts. You will learn how to read the underlying motivations of your Patrons. You will learn why archetypes work, how to use them, and how to avoid the traps that have led so many brands astray. And most importantly, you will learn how to build a brand with psychological integrity, not creative imitation.

Archetypes are the language of human meaning. It is time to speak that language fluently.

The Universal Patterns of Human Motivation

Human behavior is not random. It may appear unpredictable on the surface, but beneath the contradictions, inconsistencies, and evolving life circumstances, there are enduring psychological patterns that remain remarkably stable across time, culture, and geography. These patterns are not trends. They are not cultural fashions. They are not generational quirks. They are universal structures that shape how people make sense of themselves and the world. This is the foundation on which archetypes stand. Archetypes work because human motivation is not infinite. It is patterned. And these patterns repeat so consistently that they can be recognized in every society, mythology, religion, story system, and psychological model ever studied.

To understand why, we must begin with the simple but profound truth identified across multiple fields of psychology: humans operate through stable motivational drivers. Whether you look at Abraham Maslow's hierarchy of needs, Edward Deci and Richard Ryan's Self Determination Theory, Henry Murray's psychogenic needs, or even modern neuroscience, the same human themes appear. People want agency. People want connection. People want competence. People want stability. People want meaning. People want expression. These desires may take different forms in different contexts, but the psychological architecture beneath them remains unchanged.

Deci and Ryan's Self Determination Theory is particularly relevant. They identified three core motivational needs that predict human flourishing: autonomy, competence, and relatedness. Autonomy reflects the desire to act with freedom and intentionality. Competence reflects the desire to feel effective and capable. Relatedness reflects the desire to feel connected and valued. These three needs show up in every archetype. The Hero amplifies competence. The Explorer amplifies autonomy. The Citizen amplifies relatedness. Even the Sovereign, Creator, and Caregiver map back to these needs in different configurations. Archetypes work because they echo these basic psychological structures.

Yet another lens comes from narrative identity research, especially through the work of Dan McAdams, who argues that human beings develop identity through story. When people reflect on who they are, they do not list traits. They tell narratives. Stories about overcoming something. Stories about learning something. Stories about discovering something. Stories about finding belonging. Stories about building something. Stories about protecting others. These narrative structures mirror the archetypal structures found in mythology, folklore, and brand expression. Human identity is literary before it is logical. It is emotional before it is analytical. Archetypes speak to this narrative layer.

Evolutionary psychology also reinforces the universality of motivational patterns. Humans organized themselves in ways that maximized survival: leaders , protectors, caregivers, storytellers, explorers, innovators, connectors, morale builders, and spiritual or transformational figures. These roles are not arbitrary. They are adaptive. They allowed communities to function and survive. Archetypes map to these adaptive roles because the roles live in us biologically as well as psychologically.

Humans also gravitate toward systems of meaning that reflect these patterns. Joseph Campbell demonstrated in "The Hero with a Thousand Faces" that stories across cultures follow consistent patterns despite having no contact with one another. Heroes receive calls to action. They resist. They face trials. They transform. They return changed. This structure appears in the mythology of Greece, Nigeria, China, Polynesia, Indigenous America, and dozens more. That is not coincidental. That is human psychology made visible through story.

These universal patterns matter deeply in branding because brands exist inside the same psychological landscape. When a brand expresses an archetype, it is not inventing meaning. It is tapping into meaning that already exists within people. A brand is easier to understand when it aligns with a known motivational pattern. People instinctively know what to expect from a brand driven by an archetype because the patterns are familiar, even if the person has never studied archetypes or psychology. The recognition is intuitive.

This intuition is what gives archetypes their power. They bypass the analytical brain and speak directly to the emotional pattern recognition system that psychologist Daniel Kahneman refers to as System One. People do not need to process the brand logically to understand it. They feel it. They sense it. They categorize it effortlessly. Archetypes leverage this natural processing pathway. Misaligned archetypes disrupt it.

When a brand aligns with a universal motivational pattern, the person perceives it as coherent and trustworthy. They understand the brand's role in their life. They understand the emotional contract. They understand the expectations. They understand the promise. They understand the brand's behavior without needing long descriptions or brand books. Coherence becomes intuitive.

When a brand misaligns with universal motivational patterns, the person senses friction. The brand feels confusing, inconsistent, or insincere. Even without knowing why, the person feels something is off. The narrative structure does not match the behavior. The brand speaks in one pattern but acts in another. This is why archetypes must be chosen based on a human truth and brand capability, not aspiration or creativity.

Understanding the universal patterns of human motivation is the first step in understanding why archetypes matter. They are not invented tools. They are reflections of the deepest psychological structures of human identity, behavior, and meaning making.

Jung, Campbell, and the Roots of Behavioral Storytelling

Archetypes did not begin as branding tools. They were born in the study of the human mind, long before modern marketing existed. To understand why archetypes are so powerful in shaping perception and behavior today, we must return to their origins. Not the oversimplified versions that appear in workshops and Pinterest graphics, but the real lineage. The years of observation, research, pattern recognition, cross-cultural analysis, and psychological synthesis conducted by Carl Gustav Jung and later expanded by Joseph Campbell. Archetypes matter because they reflect the universal, persistent ways humans understand meaning. Their roots run deeper than storytelling. They run through the architecture of the psyche itself.

Carl Jung began identifying archetypes during his clinical work in the early twentieth century. While working alongside Sigmund Freud, Jung noticed that his patients' dreams contained symbolic structures that were shockingly similar to motifs found in global myth and religious narratives. These patients had no exposure to one another's stories. Many had no familiarity with the myths Jung recognized. Yet the psychological material that surfaced seemed to follow the same narrative templates. Jung's curiosity widened. Why did people from different backgrounds dream in the same symbolic patterns? Why did the unconscious mind produce imagery consistent with ancient mythology?

To answer this, Jung embarked on a long journey of comparative study. He analyzed medieval alchemical manuscripts, which he believed encoded psychological transformation through symbolic metaphor. He studied Egyptian, Greek, and Roman mythologies. He examined Christian iconography and the symbolic structures of Eastern religions. He read widely across anthropology, theology, folklore, and ritual tradition. He compared Indigenous American stories with African cosmologies and Polynesian creation myths. Everywhere he looked, he found the same figures. The wise mentor. The transformative journey. The trickster who disrupts the order. The nurturing, protective force. The destructive shadow. The miraculous rebirth. These patterns appeared with such consistency that Jung concluded they were not learned. They were innately part of the human condition.

Jung published these ideas in works such as "Symbols of Transformation," "Psychological Types," and "The Archetypes and the Collective Unconscious." In them, he argued that beneath the personal unconscious lies a deeper layer shared across humanity. Not in content, but in structure. This is the collective unconscious. It is the psychological reservoir that contains archetypal patterns, which are expressed through stories, art, dreams, rituals, and cultural behaviors. Jung did not claim this lightly. His evidence came from clinical repetition, mythological comparison, symbolic patterning, and cross-cultural resonance. The probability that separate cultures invented identical symbolic structures independently is extraordinarily low unless the patterns originate from something universal within human cognition.

Modern research supports this. Neuroscience has shown that the brain organizes information through schemas, fundamental patterns that shape perception and prediction. Cognitive linguists such as George Lakoff have shown that humans rely on metaphorical structures that mirror mythic motifs. Anthropologists such as Claude Lévi-Strauss identified the same binary oppositions and narrative patterns across global cultures. Evolutionary psychologists argue that archetypal roles reflect adaptive survival needs. The leader, the caregiver, the warrior, the trickster, the creator. These roles served evolutionary functions and persisted as psychological structures.

Jung's work laid the foundation, but it was Joseph Campbell who expanded it into a global map of storytelling. In "The Hero with a Thousand Faces," Campbell analyzed myths from dozens of cultures and demonstrated that they followed a remarkably consistent narrative arc. Campbell's "monomyth," often called the Hero's Journey, was not a formula invented for screenwriting. It was an observation drawn from the study of Indo-European myth cycles, Indigenous American stories, Mesopotamian epics, African folklore, and Buddhist teachings. Campbell showed that humanity has always understood transformation through a single psychological pathway. Departure. Initiation. Return. This is not merely a narrative pattern. It is a behavioral pattern, reflecting how people interpret growth, challenge, purpose, meaning, and identity.

The reason Jung and Campbell remain so influential is that they revealed something essential about human nature. People understand the world through roles and stories. These stories are not arbitrary. They reflect fundamental motivations. The Hero represents the drive toward courage and capability. The Sage represents the drive toward truth and understanding. The Lover represents the drive toward connection. The Explorer represents the drive toward expansion. These are not poetic metaphors. They are behavioral realities.

Psychologists such as Dan McAdams have since shown that identity itself is narratively structured. People do not simply accumulate experiences. They assemble experiences into stories that mirror archetypal forms. This is why archetypes persist. They explain how individuals make sense of themselves. They explain how communities preserve meaning. They explain how cultures transmit values. Archetypes endure because they are rooted in cognitive processes that are ancient, automatic, and deeply human.

Understanding this lineage is essential for modern branding. Archetypes are not creative inventions. They are not marketing constructs. They are not personality labels. They are reflections of the universal structures that govern human interpretation. When a brand aligns to an archetype, it becomes legible in the deepest sense. People recognize its role instinctively. They understand what the brand promises emotionally. They understand how the brand fits into their own narrative. This recognition does not require explanation. It does not require education. It is innate.

This is why archetypes work. It's not because they are clever and result in clever creative. It's because they are true.

How Archetypes Shape Perception

If archetypes began in myth, then the next logical question is why they matter in markets. Why something born from ancient storytelling still shapes how people respond to brands. Why narrative motifs written thousands of years ago appear again in the way people choose products, form loyalty, and interpret the identity of a business. The answer is simple but profound. Human beings have not changed. Our tools and technologies have changed. Our environments have changed. But our psychological architecture remains almost identical to the people who created myth in the first place. We still understand the world through the same patterns of meaning. We still make sense of identity using story. We still categorize behavior into roles. Brands enter the psyche the same way myths did: through archetypal pattern recognition.

Myth did not begin as entertainment. Myth was humanity's first operating system. Stories existed to explain the world, to transmit moral codes, to teach survival, to structure community, and to define roles. Every mythic figure represented a psychological need. Every narrative represented a motivational pathway. This is why myths endure. They were not fictional tales. They were behavioral instruction manuals disguised as stories. They taught people how to act, how to understand themselves, and how to interpret the actions of others.

When modern brands enter the world, they are interpreted through the same psychological mechanisms. People do not analyze brands through rational frameworks. They interpret them through story roles because story is the native language of meaning. When a brand behaves courageously, we recognize the Hero. When it behaves disruptively, we recognize the Rebel. When it behaves with emotional depth, we recognize the Lover. These recognitions occur instinctively because the patterns are ingrained. The unconscious mind sorts brands the same way it sorts characters in myth.

This is why archetypes shape perception without needing explanation. Patrons do not need to know the terminology to feel the truth behind it. They intuitively understand the emotional contract because it mirrors the patterns they have been exposed to all their lives. Myths conditioned humanity to interpret motivation quickly. Brands benefit from that conditioning when they align with an archetype.

Behavioral science reinforces this connection between mythic structure and decision making. Kahneman's System One thinking shows that the brain uses fast, intuitive judgments to categorize information. It takes shortcuts. Archetypes are those shortcuts. They allow the brain to interpret a brand's role without processing every detail. The more consistent the archetype, the easier it is for the brain to create meaning. This is why brands aligned to a clear archetype feel coherent even before someone consciously thinks about them.

Story also plays a central role in identity formation. McAdams' work on narrative identity shows that people organize their lives around internalized stories. They use these stories to understand who they are, what they value, and where they are going. Brands enter these stories as supporting characters. A person chooses a Hero brand when they see themselves as someone who wants to grow. They choose a Sage brand when they see themselves as someone who seeks understanding. They choose a Citizen brand when they see themselves as someone who values humility and fairness. Brands become mirrors. The archetype tells the person what kind of story the brand helps them live. (Note: the labels Hero, Sage, and Citizen are archetypes. I unpack their full meaning later in the book.)

Archetypes also determine the emotional impact a brand can have. Mythic patterns activate specific emotions: courage, awe, safety, joy, desire, wisdom, or transformation. These emotional states are not neutral. They shape behavior. Antonio Damasio's research proved that emotion drives decision making long before logic enters. Archetypes activate emotional states quickly and reliably because the patterns behind them are familiar. A Hero brand triggers motivation. A Caregiver triggers comfort. A Jester triggers joy. A Sovereign triggers trust. A Creator triggers imagination. A Rebel triggers energy. These emotional triggers are not accidents. They are inherited from mythic structures that have shaped human meaning for centuries.

The link between myth and market becomes even clearer when we examine cultural persistence. Story patterns survive because they work. They help societies function. Similarly, archetypes survive in branding because they help brands make sense to a fragmented world. Markets are noisy. Competition is overwhelming. Attention is scarce. Archetypes create simplicity. They compress meaning into recognizable patterns. They allow people to understand a brand's role instantly. They eliminate confusion by tapping into assumptions the mind already holds.

Modern marketing often imagines itself as sophisticated and data driven, but the psychological mechanisms it depends on are ancient. The same patterns that shaped how people perceived kings, shamans, storytellers, hunters, nurturers, and tricksters now shape how they perceive brands. Myth created categories of meaning. Archetypes inherited those categories. Branding applies them.

This is why brands that try to avoid archetypes often feel unanchored. They lack narrative gravity. Patrons cannot place them within the emotional landscape of their own identity. A brand without archetypal alignment becomes like a character without a role. People do not know how to relate to it, so they simply do not.

Archetypes shape perception because perception itself is archetypal. The brain relies on ancient story patterns to make sense of unfamiliar information. Brands are not exempt from this. They are interpreted through the same behavioral templates that shaped humanity's earliest stories.

When a brand aligns with mythic structure, it becomes understandable.

When it misaligns, it becomes forgettable.

When it contradicts mythic structure, it becomes distrusted.

This is the bridge from myth to market. Archetypes endure because the human mind has not evolved past its need for them. And in branding, that need becomes a strategic advantage.

Archetypes Help Brands Rise Above the Noise

Archetypes matter in modern branding because they give structure to meaning in a world drowning in noise. They give brands a clear psychological role at a time when most brands feel interchangeable. They create intuitive understanding in a landscape where attention is fractured and patience is thin. Archetypes matter today precisely because the conditions of modern life have amplified the need for clarity, consistency, and emotional resonance. But to truly appreciate their relevance in branding, we must understand the psychological mechanisms that make them indispensable.

Human beings assign meaning through pattern recognition. We are wired
to interpret the world through stories, roles, and symbolic structures. These
mechanisms allow the mind to process information faster than language alone.
They allow us to categorize people and experiences instantly. When a brand
behaves in alignment with an archetype, the mind registers it without effort.
It recognizes the brand's motivation, its promise, and its role in the person's
life. This recognition happens intuitively because archetypes match the deep
structures of human cognition revealed by Jung, Campbell, McAdams, and
modern behavioral science.

The modern marketplace intensifies the need for this kind of intuitive
interpretation. Technological acceleration has erased the boundaries that once
separated categories. A person might encounter hundreds of brand signals
in a single day: paid ads, organic content, packaging, social posts, ambient
experiences, AI recommendations, reviews, influencer content. Very few of
these signals are processed consciously. Kahneman's System One brain handles
almost all of them. It looks for patterns. It looks for shortcuts. Archetypes serve as
those shortcuts. They compress meaning into something the mind can interpret
immediately. When a brand behaves consistently with one archetype, the mind
knows where to place it. This reduces cognitive load and builds trust.

Trust is the currency of the modern brand. It is rare, fragile, and easily lost.
Archetypes strengthen trust by creating expectations the brand can meet
repeatedly. People do not trust brands because they admire them. They
trust brands because the brands operate in a way that people understand.
Understanding comes from predictability. Predictability comes from consistent
motivation. Archetypes give brands a stable motivational center. When a brand
acts with the same underlying motivation across every touchpoint, the person
experiences psychological coherence. This coherence becomes loyalty because it
feels safe.

Archetypes also matter because they speak to identity. In a world where people
curate their lives through digital environments, social platforms, and virtual
networks, identity has become fragmented. McAdams' research shows that
identity is constructed narratively. People see themselves through the stories they
tell about their lives. Brands become part of these stories when they represent
meaningful roles. A person chooses a Hero brand not because they like the
product, but because the brand reinforces their identity as someone capable of

rising to challenge. They choose a Lover brand because it reinforces their desire for emotional depth. They choose an Explorer brand because it affirms their need for freedom.

In modern branding, identity alignment matters as much as functional value. Sometimes more.

Archetypes create identity alignment by offering brands a clear narrative role. Not just a message, but a meaning. Not just a function, but a feeling. Not just a promise, but a psychological contract. People choose brands that help them reinforce who they are or who they want to become. Archetypes provide the structure that makes this alignment possible.

Another reason archetypes matter is that modern brands must scale across channels, teams, cultures, and experiences. Without a unifying behavioral system, brands drift. They become inconsistent across departments. Marketing speaks one language. Product speaks another. Operations speaks a third. Leadership contradicts them all. Archetypes eliminate this fragmentation by anchoring the entire brand ecosystem to a single motivational truth. This allows teams to make decisions without guesswork. It simplifies execution. It reduces conflict. It creates coherence at scale.

Archetypes also matter because digital environments demand authenticity. People can identify insincerity immediately. Brands that perform identities rather than embody them fracture trust. Archetypes prevent this by forcing brands to act from genuine motivational centers. When a brand chooses an archetype because it aligns to the needs of people, brand capabilities, and market conditions, authenticity emerges naturally. When brands choose archetypes based on creative aspiration, aesthetic preference, or trendy language, they violate authenticity and collapse under scrutiny.

Most importantly, archetypes matter because they return branding to humanity. Modern marketing tries to optimize everything. Data, funnels, segments, performance metrics, AI modeling. But meaning cannot be optimized. Human emotion cannot be A/B tested into existence. Loyalty cannot be manufactured through tactics alone. Archetypes remind brands that meaning comes from alignment with deep human needs. Growth comes from truth. Loyalty comes from emotional resonance. Resonance comes from psychological coherence.

Archetypes endure because human psychology endures. And in a world of superficial metrics and short-term tactics, archetypes offer something rare: a system for building brands that feel human, honest, and deeply connected to the people they serve.

That is why they matter in modern branding. Not because they are fashionable. Not because they are clever. But because they are human. And that makes them timeless.

Why This Book Reclaims Archetypes as Behavioral Tools

Archetypes have never been the problem. The problem is how the industry has stripped them of their psychological depth, diluted them into personality labels, and repackaged them as creative shortcuts. Archetypes were born from the study of human behavior, identity, and meaning. They were developed to explain why humans think the way they do, why certain patterns of behavior repeat across cultures, and why specific roles hold such emotional gravity. But somewhere along the journey, branding and advertising turned them into lightweight frameworks used to decorate decks rather than guide strategic decisions. This book exists to correct that mistake. It reclaims archetypes by returning them to their original purpose: tools for understanding behavior.

Archetypes lost their power in the creative industry because they were separated from their psychological roots. Agencies began teaching archetypes as if they were flavor profiles or tone-of-voice kits. The Hero became a list of adjectives. The Lover became a color palette. The Magician became a mood. The Rebel became a style of copywriting. None of these interpretations reflect the real architecture of archetypes. Jung did not identify these patterns to help professionals choose a font. Campbell did not map the mythic journey so that brands could create better taglines. Archetypes were never about aesthetic expression. They were always about motivational alignment.

Returning archetypes to their behavioral origins matters because brands are behavioral systems. They interact with Patrons through action, not cosmetics. A brand builds meaning through repeated behavior. Through what it reinforces, what it challenges, what it protects, and what it promises. When an archetype is applied correctly, it shapes this behavior at every level: communication, experience, service, design, culture, and decision making. When applied incorrectly, it becomes nothing more than a decorative layer on top of inconsistent behavior.

This book reclaims archetypes because modern brands cannot afford inconsistency. The speed of communication, the multiplicity of channels, and the visibility of every action require brands to be anchored to something deeper than taste. Taste changes. Trends evolve. Platforms vanish. But human motivation does not change. The underlying patterns of need, identity, and meaning that Jung uncovered still operate today. Archetypes give brands a stable psychological center in a world that demands coherence.

Archetypes also need to be reclaimed because most teams misunderstand where they fit in the strategic process. Many brands begin with archetypes when they should end with them. They choose an archetype before understanding their audience, or "Patrons" as I have labeled them in my book, The Bullhearted Brand. Before understanding their brand's true capabilities. Before understanding their competitive environment. This leads to misalignment. Archetypes must emerge from truth, not aspiration. The Golden Lasso Framework, as introduced and explained in The Bullhearted Brand, exists to ensure this alignment, and any other brand strategy framework can follow suit. This book positions archetypes precisely where they belong: as the output of deep understanding, not the input for creative exploration.

Reclaiming archetypes also means reclaiming their purpose. Archetypes were designed to explain human motivation. They were meant to illuminate the needs that guide behavior. In branding, this makes them indispensable. Brands are not chosen for functional value alone. They are chosen because they represent something meaningful. Something emotional. Something resonant. Archetypes reveal what that meaning is. They help brands understand which psychological tension they resolve. They clarify the emotional contract between brand and Patron. They turn vague positioning statements into identities rooted in human truth.

This book also reclaims archetypes because their misuse has caused real harm. When brands use archetypes as personality costumes, they drift into inauthentic behavior. They act like what they think an archetype should look like instead of acting from the archetype's motivational core. Patrons sense this immediately. Humans are exquisitely good at detecting when a brand performs identity instead of embodying it. Inauthenticity erodes trust. Eroded trust destroys loyalty. And loyalty is the only competitive advantage modern brands still have.

Archetypes must be reclaimed as behavioral tools because behavioral clarity is what modern brands need most. In a landscape where every category is crowded, where differentiation is thin, and where people have infinite choice, the brands that stand out are the ones that behave consistently. The ones that align with a single motivation. The ones that reinforce a clear emotional promise. Consistency builds memory. Memory builds meaning. Meaning builds loyalty. Archetypes build consistency.

Finally, this book reclaims archetypes because the industry is ready for a more mature system. One that respects psychological rigor. One that honors the depth of Jung's work. One that understands the lineage from myth to identity, from motivation to meaning, from behavior to brand. Archetypes deserve more than superficial treatment. They deserve to be practiced with the seriousness and integrity that their origins demand.

This book restores archetypes to their rightful place. Not as aesthetics. Not as personalities. But as psychological engines that shape how brands behave, how people choose, and how meaning is created. Archetypes are behavioral tools. And when understood at this depth, they become one of the most powerful strategic frameworks a brand can use.

CHAPTER 02

Understanding People

Branding has always been about people. Not markets. Not platforms. Not touchpoints. People. But somewhere along the evolution of modern marketing, the industry forgot this. It replaced human insight with segments. It replaced lived experience with datasets. It replaced emotional nuance with demographic categories. The result is a landscape filled with brands that know everything about their customers except who they actually are.

This chapter restores that truth. Before archetypes can be applied, before strategy can be defined, before identity can be built, a brand must understand the psychological reality of the people they wish to engage. Not as a profile. Not as a persona sketch. As a human being living inside a world of complexity, contradictions, shifting motivations, emotional needs, and identity narratives.

That's precisely why, in The Bullhearted Brand, I re-branded the notion of target markets, audiences, and all the other clever names for groupings of people. Patrons surfaced as a much better word for those in which we seek to build a relationship. Our goal as leaders of brands or agencies is to foster patronage within groups of people. Patronage is the deal and, therefore, Patrons is the better term. Throughout this book, you will see the word Patron used interchangeably with "people," as a result.

This chapter explores the complexity of people. It examines the psychology behind why people act, why they shift, and why they choose the brands they choose. It connects research from psychologists like Erik Erikson, Dan McAdams, Antonio Damasio, Albert Bandura, and Edward Deci and Richard Ryan with theories from The Bullhearted Brand about projection, identity, and Patron behavior.

Branding Is About Connecting With People

Branding is too often described as a discipline concerned with differentiation, positioning, funnels, tactics, frameworks, and competitive advantage. It is not. At its core, branding is about one thing: connecting with people. Everything else is a mechanism to achieve that connection. Yet the industry routinely forgets this. Brands chase platforms instead of psychology. They chase categories instead of human truths. They measure demographics and call it understanding. They collect data and call it insight. But demographic information is not insight. Data without interpretation is not understanding. Behavioral truth is deeper, more nuanced, and far more human.

People are not abstractions. They are not target markets. They are not segmentation clusters created by an algorithm. They are complex, meaning-making organisms shaped by biology, culture, memory, emotion, identity, and circumstance. They have needs and paint points that brands are built to answer with products and services. They feel more than they think. Branding fails whenever it reduces people to anything other than the complex, emotionally driven beings we truly are.

The industry's overreliance on demographics is the clearest evidence of this failure. Demographics were designed for census takers, not strategists. They tell us age, income, gender, ZIP code, household size, and maybe education level. But none of this tells us what actually drives behavior. Antonio Damasio's work in neuroscience proved that emotion precedes rationality in decision making. People act based on emotional significance, not demographic traits. A forty-five-year-old father of three may behave more like a twenty-two-year-old creator when exploring hobbies. A sixty-year-old retiree may behave more like a nineteen-year-old college student when exploring freedom or reinvention. Put simply, demographics do not predict motivation.

The rise of psychographics attempted to correct this, but even psychographics often drift toward superficial categories. "Foodies." "Fitness enthusiasts." "Young professionals." These labels provide flavor but not depth. They describe preferences, not psychological structures. They describe lifestyle, not meaning. Without understanding the underlying motivations, psychographics become little more than lifestyle stereotypes used to justify creative work.

Human motivation demands more respect than this. It demands psychological literacy.

Edward Deci and Richard Ryan's Self Determination Theory revealed that human motivation revolves around three core needs: autonomy, competence, and relatedness. These needs appear regardless of demographic category. A twenty-five-year-old graphic designer and a fifty-five-year-old financial analyst may share the need for autonomy. A seventeen-year-old athlete and a seventy-year-old retiree may share the need for competence. A single mother and a corporate executive may share the need for relatedness. These truths cut deeper than demographics.

When brands align with these motivations, they resonate. When they ignore them, they vanish.

Human beings also carry layers of identity that demographics cannot capture. Dan McAdams' theory of narrative identity suggests that people understand themselves through stories that give coherence to their past, explain their present, and guide their future. These identity narratives often determine brand preference far more than any demographic attribute. A Patron who sees themselves as someone overcoming adversity gravitates toward Hero brands. A

Patron who sees themselves as someone seeking meaning gravitates toward Sage brands. A Patron who sees themselves as fun-loving gravitates toward Jester brands. These patterns emerge organically, across cultures, across generations, across social groups.

Erving Goffman's work in sociology adds another layer: contextual identity. People shift roles depending on where they are, who they're with, and what emotional state they're in. This means a single Patron may act from entirely different motivations depending on context. A Patron may behave like a Citizen at work, valuing stability and fairness, but like an Explorer on weekends, craving novelty and self-expansion. That doesn't indicate a sense of insincerity or lackadaisical commitments in humans. It further supports that we're dynamic, multi-faceted beings. Brands that rely solely on surface-level identity clustering misunderstand this fluidity. People are not fixed beings. They are adaptive and situational.

Even consumer behavior research supports the argument that demographics fail to predict meaningful behavior. Studies from the Ehrenberg-Bass Institute show that category entry points (moments of need, context, emotion, or intention) predict choice far more reliably than demographic groups. People choose based on what they're trying to accomplish emotionally in a moment, not based on their demographic profile.

This is why brands must stop treating people as static categories and begin treating them as psychological systems. A brand that understands the multi-layered nature of human motivation creates deeper resonance. It moves beyond "who they are" into "what they need," "what they fear," "what they desire," and "what story they are trying to live."

When branding aligns with human truth, connection forms. When branding aligns only with demographic assumptions, people feel unseen. When branding aligns with motivational patterns, people feel understood. That difference is everything.

Human complexity is not a problem to solve. It is the landscape a brand must navigate. Understanding this complexity is not optional. It is the foundation of modern brand strategy. And it is why archetypes, grounded in universal human motivation, are essential.

Contextual Identity, Shifting Roles, Emotional Drivers, and Life Transitions

Human beings are not static. They do not wake up each morning as the same psychological configuration they were the day before. Their motivations, values, priorities, and emotional patterns shift constantly, sometimes subtly and sometimes dramatically. This is not inconsistency. This is development. It is adaptation. It is the mind recalibrating itself in response to environment, experience, and identity needs. If a brand does not understand how and why these shifts occur, it will always misunderstand its Patron. It will speak to who the Patron used to be, not who they are now. That is where disconnect happens. That is where brands fade into irrelevance.

The first and most significant explanation for motivational shift comes from Erik Erikson's model of psychosocial development. Erikson proposed that human beings move through eight distinct psychological stages, each defined by a central motivational tension. Adolescents struggle with identity formation. Young adults seek intimacy and belonging. Midlife adults pursue contribution and generativity. Later adults seek reflection, legacy, and coherence. These stages are not theoretical abstractions. They show up in real-world behavior, including brand preference. A teenager searching for identity gravitates toward Explorer or Rebel brands that help them differentiate themselves. A new parent gravitates toward Caregiver or Sovereign brands because safety, order, and security become emotionally dominant. A midlife professional seeking meaning gravitates toward Sage or Creator brands because understanding and contribution become more important than status or novelty.

If a brand assumes that all Patrons in a demographic behave the same way, it misses the psychological reality that two people of the same age can be in entirely different stages of identity development. A thirty-year-old who is single, experimenting with career and place, may behave like a young Explorer or Lover. A thirty-year-old with two children may behave more like a Citizen or Caregiver. The demographic is identical. The psychological state is not. Brands that ignore this nuance lose resonance.

Motivation also shifts based on life transitions, a concept supported by decades of psychological research. Transition is one of the most powerful drivers of behavioral change. Becoming a parent. Starting a new career. Moving to a new city. Ending a relationship. Facing loss. Experiencing crisis. These moments destabilize the existing identity narrative, forcing the individual to reevaluate what matters, what they need, and how they define themselves. Research from developmental psychologist Daniel Levinson and continued by contemporary scholars shows that life transitions create fertile ground for identity reformation. Brands that understand this gain enormous influence.

For example, a Patron entering college may shift from seeking safety and simplicity toward seeking belonging, identity, and emotional expression. They may be drawn toward Jester, Citizen, or Lover brands because those archetypes align with the psychological priorities of social integration and identity experimentation. Conversely, a Patron going through a period of instability may shift toward Sovereign, Caregiver, or Innocent brands that provide order, security, and clarity. The shift is not random. It is a psychological recalibration toward the needs elevated by circumstance.

Motivation is also contextual. This is where Erving Goffman's theory of self-presentation becomes crucial. People do not have a single identity. They have multiple identities that activate depending on environment. A Patron may express competence and authority at work, humility and belonging at home, adventure and independence with friends, and introversion and reflection when alone. Each "self" contains different values, different emotional needs, and different behavioral triggers. Brands that speak to only one of these selves risk missing the emotional complexity of the Patron's lived experience.

This is why brands with rigid, one-dimensional audience frameworks falter. They assume people behave consistently across all contexts. But they simply do not. A person changes roles constantly. A brand must understand not only the person's core motivation but also the motivational shifts that happen across contexts. Archetypes help because they speak to deep motivational needs that remain relevant across roles, but even archetypes must be applied with contextual insight.

Motivation also shifts based on emotional state, something extensively documented by neuroscientist Antonio Damasio. When stress increases, the brain prioritizes survival needs. When confidence increases, it prioritizes growth. When belonging is threatened, it seeks community. When control is lost, it seeks autonomy restoration. These shifts directly correlate to archetypal preferences. A stressed person may turn toward Innocent or Caregiver brands. An ambitious person may turn toward Hero brands. A disillusioned person may turn toward Rebel brands. Emotional states modulate how identity needs express themselves moment to moment.

Behavioral economics adds another layer. Research by Rucker and Galinsky shows that when individuals experience a loss of power or agency, they gravitate toward brands that symbolically restore autonomy or identity strength. This is compensatory consumption. It explains why someone experiencing career uncertainty may buy products that symbolize control or capability. It explains why someone experiencing loneliness may gravitate toward community-oriented brands. These choices are not logical. They are psychological responses to emotional imbalance.

Finally, motivation shifts because identity is an ongoing construction, not a fixed state. Dan McAdams' narrative identity theory shows that people continually update the story of who they are based on new experiences, aspirations, and challenges. Every life event becomes a narrative fragment that reshapes the meaning-making system. Brands enter that story as supporting characters. When a person's identity story changes, the role they want a brand to play changes with it.

This is why brands must understand the dynamic, shifting nature of motivation. People are not fixed points. They are moving systems. Motivation is fluid. Identity is narrative. Emotional needs rise and fall. Context reshapes behavior. Transitions rewrite priorities. Demographics do not capture any of this.

Archetypes matter because they map to universal motivations beneath these shifts. But brand strategy must also recognize the shifts themselves. The brand that understands human movement creates emotional resonance. The brand that assumes stasis becomes irrelevant before it even realizes what happened.

How Patrons Experience the World and Themselves

People do not experience brands objectively. They experience them through the lens of their own identity, their own insecurities, their own aspirations, and their own internal narrative. This is the heart of the projection layer, the psychological mechanism through which Patrons assign meaning to the brands they encounter. In The Bullhearted Brand, I defined this idea clearly: brands are not simply chosen. They are interpreted. They are filtered through belief systems, emotional histories, contextual needs, and identity stories. The projection layer is the space where the Patron's internal world meets the external brand and forms an emotional contract.

Projection is not abstract theory. It is one of the most fundamental processes in human psychology. Carl Jung identified projection as a central dynamic of the psyche. When people encounter something external that resonates with an internal truth, need, fear, or desire, they project meaning onto it. This is why symbols, stories, myths, and archetypes carry such weight. They become vessels for meaning because the mind fills them with content from within. Jung argued that individuals project unconscious material onto external figures to make sense of themselves. Brands, whether they intend to or not, serve this same function.

Dan McAdams' narrative identity research strengthens this understanding. People build their lives as stories. Not fictional stories, but psychological ones. They tell themselves stories about who they are, who they were, and who they are becoming. These stories define their motivations, their relationships, their goals, and their decisions. Brands enter those personal stories as characters. Sometimes as mentors. Sometimes as allies. Sometimes as tools. Sometimes as symbols. The role the brand plays depends entirely on what narrative the Patron brings to the interaction.

The projection layer explains why branding is not a one-to-many broadcast. It is a one-to-one psychological negotiation. A Patron does not simply see a message. They interpret it. They test it against their worldview. They decide whether it reinforces their identity, expands it, or contradicts it. Their choice is emotional first, narrative second, and rational third. This sequencing is validated by Antonio Damasio's somatic marker hypothesis, which demonstrated that emotion is the precursor to rational decision making. The brain asks, "Does this feel like me?" before it asks, "Does this make sense for me?"

Projection also explains why two Patrons can look at the same brand and walk away with completely different interpretations. The brand has not changed. The projection has. One Patron may see Patagonia as a symbol of environmental integrity. Another may see it as a badge of social identity. Another may see it as an aspirational marker of an outdoor lifestyle they want to embody. Another may see it as an expression of ethical consumerism. Patagonia did not tailor itself to each Patron individually. Each Patron projected onto the brand the meaning that fit their identity story.

The projection layer also explains the emotional intensity of brand loyalty. Loyalty is not rational. It is psychological bonding reinforced over time. When a Patron consistently projects a specific identity narrative onto a brand and the brand consistently reinforces it, trust is formed. Trust becomes loyalty. Loyalty becomes identity extension. This is why people defend certain brands with almost tribal passion. They are not defending the brand. They are defending the part of themselves that the brand validates.

Projection also reveals why misalignment is so dangerous. When a brand behaves in ways that contradict its projected meaning, the Patron experiences narrative disruption. If a brand that projects innocence behaves cynically, the break is severe. If a brand that projects rebellion becomes conformist, the Patron feels betrayed. If a brand that projects competence becomes unreliable, trust collapses. Behavioral economics calls this expectancy violation. Narrative psychology calls it identity dissonance. Branding calls it the beginning of the end.

The projection layer is where expectations live. And expectations are fragile.

This is why brands must behave with psychological coherence. They must understand not only the archetype they intend to express but the meaning that Patrons are likely to project onto them. A brand that expresses the Hero archetype will receive projections of capability, courage, discipline, and growth. If it behaves inconsistently with those traits, the Patron's projection breaks. A Lover brand will receive projections of connection, warmth, and intimacy. If its behavior becomes cold, transactional, or distant, the projection breaks. A Sovereign brand receives projections of order and stability. If it behaves chaotically or indecisively, the projection breaks.

Projection is also influenced by cultural context. Cultural psychology shows that communities share symbolic associations. For example, in individualistic cultures, the Hero archetype is often tied to personal achievement. In collectivist cultures, the Hero archetype is tied to communal responsibility. The projection shifts because the cultural identity narrative shifts. Brands must know the cultural environment in which projection occurs because meaning is co-created by culture and individual experience.

This interplay between individual and culture reinforces the need for archetypes as behavioral anchors. Archetypes reflect universal patterns, but projection shapes how Patrons interpret those patterns. Archetypes give the brand a stable motivational center. Projection gives the brand individualized meaning. Together, they create resonance.

The projection layer is ultimately where brand meaning is determined. Not in the boardroom. Not in the strategy deck. In the minds of the Patrons, filtered through their needs, their narratives, their emotional states, their contexts, and their experiences. Brands cannot force meaning onto people. They can only behave consistently enough that Patrons project meaning naturally.

The Psychology Behind Why People Choose Brands

If branding were rational, every category would have one winner. The fastest. The cheapest. The highest quality. The most convenient. But people do not choose brands rationally, and the science around human decision making leaves no room for debate on that point. Brands are chosen because they satisfy psychological needs long before they satisfy functional ones. They symbolize identity. They regulate emotion. They reinforce narrative. They create meaning. They reduce uncertainty. They provide safety, aspiration, or belonging. And all of this happens beneath conscious awareness.

To understand why people choose brands, we must begin with the role of emotion. Antonio Damasio's research in neuroscience forever removed the illusion that humans think first and feel second. In "Descartes' Error," Damasio revealed that emotion is not a barrier to rationality. It is a prerequisite. The brain uses emotional associations, or somatic markers, to evaluate choices quickly. Brands tap into these emotional markers. A Patron does not choose Patagonia because of technical specs. They choose Patagonia because it symbolizes integrity, exploration, and environmental responsibility. The emotional meaning precedes the rational justification. This is not marketing theory. This is neurological fact.

Daniel Kahneman extended this understanding by distinguishing between two systems of thought: System One, which is fast, intuitive, associative, and emotionally driven. And System Two, which is slow, analytical, and effortful. Brand choice lives almost entirely in System One. The brand that feels right wins, because System One processes meaning faster than the conscious mind can analyze. Archetypes speak directly to System One by activating universal motivational patterns. A Hero brand triggers capability. A Jester brand triggers joy. A Lover triggers connection. These triggers bypass analysis and shape preference before the Patron even realizes a decision is being made.

Identity is the second driver of brand choice, and its influence is just as strong. People select brands that align with the story they believe about themselves or the story they are trying to become. Dan McAdams' work on narrative identity demonstrated that humans experience their lives as evolving stories. These stories require symbolic reinforcement. A Patron building a story about becoming healthier chooses brands that support capability or purity. A Patron building a story about belonging chooses brands that reinforce their social identity. A Patron building a story about individuality chooses brands that symbolize freedom or rebellion. Brands become tools of identity construction. Without identity resonance, brands become commodities.

This is where social identity theory becomes relevant. Developed by Henri Tajfel and John Turner, the theory shows that people affiliate with groups to strengthen their sense of belonging and self worth. Brands function as social markers. Wearing a Harley Davidson jacket signals identity. Carrying a Stanley cup signals group affiliation. Choosing Apple signals values around creativity, technology, and status. Patrons do not choose brands in isolation. They choose brands with the unconscious desire to belong to something larger or to differentiate from something they reject. Brands act as identity flags in the landscape of social meaning.

Behavioral economics adds additional layers to this decision-making process.

Rucker and Galinsky's research on compensatory consumption revealed that when people feel a loss of control, power, or identity, they use consumption to restore balance. Someone who feels powerless may buy brands that symbolize capability. Someone who feels disconnected may buy brands that symbolize belonging. Someone who feels stagnant may choose brands that symbolize creativity or change. These choices are not frivolous. They are emotional coping strategies. Brands that ignore this dimension miss the underlying motivations that sustain loyalty.

Emotion, identity, and compensation, however, only explain part of the story. Cognitive fluency also guides brand preference. Research from psychologist Adam Alter shows that people prefer things that are easy to process. When a brand expresses a clear archetype, the brain processes it faster, more comfortably, and with greater trust. A Sovereign brand feels structured. A Jester brand feels light. A Sage brand feels reliable. These impressions emerge instantly because archetypes align with mental shortcuts the brain already uses. Brands that feel easy to understand feel more trustworthy.

Meaning is the final driver. Viktor Frankl, in "Man's Search for Meaning," argued that humans are motivated by meaning-making above all else. Modern branding rarely acknowledges this, but Patrons choose brands that reinforce a sense of meaning in their lives. This meaning may be personal, social, or moral. It may be tied to self improvement, community, purpose, or pleasure. When brands fail to offer meaning, they become disposable. When brands provide meaning, they transcend category and become part of the Patron's worldview.

Taken together, these psychological forces form the backbone of brand choice. People choose brands because they reflect who they are. Because they reinforce what they value. Because they help them navigate uncertainty. Because they support emotional needs. Because they fit the story they are trying to tell about themselves. Because they simplify decisions in an overwhelming world. Because they feel familiar and coherent.

CHAPTER 03

What Archetypes Truly Are

Archetypes sit at an odd cultural crossroads. They are ancient, but they feel modern. They are psychological, but they appear in branding decks. They are universal, but they get treated like options on a creative menu. Most people believe they understand archetypes, yet very few understand them beyond the surface. Archetypes have been reduced, repackaged, aestheticized, and oversimplified until the industry barely recognizes them anymore. The real depth behind them has been lost.

Archetypes are not decoration. They are not branding flavors. They are not moods or tones. They are not stylistic directions. They are not costumes. Archetypes are frameworks that reflect the deepest structures of human motivation. They are the architecture of meaning. They explain how people interpret the world, how they form identity, how they make decisions, and how they emotionally evaluate the brands that enter their lives.

Brands that understand archetypes at this level operate with clarity. They speak with coherence. They design experiences with intent. They build trust faster and sustain loyalty longer. But brands that misunderstand archetypes treat them like color palettes or personality exercises and wonder why consistency collapses and loyalty never forms.

This chapter is meant to strip away all misunderstanding. It explores what archetypes truly are, why they exist, how they map to human behavior, and why they remain the most durable framework for shaping brand identity. It examines the psychological mechanisms that give archetypes their power, the narrative engines that drive them, and the behavioral patterns that make them reliable across culture and time. It also explores the practical implications: how archetypes strengthen Purpose, how they fit into the Patron's emotional landscape, and how they anchor every decision a brand makes.

If a brand does not understand archetypes at this level, nothing else in this book matters.

How Archetypes Give Purpose Statements Behavioral Integrity

Brands today talk endlessly about Purpose. Every company claims to have one. Every leadership team wants to articulate a reason for being that rises above product and profit. This instinct is noble. It reflects a cultural shift toward meaning and responsibility. But Purpose without behavioral grounding is fragile. Worse, it is performative. It sounds good, but it does not translate into action. It becomes a slogan masquerading as identity.

Simon Sinek's Start With Why popularized the idea that organizations must articulate their deeper beliefs before articulating what they do. It resonated because it captured a truth most brands ignore: people want meaning, not mechanics. But Sinek never answered a more difficult question. How do you know if your Purpose will actually motivate behavior? How do you know if it aligns to a real human need? How do you know if it is psychologically coherent? How do you know if your Why resonates beyond aspiration?

This is where archetypes provide the missing half of the equation.

Purpose is direction.

Archetype is motivation.

Direction without motivation is a vehicle with no engine.

An organization can articulate a compelling Why, but if it chooses an archetype that does not reinforce that Why, the Purpose collapses. A brand cannot claim its Purpose is to "empower individuals" if it expresses the Innocent archetype, which seeks simplicity and purity rather than capability. It cannot claim its Purpose is to "inspire connection" if it expresses the Sage, which values clarity over intimacy. It cannot claim its Purpose is to "redefine the industry" if it expresses the Caregiver, which stabilizes rather than disrupts.

Purpose must be paired with the right motivational architecture.

This is not philosophical; it is psychological. Albert Bandura's research on self efficacy demonstrated that people need to experience alignment between intention and behavior to build trust. When a brand's stated Purpose does not match its archetypal behavior, patrons experience cognitive dissonance. They may not articulate it, but they feel it. And once that internal conflict emerges, trust fractures.

Archetypes provide the structure that ensures behavioral integrity. If a brand's Purpose is to champion inner strength, the Hero archetype reinforces that Purpose through discipline, encouragement, and capability building. If a brand's Purpose is to elevate understanding, the Sage archetype reinforces it through clarity, insight, and guided exploration. If a brand's Purpose is to create belonging, the Citizen or Lover archetypes reinforce it through warmth, fairness, and emotional connection. If a brand's Purpose is to challenge stagnation, the Rebel reinforces it through disruption and defiance of the status quo.

Purpose becomes even more problematic due to a misunderstanding of what defines a "good purpose." Even Sinek never placed Purpose directly in the category of a larger ding in the universe, or a philanthropic alignment. The fact is, Purpose can be simple. And more and more, I'm in the camp of simplicity of purpose being even more powerful than the broad strokes seen in many corporate strategies these days.

To put a finer tip on that point, Southwest Airlines had a very clear, simple purpose for a long time: To be the cheapest airline in the sky. The simplicity of that purpose is refreshing and easy to remember. So long as the airline built the entire organization around that focus, Southwest can own it. With a little help from The Citizen archetype, being the cheapest airline in the sky has undeniable, strong emotional ties. It's a win because archetypes reveal whether a Purpose is actually true. In this case, the accessibility of air travel is a fantastic indicator of CItizen thinking.

Leaders often confuse inspiration for truth. They write Purpose statements that reflect who they wish they were rather than who they are built to be. Archetypes strip away aspiration and reveal what is psychologically coherent. They expose the motivations a brand can consistently express across product, culture, leadership, and experience. They force discipline. They force honesty.

Archetypes also ground Purpose in cognitive schema. According to schema theory by Bartlett and later Rumelhart, the human mind processes new information by matching it to existing mental frameworks. Purpose statements that align with an archetype become easier for the Patron to understand because they map cleanly onto familiar motivational structures. Purpose statements without archetypal grounding often feel vague because the mind has no structure to attach them to.

This is why the strongest brands in the world use archetypes whether intentionally or intuitively. Their Purpose aligns with their motivational structure. Brands that struggle with Purpose do not have a messaging problem. They have a motivation problem because purpose is only as true as the behavior that expresses it. Archetypes determine that behavior.

This is the "Purpose behind Purpose." Archetypes reveal the psychological truth that makes Purpose believable, durable, and actionable. Without an archetype, Purpose is a story with no character. With an archetype, Purpose becomes a living force that shapes everything the brand does.

The Gap Between Who People Are and Who They Are Trying to Become

Archetypes are not the brand's expression of itself. They are the brand's relationship to the Patron. A Hero brand does not say "I am strong." It says, "I strengthen you." A Sage does not say, "I know." It says, "I will help you understand." Archetypes are always relational. They exist in the psychological space between Patron and brand.

If archetypes only reflected who Patrons are, they would not be powerful. They are powerful because they reflect who Patrons are becoming. People live in tension between their current state and their desired future. They navigate an emotional landscape defined by aspiration, insecurity, identity formation, and narrative evolution. Brands enter this landscape not as products, but as psychological tools. They help Patrons bridge the distance between their present and their imagined self.

This concept is supported across psychology. Dan McAdams describes identity as an "internalized and evolving life story." People interpret themselves through narrative, not data. They do not think, "I am a thirty-four-year-old mother of two." They think, "I am someone trying to grow into a more capable version of myself," or, "I am someone trying to rediscover joy," or, "I am someone trying to feel confident again." These internal stories shape decisions far more than demographics ever could.

Erik Erikson's stages of development reinforce this idea. At every stage of life, people navigate psychosocial tensions: identity versus confusion, intimacy versus isolation, generativity versus stagnation. These tensions are universal. They shape behavior. They influence brand choice. A Patron experiencing identity formation seeks brands that reinforce exploration or empowerment. A Patron experiencing isolation seeks brands that reinforce connection. A Patron experiencing stagnation seeks brands that reinforce transformation or clarity. The brand's archetype becomes the emotional companion in this developmental journey.

Edward Deci and Richard Ryan's Self Determination Theory adds another dimension: the pursuit of autonomy, competence, and relatedness. Patrons choose brands that help them achieve the psychological needs they feel deprived of. Someone lacking autonomy seeks Explorer or Rebel brands. Someone lacking competence seeks Hero or Sage brands. Someone lacking relatedness seeks Lover or Citizen brands. The archetype becomes a symbolic solution to an emotional deficit.

This is why a brand must understand the gap between the Patron's current emotional state and their desired one. The gap is where brand meaning is created. When a Patron chooses a brand, they are not choosing the product alone. They are choosing the identity that product helps them construct. They are choosing the emotional relief it provides. They are choosing the story it reinforces.

Patrons project their narrative onto brands. This projection process, rooted in Jungian psychology, is not superficial. When a Patron feels lost, they project clarity onto Sage brands. When they feel constrained, they project freedom onto Explorer brands. When they feel small, they project power onto Hero brands. When they feel disconnected, they project safety onto Lover or Citizen brands. The brand becomes a symbolic extension of the Patron's psychological needs.

Brands that understand this build emotional relevance. Brands that ignore it build noise.

The gap between who people are and who they want to be is not a flaw in the human psyche. It is the engine of growth. Brands become meaningful when they help close that gap.

Understanding the Patron is not about profiling. It is about empathy. It is about recognizing the story the Patron is living and the one they hope to live next. When brands meet Patrons in that space, the connection becomes profound.

PART

II

Archetypes & Their Quadrants

CHAPTER 04

Understanding the Structure of Archetypes

Archetypes are often introduced as if they are a collection of twelve interesting personalities, each with its own flavor and creative identity. But archetypes have never been about personality. They are about motivation. They are about the deep, instinctive forces that drive human behavior long before thought becomes conscious. Jung did not discover archetypes by listing adjectives. He discovered them by examining the patterns that appeared again and again across cultures, dreams, rituals, literature, and human behavior. When you study these patterns long enough, you begin to see that archetypes do not float freely. They cluster. They organize themselves into psychological territories. They take on shape, direction, and gravity.

This is why archetypes require a structural understanding. When we present them visually in a diagram (fig A, on the next page), the point is not decoration. The point is clarity. The diagram exists because archetypes live within a framework. They are organized into four psychological quadrants, each representing a primary direction of human motivation. This structure is not a modern invention. Its roots can be found in Jung's typological work, in Campbell's analysis of global myth, in Erikson's developmental stages, and in contemporary motivational research. When you observe human behavior across time, the same motivations appear: the desire to change one's world, the desire to find belonging, the desire to create stability, and the desire to seek personal meaning. These four motivations represent the universal directions of the human psyche. Everything else is nuance.

The quadrants form the outer architecture. The archetypes themselves form the inner detail. The quadrants explain why someone behaves the way they do. The archetypes explain how they express that motivation. It is the difference between identifying someone as a person who seeks stability and identifying them as a Sovereign, a Creator, or a Caregiver. The quadrant is the compass; the archetype is the path the person chooses to walk. Branding must honor this structure. Without it, archetypes become random labels instead of psychological tools.

The Four Quadrants and the Tension Between Them

Every quadrant expresses a fundamentally different motivational orientation. Some people are driven by the force of outward change, the impulse to confront the world and push it forward. Others are driven by inward change, the search for truth, meaning, clarity, or inner alignment. Some are driven by the need for stability and structure, the instinct to create order. Others are driven by the need for connection, the instinct to build community and emotional safety. These tensions exist in every psyche, and the quadrants reflect them in clean, psychological terms.

The quadrant of Change the World represents the human drive toward external transformation. It is fueled by ambition, challenge, disruption, and impact. It is not subtle. It moves outward with force, and it thrives in conflict and adversity.

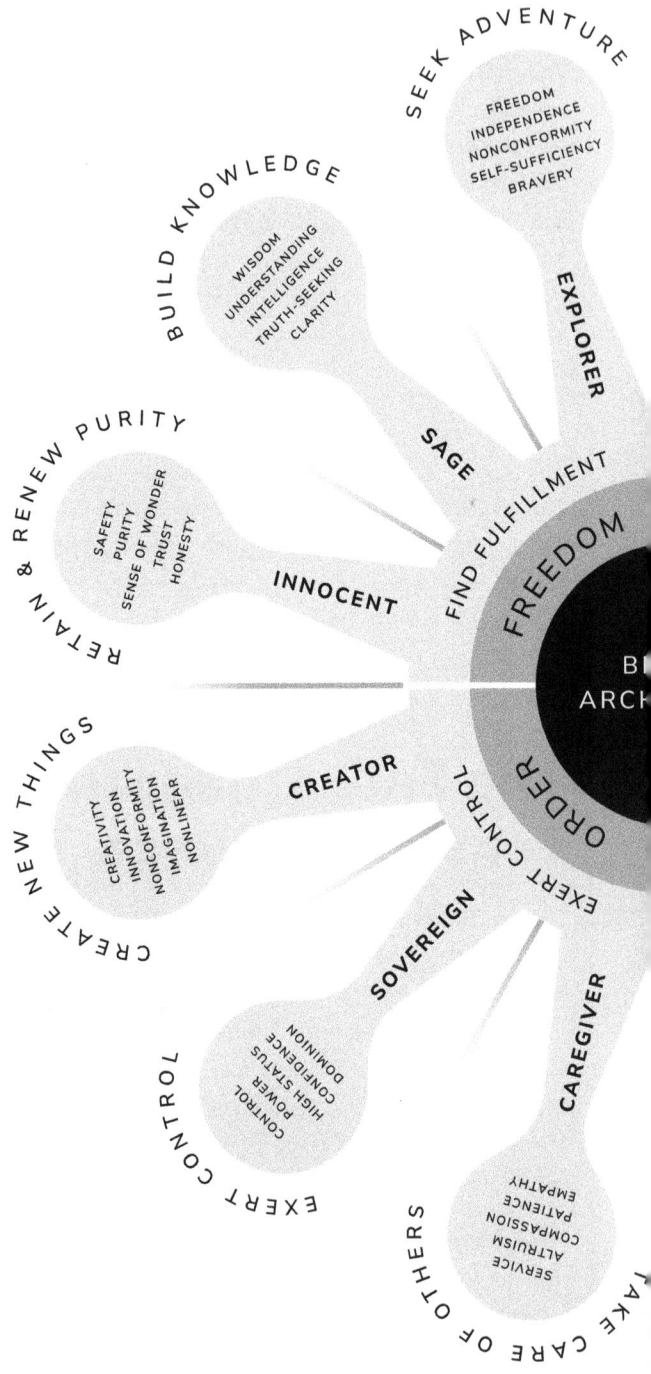

fig A. Archetypes Diagram

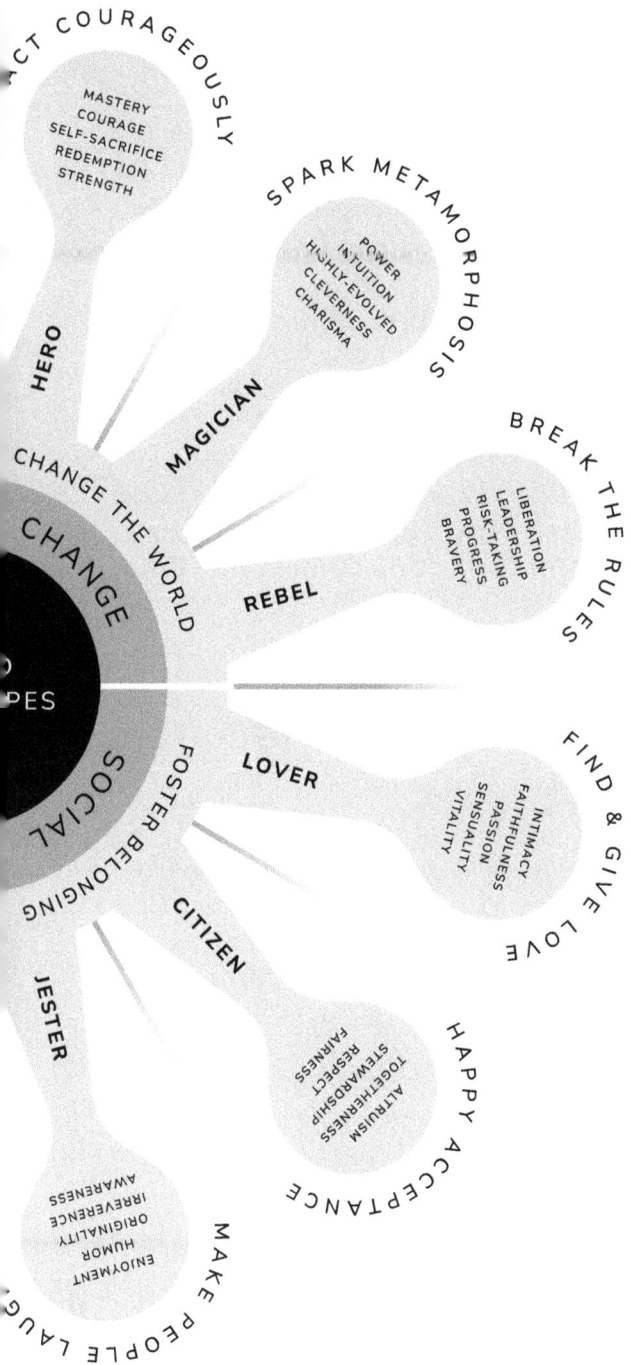

ACT COURAGEOUSLY

MASTERY
COURAGE
SELF-SACRIFICE
REDEMPTION
STRENGTH

SPARK METAMORPHOSIS

POWER
INTUITION
HIGHLY-EVOLVED
CLEVERNESS
CHARISMA

HERO

MAGICIAN

CHANGE THE WORLD

BREAK THE RULES

CHANGE

LIBERATION
LEADERSHIP
RISK-TAKING
PROGRESS
BRAVERY

PES

REBEL

SOCIAL

FOSTER BELONGING

LOVER

FIND & GIVE LOVE

INTIMACY
FAITHFULNESS
PASSION
SENSUALITY
VITALITY

CITIZEN

JESTER

ALTRUISM
TOGETHERNESS
STEWARDSHIP
RESPECT
FAIRNESS

HAPPY ACCEPTANCE

ENJOYMENT
HUMOR
ORIGINALITY
IRREVERENCE
AWARENESS

MAKE PEOPLE LAUGH

Opposite it is the quadrant of Find Fulfillment, which moves inward toward introspection, meaning, truth, and personal wholeness. These two quadrants represent the eternal tension between outer purpose and inner purpose, between changing the world and understanding oneself.

The other axis reflects the tension between stability and relational harmony. The quadrant of Exert Control focuses on building structure, creating order, enforcing clarity, and establishing a stable environment. It is the impulse to make things predictable and safe. Opposite it is Foster Belonging, which creates stability not through structure but through connection, kindness, and collective cohesion. One secures the world through rules. The other secures it through relationship.

These oppositions matter because brands cannot live in two opposing motivational directions without collapsing. A brand cannot promise bold disruption and inner tranquility at the same time. It cannot promise strict control and open emotional connection simultaneously. When brands try to mix quadrants, they create psychological dissonance. Patrons feel that something is off, even if they cannot articulate why. The mind is wired to detect motivational conflict. Quadrants exist to prevent it.

A High Level View of the Twelve Archetypes

Once the quadrants provide the motivational shape, the archetypes express the nuance of that motivation. Each quadrant contains three archetypes that share the same central drive but manifest it differently. This is where the richness comes in. The twelve archetypes are not redundant because each one reflects a distinct behavioral pattern, a different way of expressing the same core desire.

In the quadrant of Change the World, the Hero expresses transformation through courage and discipline, the Magician through insight and possibility, and the Rebel through defiance and disruption. They all seek change, but each uses a different psychological method.

In Foster Belonging, the Lover creates intimacy, the Citizen creates fairness and community, and the Jester creates social cohesion through joy. They all strengthen connection, but with different emotional textures.

In Exert Control, the Sovereign creates order through leadership and structure, the Creator through craft and vision, and the Caregiver through protection and nurturance. All three create stability, but each one uses a different form of authority.

And in Find Fulfillment, the Sage seeks truth, the Explorer seeks freedom, and the Innocent seeks purity and renewal. Each one turns inward, but toward different forms of meaning.

Together, the quadrants and the twelve archetypes form a complete map of human motivation. When a brand chooses an archetype, it is choosing both a motivation and a method. It is choosing a role in the Patron's psychological life. That is why the structure matters.

A Note on Jung's Shadow Archetypes and Why They Are Excluded From Branding

Jung understood that every archetype has a dark form. Wherever there is human motivation, there is also the potential for distortion. A Hero can become a Tyrant. A Lover can become an Addict. A Sovereign can become an Oppressor. A Magician can become a Manipulator. Jung catalogued these shadow forms not as characters to emulate but as diagnostic tools. They revealed where the psyche collapses, inflates, or loses integration. They showed what happens when a psychological drive becomes corrupted by fear, repression, trauma, or imbalance.

But in branding, these archetypes have no role. Not because they are uninteresting, but because they are inherently unethical.

Shadow archetypes destabilize trust. They violate psychological safety. They manipulate vulnerability. They generate anxiety, not meaning. A brand aligned to a shadow motivation becomes harmful by design. It erodes identity instead of reinforcing it. It exploits emotional need instead of supporting it. It fractures narrative rather than strengthening it.

More importantly, shadow archetypes destroy coherence. They contain internal contradictions that no brand can sustainably express. A Tyrant demands obedience. A Manipulator hides intention. A Destroyer seeks collapse. These are not brand behaviors. They are psychological breakdowns.

The presence of shadow archetypes in Jung's work serves a different purpose in this book. They remind us that archetypes must be practiced with discipline. They warn against inflation, distortion, and the temptation to chase attention through performative edginess. They underscore the importance of choosing an archetype that represents the best, healthiest version of a brand's motivation.

Brands should embody clarity, not chaos. They should strengthen identity, not fracture it. They should anchor meaning, not destabilize it. That is why the twelve archetypes used in this system are the healthy expressions of human motivation. They create alignment, coherence, and emotional resonance. They live within the quadrants as the stable structures of human meaning. And they form the backbone of the chapters that follow.

CHAPTER 05

Quadrant: **Change the World**

The Change the World quadrant is powered by archetypes who refuse to accept the world as it is. They believe that improvement begins with disruption, possibility, and courage. These brands do not polish the status quo. They challenge it.
The Hero confronts adversity to strengthen others. The Magician transforms perceptions to reveal new potential. The Rebel exposes broken systems and forces culture to reckon with truth. Together, these archetypes reshape categories through boldness, vision, and conviction.

What makes this quadrant especially magnetic is not only its energy, but what it counterbalances. When people feel suffocated by excessive control, overwhelmed by conformity, or exhausted by monotony, they seek archetypes that restore autonomy and possibility. Self Determination Theory, developed by Edward Deci and Richard Ryan, identifies autonomy as a core psychological need. When that need is suppressed, individuals pursue brands that reignite freedom, capability, and imagination. This is why customers flock to Hero, Magician, and Rebel brands during periods of cultural stagnation or personal constraint.

Research in compensatory consumer behavior shows that when individuals feel restricted or powerless, they gravitate toward brands that signal strength, disruption, and change. The Change the World quadrant satisfies this craving. These archetypes counterbalance the emotional weight of rigid structure by offering movement. They counterbalance the isolation that comes from intense self reflection by offering collective action. They counterbalance the safety of belonging by reigniting ambition and individuality. The quadrant appeals to customers who have outgrown stability and are ready for momentum.

Brands in this quadrant must wield their influence carefully. Transformation carries responsibility. These archetypes are capable of shifting markets, movements, and culture itself. When used with integrity, they elevate entire industries. When used without discipline, they destabilize. The Change the World quadrant represents brands that push humanity forward, not through noise or novelty, but through purpose driven transformation.

A hero is an ordinary individual who finds the strength to persevere and endure in spite of overwhelming obstacles.

– Christopher Reeve

The Hero

People love to call themselves a Hero brand. It sounds bold. It sounds confident.
It sounds powerful. The problem is that most of the brands claiming the
Hero archetype are not Heroic at all. They are motivational at best and self
congratulatory at worst. They talk about winning, about inspiration, about
greatness, but they skip the essential part of the Hero story. The struggle.
The confrontation. The growth. The work. The Hero archetype is not rooted
in confidence. It is rooted in capability that is earned. And that distinction is
everything.

The Hero is one of the oldest and most persistent patterns in human psychology.
Carl Jung described archetypes as universal templates of thought and behavior
that emerge across cultures without instruction. He identified the Hero as the
part of the psyche that confronts adversity in order to transform. Not transform
circumstances. Transform the self. The Hero archetype is not about defeating
something external. It is about integrating something internal. That is why
humans respond so strongly to Hero stories. They mirror the battles we all
experience within ourselves.

Joseph Campbell expanded on Jung's work in his landmark book The Hero with a
Thousand Faces. Campbell analyzed myths from cultures around the world and
demonstrated that the Hero story follows a consistent arc. The Hero receives a call
to action. The Hero resists the call. The Hero enters an unknown world. The Hero
faces trials. The Hero receives guidance. The Hero experiences a symbolic death.
The Hero returns changed. This is not a formula for stories. It is a formula for
human growth. Campbell documented the developmental journey that humans
have lived for millennia. Brands that use the Hero archetype are stepping into this
ancient psychological current. But to do it correctly, they must understand what
makes the Hero compelling in the first place.

One of the strongest scientific foundations of the Hero archetype comes from
the work of Albert Bandura. Bandura was a Stanford psychologist and one of the
most influential researchers in the history of behavioral science. He introduced
the concept of self efficacy, which is a person's belief in their ability to succeed

in a specific situation. Bandura proved through decades of research that belief in capability is a stronger predictor of action than ability itself. This is the engine that makes the Hero archetype powerful in branding. A Hero brand increases the Patron's belief in themselves. It shows them they can do something difficult. It demonstrates that capability is possible. Bandura would argue that if a brand raises self efficacy, it changes behavior. And this is exactly what the Hero archetype exists to do.

The Hero archetype is reinforced by the work of Edward Deci and Richard Ryan, two psychologists who developed Self Determination Theory. Deci and Ryan found that human motivation depends on three psychological needs: autonomy, competence, and relatedness. The Hero archetype primarily engages the need for competence. People want to feel capable. They want to feel that effort leads to progress. They want to feel that improvement is possible. When a brand frames struggle as worthwhile and demonstrates that capability can be learned, it satisfies this deep motivational need. A brand aligned with the Hero archetype does not promise comfort. It promises that the work will matter.

Another major contribution comes from Dan McAdams, a researcher who helped establish the field of narrative identity. McAdams found that humans construct meaning by forming personal narratives. One of the most common and powerful identity structures is the story of overcoming adversity. People see themselves as characters who face obstacles and grow from them. This is why Hero stories resonate so deeply. They provide a template for personal meaning making. Hero brands tap into that template by positioning the Patron as someone who can rise, endure, grow, and change.

The motivations of the Hero archetype reflect these psychological patterns. Hero brands are driven by a desire to create meaningful impact. They seek challenge, not avoidance. They value effort, not ease. They believe that change is earned. They operate through demonstration rather than assertion. Hero brands do not attempt to rescue people. They attempt to strengthen them. And that distinction separates them from the Caregiver archetype, which provides comfort, and the Sovereign archetype, which provides order.

A Patron who responds strongly to a Hero brand often identifies with effort. They may feel underestimated. They may seek mastery. They may crave direction or discipline. They may want a clear path toward improvement. Hero brands give them a structure that channels that motivation. They give them a story in which their struggle becomes purposeful.

Cultural stories provide clear examples of the Hero archetype in action. King Arthur represents the noble Hero who seeks justice and order. Harry Potter represents the reluctant Hero who grows through loss and mentorship. Wonder Woman represents the principled Hero who intervenes where others do not. Each of these characters faces adversity that becomes transformative. None of them begin as extraordinary individuals. They become extraordinary through the struggle.

In the world of branding, Nike stands as the clearest expression of the Hero archetype. Nike does not sell athletic wear. It sells the belief that ordinary people can do something difficult. Nike's messaging focuses on effort, grit, and personal capability. Their brand is a living representation of Bandura's research on self efficacy. When Nike tells people to "just do it", they are activating a psychological shift. They are increasing the Patron's belief in their own ability.

Microsoft expresses the Hero archetype through empowerment. Their Purpose is to empower every person and organization to achieve more. This is competence based motivation at global scale. Microsoft's platforms exist to strengthen human capability. They allow people to build, create, solve, and grow in ways that would otherwise be impossible. The Hero archetype is present in that push toward greater ability.

Sea Shepherd represents the Hero archetype at its most literal. Their mission is interventionist and sacrificial. They confront threats directly and risk significant consequences to protect marine wildlife. This is Hero behavior in the Jungian sense. Confrontation. Sacrifice. Transformation. Few brands activate the Hero archetype with such intensity or purity.

The strengths of the Hero archetype stem directly from its psychological roots. Hero brands create momentum because they offer clear direction. They build trust because they demonstrate ability rather than claiming it. They create identity transformation because they provide a narrative structure that people adopt. They form communities because shared struggle creates loyalty. And they stand out because most brands attempt to avoid tension while Hero brands move toward it.

The challenges of the Hero archetype are equally real. A Hero brand can easily slide into ego driven behavior. They may frame every situation as a battle and exhaust their audience with constant intensity. They may create internal cultures that produce burnout. They may alienate Patrons who do not identify with struggle. And they may misidentify or manufacture adversaries, which immediately undermines credibility.

The Hero archetype is also one of the most misunderstood in branding. Many brands confuse inspiration with heroism, but inspiration without struggle is the Innocent. Some believe that Hero automatically implies athletics, but athletics is only one context in which the archetype appears. Others believe that motivational language is Heroic, but words are meaningless without demonstrated capability. Some brands position themselves as rescuers, but that is the Caregiver, not the Hero. Rescue removes effort. Heroism requires it.

A brand must approach the Hero archetype with discipline. It must identify a real adversity that the Patron faces. It must demonstrate real capability to help them overcome it. It must show the work. It must elevate the Patron rather than overshadow them. And it must commit to consistency because the Hero archetype collapses the moment it becomes performative.

This is the psychological and strategic foundation of the Hero archetype. It is not energy. It is not hype. It is not language. It is a disciplined approach to helping people become more capable. When a brand commits to that principle, it earns the right to call itself a Hero brand.

Motivations of the Hero Archetype

The Hero archetype is driven by a core psychological truth. Humans want to feel capable. This drive appears across cultures and across time. It is present in the developmental theories of Carl Rogers, in the motivational frameworks of Edward Deci and Richard Ryan, and in the identity formation research of Dan McAdams. Capability is not a luxury for most people. It is a need. It determines how they see themselves and what they believe they can do. The Hero archetype exists because this need exists.

At its core, the Hero is motivated by a desire to confront and overcome. The Hero seeks challenge because challenge validates effort. Challenge reveals growth. Challenge creates identity. The Hero does not want an easy path. An easy path robs the Hero of meaning. The Hero wants a path that makes them stronger.

This is why Hero brands often feel more intense or energetic than other archetypes. They carry an urgency that comes from purpose driven effort. They see a problem, a limitation, a threat, or a gap, and they move toward it. They want to improve something. They want to strengthen someone. They want to elevate a community or an industry. Hero brands believe progress requires friction. They are comfortable inside that friction because friction creates competence.

Hero brands are motivated by clarity. They want a defined opponent. The opponent does not have to be a person or a competitor. It can be a mindset, a limitation, a standard, or a threat. Nike's opponent is doubt. Microsoft's opponent is limitation. Sea Shepherd's opponent is destruction. The specific form of the opponent does not matter as much as the psychological need for one. The Hero archetype requires resistance. Without resistance, there is nothing to overcome.

Another core motivation of the Hero archetype is the desire to strengthen the Patron. This is where Hero brands separate themselves from Sovereign brands or Outlaw brands. The Sovereign wants to lead. The Outlaw wants to disrupt. The Hero wants to empower. Hero brands operate as guides, coaches, trainers, mentors, or allies. Their goal is not to display their own strength. Their goal is to help the Patron find theirs.

This is reinforced by Self Efficacy Theory. Albert Bandura's research showed that people develop belief in their own capability through four primary experiences. Mastery experiences. Vicarious experiences. Social persuasion. And emotional regulation. Hero brands activate each of these pathways. They show mastery through demonstration. They show vicarious success through stories of others. They persuade through messaging. And they help regulate emotional states by framing struggle as normal, expected, and even valuable.

Hero brands are also motivated by progress. They are unsatisfied with stagnation. They want to push forward. They want to improve. They want to grow. They measure success by advancement, not stability. This is why Hero brands often appeal to people who identify with growth oriented mindsets. They give people an arena in which to push themselves.

Finally, Hero brands are motivated by responsibility. They feel a duty to step in. They see circumstances where effort is required, and they act. This responsibility driven behavior is tied to moral identity theory in psychology. Individuals and groups who adopt a principled identity feel compelled to work toward a greater good. Hero brands often carry this sense of duty. They see something broken and believe it is their obligation to attempt to fix it.

These motivations make the Hero archetype one of the most dynamic and demanding in brand strategy. It is not passive. It is not gentle. It is not quiet. It is not self congratulatory. It moves forward. It pushes. It builds. It strengthens. Hero brands take action where others hesitate. And when done correctly, they draw audiences who want to take action alongside them.

Strengths of the Hero Archetype

Courage Unbounded

Hero brands are defined by their willingness to confront what others avoid. Their courage is not performative and it is not reckless. It is the discipline to move toward challenges with clarity and conviction, even when the path is uncertain. Customers gravitate to Hero brands because they demonstrate strength in moments when everything else feels unstable. Courage becomes an emotional stabilizer. Patrons trust brands that act decisively, especially in categories weighed down by indecision, bureaucracy, or complacency. The Hero steps into the tension and shows the market what momentum looks like.

This courage also inspires internal culture. Teams inside Hero brands understand that bold action is expected rather than feared. They take initiative because the brand identity gives them permission to move. This creates a culture of forward motion that compounds over time. A Hero brand does not wait to see what competitors will do. It establishes new standards by taking risks others hesitate to take. When courage becomes cultural, the brand becomes the engine of change rather than a respondent to it.

Moral Clarity

Hero brands possess an unmistakable moral center. They know what they stand for and what they stand against, and they communicate this with precision. In a world where many brands dilute their values for broader appeal, the Hero remains unwavering. Their moral clarity becomes a beacon for customers seeking direction in complicated categories. People follow Hero brands because they trust their integrity. They believe the brand will make difficult decisions ethically rather than opportunistically.

This clarity extends into actions, not just messaging. Hero brands align their operations, partnerships, and internal expectations with their stated values. When they confront industry injustice, unsafe practices, or inequity, they do so with purpose rather than posturing. Their moral stance shapes loyalty because customers sense that the brand's convictions are real, not borrowed. Moral clarity gives the Hero brand a level of credibility competitors cannot manufacture. It becomes the anchor that grounds the brand's strength.

Resilience

Hero brands endure. They maintain momentum even when faced with obstacles that would exhaust or derail other archetypes. Their resilience comes from a deep belief that challenges exist to be overcome rather than avoided. This attitude influences everything from customer service to crisis response. Even when external circumstances shift dramatically, Hero brands return with steadiness and resolve. Customers admire this resilience because it mirrors their own aspirations for perseverance. They feel aligned with the brand's strength and stay loyal because of it.

Operationally, resilience shapes decision making. Hero brands do not crumble under pressure. They respond with adaptability, strategic persistence, and emotional discipline. Teams feel supported because leadership remains composed in difficulty. This steadiness protects the brand's identity from fragmentation during turbulent times. Resilience becomes a quiet form of reassurance. The Hero proves its strength not by avoiding hardship, but by moving through hardship with intention.

Inspiration for All

Hero brands elevate people. They turn aspiration into action by showing customers what is possible beyond their current limitations. Inspiration is not an emotional high. It is a strategic tool that expands a customer's sense of capability.

When a Hero brand communicates, it activates belief. Patrons feel something shift internally. They see themselves as able to do more, become more, pursue more. The Hero makes improvement feel attainable rather than abstract, which creates an emotional bridge between the brand and its audience.

This inspiration also builds community. Hero brands attract people who crave progress and growth, creating groups unified by shared striving rather than shared status. The brand becomes a rallying point that brings people together because of what they believe in, not because of what they own. Inspiration becomes the connective tissue that transforms a customer base into a movement. When a Hero brand leads with belief, it earns followers who willingly climb alongside it.

Selflessness

Hero brands direct their strength toward the good of others. Their actions prioritize service, protection, or empowerment rather than self glorification. Customers sense this and interpret it as integrity. A Hero brand does not fight for the sake of dominance. It fights for the sake of the people it serves. This selflessness increases trust because customers feel the brand's intentions are aligned with their well being rather than the brand's ego. Selflessness becomes a credibility amplifier.

Internally, selflessness shapes culture. Teams understand that their work has purpose beyond performance metrics. They see themselves as contributors to something larger than individual success. This creates a sense of camaraderie and meaning that strengthens morale. Externally, selflessness shows up in how the brand responds to crises, supports communities, and upholds its responsibilities. When customers see a brand consistently act with generosity and responsibility, loyalty deepens. The Hero earns its identity by elevating others.

Challenges of the Hero Archetype

Overidentification with Struggle

Hero brands often become so attached to the narrative of overcoming adversity that they manufacture unnecessary tension. They frame every initiative as a battle, every update as a victory, and every setback as a test of character. This constant dramatization exhausts customers. Over time, the brand feels intense instead of inspiring, heavy instead of uplifting. When every message is about grit, the tone becomes predictable and emotionally demanding. Patrons who are already overwhelmed by the world may disengage because they do not want the burden of perpetual struggle reinforced in their brand relationships.

Internally, this overidentification creates pressure that destabilizes teams. Employees may feel obligated to operate in crisis mode even when none exists, turning passion into fatigue. Cultures built on hardship eventually normalize burnout because working without strain feels like underperformance. A Hero brand must learn that resilience does not require manufacturing adversity. Real heroism is measured by impact, not by how loudly the struggle is communicated.

Ego Driven Posturing

The Hero's confidence becomes a liability when it slides into ego. Some Hero brands begin to believe they are the savior of their category, the moral authority of their industry, or the gold standard against which all others should be measured. This posture alienates customers who interpret the tone as self congratulatory rather than uplifting. When the brand positions itself as the hero of the story instead of the Patron, the emotional contract breaks. Customers want to feel strengthened by the brand, not overshadowed by it.

Ego driven behavior also weakens internal trust. Teams feel pressure to perform at superhuman levels because the brand's identity demands constant heroics. Critique becomes difficult because leadership associates disagreement with disloyalty. When ego shapes culture, humility disappears. This prevents the brand from learning, adjusting, or accepting nuance. A Hero brand must stay grounded. True strength elevates others rather than glorifying itself.

Perfectionistic Intensity

Hero brands often develop a perfectionistic intensity that contaminates their culture and communication. The identity demands excellence, but the expectation can become extreme. Teams may feel that anything less than flawless execution diminishes the brand's strength. This mindset creates a culture of pressure that discourages experimentation, risk taking, or honest conversations about failure. Instead of developing resilience through iterative growth, the brand creates fear around imperfection.

Externally, perfectionism stifles relatability. Customers do not bond with flawless brands. They bond with brands that demonstrate humanity while achieving excellence. When a Hero brand refuses to show vulnerability, it loses emotional access. The audience may admire the brand, but they do not feel close to it. Authentic heroism requires acknowledging limits, not denying them.

Aggressive Tone

Hero brands can become unintentionally aggressive in their messaging. Their language may lean too heavily on intensity, pressure, or demands for action. What is meant to motivate may instead overwhelm. Customers begin to feel pushed rather than empowered. Aggression weakens the brand's inspirational effect because it shifts the emotional experience from confidence to defensiveness. People push back when they feel pushed.

Aggressive tone also narrows the audience. Not all customers identify with the energy of relentless drive. Some value calm, joy, or exploration. When the Hero insists that only struggle produces meaning, it invalidates other forms of fulfillment. This alienates segments who prefer empowerment through curiosity or delight rather than confrontation. A Hero brand must learn how to calibrate intensity so it invites rather than intimidates.

Misplaced Conflict Creation

Hero brands sometimes create or exaggerate an enemy simply to maintain narrative tension. This is one of the most common missteps in the archetype. When the brand positions itself in constant opposition, it may accidentally villainize competitors, the category, or even customers who do not share its worldview. This makes the brand feel combative rather than courageous. Customers want clarity, not conflict for entertainment's sake.

Internally, misplaced conflict creates fracture. Teams become hyper competitive or emotionally charged because the brand's tone normalizes confrontation over collaboration. The organization becomes addicted to drama. This damages long term stability because perpetual conflict replaces sustained strategy. The Hero must learn to fight only when a real battle exists. Without discipline, the brand becomes known for noise instead of impact.

Archetype in Practice: People & Characters

King Arthur

King Arthur remains one of the most enduring Hero figures because his story reflects a universal psychological structure. He is not born into unchallenged power. He earns authority through worthiness. The moment he pulls the sword from the stone is not a display of magic. It is a demonstration of character. That is critical in Hero narratives. Capability is revealed through a test. Jung identified this pattern as the confrontation with the Shadow, the moment in which an individual proves their inner strength by meeting a significant challenge. Arthur's rise is defined by repeated trials. He faces betrayal, conflict, and responsibility that strain his capacity. The Hero archetype is not expressed through victory alone. It is expressed through the integrity required to achieve it.

Arthur's leadership style also reflects a fundamental aspect of the Hero archetype. He is responsible for more than himself. He carries a duty to protect and elevate the people he leads. In this sense, Arthur demonstrates what Campbell describes as the Hero's return, where the transformed individual brings new wisdom or capability back to their community. Arthur's victories matter not because he wins, but because his victories strengthen others. Hero brands follow the same path. They do not center themselves. They center the people they serve and elevate them through demonstrated action.

Harry Potter

Harry Potter exemplifies the reluctant Hero. He does not seek glory. He does not desire the role. He is pulled into conflict by forces larger than himself. This aligns with Campbell's initial stages of the monomyth, which include the call to adventure and the refusal of the call. Harry's reluctance makes him relatable. His Heroism emerges not from confidence but from repeated decisions to act despite fear. This reflects an important psychological truth. Courage is not the absence of fear. Courage is the willingness to move forward while fear remains. Hero brands must understand this distinction. They do not inspire people by pretending struggle does not exist. They inspire by validating the struggle and showing that progress is possible within it.

Harry's growth also mirrors Bandura's self efficacy pathways. He experiences mastery through the challenges he overcomes. He gains vicarious reinforcement through Dumbledore, Sirius, Lupin, and others who model capability. He receives social persuasion from mentors who reinforce belief in his abilities. And he learns emotional regulation through repeated exposure to stress and adversity. These factors build confidence through lived experience, not optimistic language. Hero brands must operate the same way. They help patrons build belief based on demonstrated progress, not slogans.

Wonder Woman

Wonder Woman embodies the principled Hero archetype. She engages in conflict not for personal gain but because she feels a moral obligation to intervene. Moral identity theory suggests that when individuals see themselves as responsible for upholding certain values, they act even when the action carries significant cost. Wonder Woman consistently steps into danger because she believes in the protection of others. She represents the Hero who assumes responsibility in the absence of authority or consensus.

Her Heroism is also grounded in purposeful struggle. She trains. She endures. She faces trials that test her judgment, strength, and resilience. Her power is not presented as a shortcut. It is the result of discipline. This mirrors the core of the Hero archetype. The Hero grows through intentional effort. Brands expressing this archetype must demonstrate effort and consistency. Wonder Woman's narrative offers a credible template for how the Hero archetype handles power. It is always channeled toward service, not dominance. The Hero strengthens others by leading through example.

Archetype in Practice: Brands

Nike

Nike is the modern benchmark for the Hero archetype. The brand's entire identity is built on the belief that ordinary people can achieve extraordinary outcomes through effort. This is not abstract positioning. It is grounded in the psychological principles of self efficacy. Albert Bandura demonstrated that belief in one's capability directly influences performance. Nike activates this belief through consistent demonstration of struggle, resilience, and growth. Their advertising rarely shows ease. It shows friction. It shows athletes, both elite and everyday, confronting challenges and enduring them. This visual demonstration reinforces the concept that progress is earned, not gifted.

Nike further embodies the Hero archetype through its commitment to elevating the Patron. The narrative is never about the brand saving the individual. It is about the individual discovering their own capability. The brand positions itself as the guide, not the protagonist. This follows Campbell's structure where mentors empower Heroes to complete their journey. Nike's community initiatives, from running clubs to training programs, reinforce the same principle. Capability emerges through effort and support, not shortcuts. This consistency is what makes Nike a textbook example of the Hero archetype.

Microsoft

Microsoft expresses the Hero archetype through empowerment at scale. The company's Purpose, to empower every person and organization to achieve more, is an explicit commitment to strengthening human capability. This aligns directly with Self Determination Theory. Edward Deci and Richard Ryan found that competence is one of the three essential human psychological needs. Microsoft's platforms and tools are designed to increase competence, reduce barriers, and allow people to accomplish tasks that were previously out of reach.

This approach reflects the Hero archetype's focus on capability, not rescue. Microsoft does not remove the challenge. It equips people to meet the challenge. The company demonstrates this through product evolution, accessibility features, and educational programs designed to elevate user skill. In this sense, Microsoft models the Hero's role as the guide. Like the mentors described by Campbell, the brand provides support, structure, and tools that enable people to rise. The result is a brand identity rooted in strengthening others, which is the defining behavior of the Hero archetype.

Sea Shepherd

Sea Shepherd represents the Hero archetype in its most literal and uncompromising form. The organization confronts direct threats to marine wildlife by physically intervening. This behavior aligns with Jung's description of the Hero confronting the Shadow. The Shadow represents the forces that destabilize or harm the world. The Hero moves toward that danger, not away from it. Sea Shepherd's actions require sacrifice, risk, and confrontation. These are the hallmark traits of the Hero archetype.

The organization also reflects the Hero's responsibility driven motivation. Moral identity theory explains that individuals or groups with strong internalized values feel obligated to act on those values even when doing so is costly. Sea Shepherd demonstrates this commitment through its willingness to incur operational and legal risk for the sake of its mission. This creates credibility because the sacrifice is real. Hero brands gain trust when their actions show that their commitments are not symbolic. Sea Shepherd proves that the Hero archetype is most powerful when the brand's behavior matches its stated purpose without compromise.

The world is full of magic things, patiently waiting for our senses to grow sharper.

– W. B Yeats

The Magician

The Magician is often flattened into a symbol of creativity or mystique, but the true Magician archetype is neither whimsical nor performative. At its core, the Magician represents one of the oldest human impulses: the desire to understand how the world works and the belief that understanding can reshape reality. The Magician archetype is rooted in mastery. Not mastery of people, but mastery of systems. The Magician looks beneath the surface, finds the underlying pattern, and uses that insight to create transformation. This is why Magicians have existed in every culture throughout history. They are the thinkers, healers, scientists, and visionaries who reveal possibilities others cannot see.

The psychological roots of the Magician lie not in spectacle but in cognition. Humans experience the world through interpretation, not observation. Everything we perceive is filtered through mental models that define meaning. When those models shift, our experience shifts. Cognitive psychologists call this reframing. Change the frame and you change the reaction. Change the reaction and you change the behavior. The Magician archetype is the embodiment of reframing. Magician brands do not persuade. They reveal. They take what already exists and present it in a way that transforms understanding.

Anthropologists have long noted that societies rely on individuals who can interpret the unseen. Early healers who understood herbal medicine, navigators who understood the stars, metallurgists who transformed ore into tools, and scholars who translated forgotten knowledge all played the role of the Magician. Their power came from understanding forces others could not grasp. This is consistent across cultures. The Magician is not defined by manipulation but by insight. They convert complexity into clarity.

Modern research reinforces this. Studies in meaning making show that humans create psychological coherence by linking events to interpretive narratives. When events lack meaning, they create anxiety. When meaning is supplied, anxiety diminishes and action becomes possible. The Magician archetype taps directly into this process. It gives Patrons a new way to interpret themselves, their challenges, or their potential. That transformation is emotional, cognitive, and behavioral.

The Magician archetype also expresses the human desire for potential. People want to believe change is possible. They want to believe constraints can be overcome. They want to believe the future can be different from the past. Magician brands channel this hope into action. They do not offer escape. They offer transformation through understanding. They give Patrons the sense that something powerful is possible because the rules of the system have been revealed.

This is why Magician brands often feel visionary. They operate with clarity that others have not yet reached. They see a world others do not see yet and bring it into view. But the Magician archetype is not about predicting the future. It is about revealing potential already present in the system. It is about translating complexity into possibility.

True Magician brands do not decorate themselves with mystery. They do not use confusion as a tool. They do not posture or perform. They demonstrate mastery through clarity, precision, and insight. They give Patrons access to a new way of understanding their world. And when a brand changes what people believe is possible, it changes what people do.

The Magician archetype is powerful not because it entertains or surprises. It is powerful because it transforms meaning. And meaning, once changed, changes everything else.

Motivations of the Magician Archetype

The Magician archetype is motivated by transformation. Their central drive is to unlock potential, reveal hidden truths, and alter the way people see themselves or their environment. They seek change at a fundamental level. Not superficial change. Not cosmetic change. Meaningful change that reconfigures understanding and leads to a different outcome.

One of the core motivations of the Magician is the pursuit of knowledge. The Magician wants to understand how things work beneath the surface. This is reflected in Jung's analysis of the archetype as a figure who operates between consciousness and the unconscious, translating insight into action. Magician brands demonstrate this motivation by showing mastery of a system, whether scientific, technological, social, or emotional. They do not guess. They study. They experiment. They refine. They pursue understanding as a path to transformation.

Another key motivation of the Magician is empowerment. Like the Hero, the Magician wants to strengthen others, but the method is different. The Hero strengthens through effort. The Magician strengthens through insight. The Magician believes that revelation can be transformative. When a person sees the world differently, they behave differently. This is supported by research in cognitive behavioral psychology, which shows that reframing beliefs leads to sustained behavioral change. The Magician archetype is built on this psychological mechanism.

The Magician is also motivated by possibility. They see potential in places where others see limitation. They believe that obstacles can be dissolved through understanding. They believe that existing structures can be rearranged to produce new and better outcomes. Magician brands speak to the Patron's desire for progress through transformation. They activate curiosity and imagination, creating a vision of what could be rather than what has been.

Magician brands are motivated by precision. Transformation requires accuracy. It requires clarity. It requires knowledge applied with intention. The Magician archetype does not rely on brute force. It relies on mastery. This distinguishes it from the Hero, who conquers through discipline, and from the Rebel, who challenges through disruption. The Magician changes reality through understanding.

Finally, the Magician is motivated by meaning. They want to create significance. They want to help people interpret their world in a way that feels coherent and purposeful. This connects to the psychological need for meaning making, which studies show is one of the most powerful drivers of human behavior. The Magician archetype uses transformation to produce meaning and uses meaning to produce transformation.

Strengths of the Magician Archetype

Wisdom and Insight

Magician brands see what others overlook. Their strength lies in synthesizing patterns, truths, and connections that remain invisible to the rest of the category. This insight is not mystical. It is the result of disciplined attention, curiosity, and a deep understanding of human behavior. Customers perceive Magician brands as perceptive because the brand speaks directly to underlying motivations, fears, and desires rather than superficial needs. This creates a sense of resonance. Patrons feel as though the brand understands them on a deeper level than competitors. Wisdom becomes a form of intimacy.

This insight also gives Magician brands market advantage. They recognize opportunities before others can articulate them. They decode emerging cultural or behavioral shifts and transform them into experiences that feel intuitive and inevitable. Insight fuels foresight. Customers trust the brand's intuition because it consistently reveals something meaningful. Magician brands do not simply follow the market. They anticipate it. And in doing so, they earn a reputation for clarity in a world clouded by complexity.

Transformation

Magician brands exist to facilitate transformation. They take customers from one emotional, functional, or psychological state to another. This movement is the core of their value. They help Patrons become something more capable, more confident, or more whole. Transformation becomes the narrative engine that drives identity, loyalty, and differentiation. Customers do not just buy from a Magician brand. They evolve through it. The brand becomes an agent of change rather than a provider of goods.

Transformation also strengthens storytelling. Every product or experience becomes a chapter in a larger journey of becoming. This gives the brand thematic cohesion that competitors struggle to match. The Magician promises not output, but outcome, and that promise is incredibly compelling. Transformation is also emotionally sticky. People remember the brands that changed them. They carry those brands forward because the transformation becomes part of their self story.

Visionary Thinking

Magician brands think expansively. They envision possibilities beyond the limits of current reality. This visionary mindset helps them create offerings that feel ahead of their time or perfectly tuned to what the world will need next. Vision gives the brand ambition and clarity. It sets the Magician apart from brands that iterate on what already exists. Instead of asking how to improve, the Magician asks how to reimagine. Customers feel this expansiveness and associate the brand with progress, inspiration, and potential.

Internally, visionary thinking fuels innovation. Teams are encouraged to think in terms of what could be rather than what is. This mindset emboldens creativity and encourages experimentation without fear. Vision becomes a cultural operating system. A Magician brand that consistently reveals new possibilities earns thought leadership status, not by declaring it, but by demonstrating it. Vision is not a tagline. It is a pattern of behavior.

Healing and Restoration

Magician brands restore what has been diminished or broken. Their strength lies in renewal, whether emotional, physical, or experiential. They provide clarity where there was confusion, empowerment where there was insecurity, and possibility where there was stagnation. This healing does not have to be literal or therapeutic. Sometimes it is the emotional relief of a simpler experience, a clearer narrative, or a product that resolves a persistent frustration. Healing becomes a subtle but powerful differentiator because it satisfies needs customers often cannot articulate.

This restorative quality gives the brand a comforting aura. Patrons feel better after interacting with a Magician brand than they did before. The experience feels cleansing or elevating. This emotional shift deepens loyalty because people remember the brands that help them recover, reset, or rise. Healing becomes a strategic asset because it makes the brand indispensable during moments of transition, uncertainty, or fatigue. A Magician who can restore energy becomes a companion through life's complexity.

Mastery

Mastery is the Magician brand's source of authority. These brands are not dabblers. They are experts. Their execution feels precise, intentional, and refined. Mastery signals discipline and depth. Customers trust the Magician because its products or experiences consistently demonstrate competence far beyond the baseline. Mastery is proof that the brand understands not only what it is doing, but why it is doing it. This level of skill creates emotional security for the Patron.

Mastery also shapes the internal culture. Teams strive toward high standards because the brand identity demands it. There is pride in precision. Pride in craft. Pride in doing something beautifully rather than acceptably. This consistency builds brand equity. When a Magician brand delivers mastery over time, it establishes itself as the unquestioned expert in the category. Competitors may attempt imitation, but imitation without mastery becomes obvious. The Magician earns loyalty by doing what few are capable of doing well.

Challenges of the Magician Archetype

Illusion Over Substance

Magician brands are masters of perception, but that mastery becomes a liability when the brand leans too heavily on symbolism, narrative, or aspirational messaging without supporting it with real value. Illusion replaces substance when storytelling becomes a smokescreen for weak offerings, underdeveloped systems, or shallow insight. Customers may initially be captivated by the brand's mystique, but mystique fades quickly when the experience does not match the promise. In a world where consumers expect transparency, illusion without integrity is not seen as charm. It is seen as deception.

This pattern also weakens internal alignment. Teams may begin prioritizing aesthetic, metaphor, or visionary language over the operational rigor required to sustain the brand's promise. Creative energy is spent on crafting a feeling rather than building the reality that feeling depends on. Over time, the illusion collapses under the weight of customer expectation. The Magician must ground its magic in mastery and ensure that every act of enchantment is supported by real excellence. Without substance, the brand becomes a mirage that evaporates when examined closely.

Elitist Insight

Magician brands can drift into elitism when their depth of knowledge causes them to dismiss the perspectives of those who think differently. Insight becomes superiority. The brand begins speaking in ways that feel inaccessible or coded, alienating customers who do not share the same intellectual or cultural frameworks. When a brand positions itself as enlightened rather than enlightening, it creates emotional distance. Customers may admire the brand from afar but feel uninvited to participate or co create meaning with it.

Elitism also damages collaboration. Teams may silo themselves into expertise bubbles, believing that only those with specialized understanding can contribute meaningfully. This limits innovation because great insights often emerge from unexpected intersections of diverse viewpoints. When the Magician values its own intellect too highly, it restricts the very alchemy that makes it powerful. The brand must remember that insight is most impactful when it is shared generously, not guarded as superiority.

Detachment from Reality

Visionary thinking can drift into detachment when the Magician becomes so focused on what could be that it loses contact with what is. This creates a divide between aspiration and execution. The brand may articulate extraordinary futures that it has no operational ability to deliver. Customers notice this gap quickly. What first feels inspiring begins to feel impractical. The Magician becomes the brand that dreams beautifully but struggles to act reliably.

Internally, this detachment creates frustration. Teams feel pulled toward ambitious visions that lack grounding, clarity, or feasibility. They may struggle to prioritize because the brand constantly shifts its focus toward the horizon rather than the next meaningful milestone. Detachment weakens credibility. For a Magician to remain powerful, its vision must be connected to the present in ways that make transformation tangible. Imagination without execution leads only to disillusionment.

Dependency on Inspiration

Magician brands rely heavily on inspiration as both creative fuel and strategic direction. But inspiration is unpredictable. When a brand depends on moments of insight rather than disciplined systems for innovation, its output becomes inconsistent. Peaks of brilliance are followed by long valleys of stagnation. Customers feel this inconsistency. They experience periods of awe followed by long periods of nothing. The brand becomes unpredictable, not mystifying.

Dependency on inspiration also leads to burnout within the organization. Teams chase moments of creative spark rather than developing repeatable processes that generate excellence. Without structure, the brand becomes emotionally and operationally fragile. When the magic does not show up, there is no backup plan. The Magician must learn that inspiration is a catalyst, not a strategy. Sustainable magic requires discipline.

Overcomplication

Magician brands often complicate what should be simple. Their desire for depth, symbolism, or conceptual elegance can result in messaging, products, or experiences that feel overly intricate. Customers may appreciate the beauty of the idea but struggle to understand the offering or its relevance. Overcomplication weakens utility and damages clarity. People do not want to decode a brand. They want to experience it.

Internally, this complexity slows momentum. Decision making becomes tangled in layers of conceptual framing and philosophical debate. Execution suffers because the brand overthinks instead of acts. Overcomplication is the shadow side of intelligence. It replaces clarity with cleverness and alienates both customers and employees. The Magician must remember that simplicity is not the enemy of depth. It is the pathway to impact.

Archetype in Practice: People & Caracters

Merlin

Merlin is one of the oldest and clearest expressions of the Magician archetype. He is not a warrior. He is a guide. His power comes from knowledge, not force. In Arthurian legend, Merlin understands the forces that shape destinies and events. He interprets signs, reveals meaning, and provides wisdom that helps Arthur become a just and capable leader. Merlin's influence aligns with Jung's description of the archetype as a figure who bridges consciousness and the unconscious. He operates in realms others cannot perceive and translates insight into action.

Merlin also embodies the Magician's role in transformation. He does not change Arthur through command. He changes him through revelation. He shows Arthur who he can become and provides the knowledge necessary to fulfill that potential. Merlin is a model for how the Magician archetype must behave. Transformation happens through guidance and understanding, not through dominance.

Marie Curie

Marie Curie represents the Magician archetype grounded in scientific mastery. Her work did not simply advance knowledge. It reframed humanity's understanding of energy, matter, and the unseen forces within the physical world. Curie's discoveries about radioactivity fundamentally transformed science and medicine. Her path reflects the Magician's motivation to uncover deeper truths. Curie pursued knowledge with precision, discipline, and a relentless desire to understand the invisible forces shaping reality.

Curie also demonstrates the Magician's role in empowering others. Her research created new possibilities that changed the trajectory of entire fields. She transformed what scientists believed was possible and expanded the boundaries of human capability. This is the Magician archetype expressed through rigorous inquiry. Transformation rooted in insight rather than imagination.

Steve Jobs

Steve Jobs exemplifies the modern Magician in the realm of technology and design. His genius was not rooted in engineering alone. It was rooted in the ability to see potential where others saw limitation. Jobs reframed what technology could be. He saw computers not as tools for specialists but as extensions of human creativity and emotion. This reframing reflects the Magician's psychological power. Jobs changed how people interpreted technology and therefore changed how they engaged with it.

Jobs also embodied the Magician's precision. He was known for obsessive attention to detail. Transformation requires accuracy, and Jobs understood that every aspect of an experience contributes to meaning. His work at Apple consistently revealed new possibilities by simplifying complexity and presenting technology in a form that felt intuitive. Jobs demonstrated what the Magician archetype looks like when applied to innovation. Insight becomes transformation. Transformation becomes progress.

Archetype in Practice: Brands

Snickers

Snickers expresses the Magician archetype by transforming emotional and physiological states through a simple and accessible action. The brand's long running campaign, centered on the idea that people are not themselves when hungry, reflects cognitive reframing. Snickers shifts the interpretation of hunger from a physical inconvenience to a change in personality or identity. This reframing is grounded in psychological research that shows hunger influences emotional regulation and cognitive performance. Snickers inserts itself as the solution that restores the true self.

The power of this positioning is that it transforms how people understand a common experience. Snickers does not compete on ingredients or flavor complexity. It competes on meaning. It offers transformation. A return to equilibrium. A recovery of identity. This is the Magician archetype applied to a mass market product. Small shift. Big effect. Transformation that feels immediate and believable.

Red Bull

Red Bull embodies the Magician archetype by positioning itself as a catalyst for energy and possibility. The brand does not focus on flavor or calories. It focuses on transformation of state. Red Bull offers Patrons a shift from fatigue to capability. This positioning uses the psychological principle of state dependent performance. Energy levels influence confidence, focus, and physical output. Red Bull ties its brand directly to that shift.

The brand's communication reinforces this transformational identity by highlighting extreme sports, adventurous behavior, and creative achievement. Although the Magician archetype does not rely on spectacle, Red Bull uses spectacle as evidence of transformation. The brand communicates that Red Bull unlocks potential, expands limits, and enables action. This connects directly to the Magician's motivational structure. Transformation is the product.

Spanx

Spanx is a powerful example of the Magician archetype expressed through confidence transformation. The brand shifts the Patron's perception of their body and appearance, which directly influences self esteem and performance. Research in psychology consistently shows that self perception affects behavior, posture, communication, and emotional expression. Spanx taps into this connection by framing its products as tools for empowerment rather than concealment.

Spanx does not promise invisibility. It promises transformation of how a person feels. The brand elevates confidence by reshaping experience, not identity. This aligns with the Magician archetype's role in altering perception to create new outcomes. The transformation is visible, emotional, and behavioral. It gives the Patron a new way to interpret themselves. Spanx achieves this without theatrics. It delivers a practical outcome with psychological significance.

Rebel children, I urge you, fight the turgid slick of conformity with which they seek to smother your glory.

– Russell Brand

The Rebel

The Rebel archetype is one of the most powerful forces in culture because it emerges not from desire but from necessity. The Rebel appears when systems become too rigid, too controlling, or too indifferent to the people they govern. Rebellion is not chaos. It is a psychological correction. When autonomy is restricted or when individuals feel unseen or unheard, the natural response is resistance. The Rebel archetype captures this instinct. It is the energy that pushes back against pressure and insists on an alternative. The Rebel does not accept the world as it is. The Rebel demands the world reckon with what it has ignored or suppressed.

Sociologists studying social movements have shown that rebellion is rarely irrational. It emerges when structural tension reaches a tipping point. When expectations, norms, or institutions prevent people from expressing their identity or agency, rebellion becomes both adaptive and necessary. This is the psychological foundation of the Rebel archetype. It is not a desire to break rules. It is a response to rules that no longer deserve obedience.

Reactance theory, one of the most well established concepts in psychology, explains this dynamic clearly. When individuals perceive their freedom to choose as threatened, they experience a motivational surge to restore that freedom. Resistance is not a flaw. It is a protective response. The Rebel archetype channels reactance into purpose. It converts frustration into liberation. It gives people a path to reclaim agency.

Throughout history, Rebels have sparked progress. They challenge norms that have calcified into barriers. They expose contradictions that polite society prefers to ignore. They call out the gap between what institutions claim and what institutions deliver. This is the role the Rebel plays in myth, literature, and culture. Not destruction for pleasure, but destruction for renewal. The Rebel archetype holds the belief that something better is possible and that change requires confrontation.

Cultural narratives reflect this. Characters who embody the Rebel archetype do not rebel for spectacle. They rebel because conformity has a cost. They reveal hidden weaknesses in the system. Their defiance creates pressure that forces adaptation. They disrupt not to destabilize, but to restore fairness, autonomy, or agency.

The Rebel archetype in branding follows the same psychological path. Rebel brands give Patrons permission to break from structures that feel outdated or oppressive. They offer alternative paths. They stand beside the Patron, not above them. They amplify the frustration people already feel and give it direction. Rebel brands do not push rebellion onto people. They articulate the rebellion people already experience internally.

The Rebel archetype is powerful because it is honest. It names what others avoid. It rejects what others tolerate. It speaks to people who feel restricted by norms that do not reflect their values. And it empowers them to choose differently. Rebellion is a form of self expression. It is a way to reclaim authorship of one's life. Rebel brands tap into that desire for independence with clarity and conviction.

A true Rebel brand does not manufacture outrage. It identifies genuine tension and challenges the system that produces it. It does not rebel for attention. It rebels because the status quo demands questioning. When done correctly, the Rebel archetype becomes a catalyst for change, both cultural and personal.

Motivations of the Rebel Archetype

The Rebel archetype is motivated by the desire for liberation. Rebel brands want to remove restraints, break barriers, and eliminate restrictions that limit human potential or freedom. They are driven by dissatisfaction with the status quo. The Rebel is uncomfortable with stagnation. They see complacency as a form of decay.

Another core motivation of the Rebel is justice. Although not always expressed through moral language, Rebel brands often identify systems that treat people unfairly or inefficiently. Their rebellion is purposeful. They challenge norms because those norms no longer serve the Patron. This is supported by research in moral cognition, which shows that perceived injustice creates strong emotional and behavioral responses. Rebel brands channel those responses into action.

The Rebel is also motivated by autonomy. Self Determination Theory identifies autonomy as one of the three essential human needs. When autonomy is restricted, people resist. The Rebel archetype embodies this resistance. It appeals to Patrons who feel constrained or undervalued. Rebel brands offer a sense of agency. They do not guide or transform like the Hero or Magician. They liberate.

The Rebel is motivated by disruption. This is not disruption for entertainment. It is disruption for progress. The Rebel believes that change requires confrontation. They are comfortable being the catalyst that forces the system to adapt. They carry the psychological confidence to challenge dominant structures.

Finally, the Rebel is motivated by identity. People often use rebellion as a way to assert individuality. Research on adolescence and adult identity development shows that rebellion can be a method for declaring independence, especially when external control is perceived as intrusive. Rebel brands understand this and position themselves as tools for self expression.

Strengths of the Rebel Archetype

Courageous Defiance

Rebel brands earn their power through unapologetic defiance. They refuse to accept the norms, limitations, or broken assumptions of their category. This defiance is not mindless opposition. It is principled. When a system becomes complacent or corrupted, the Rebel becomes the challenger who articulates what everyone else feels but has been conditioned not to say. Customers gravitate to this courage because it gives voice to their own frustrations. When a brand stands up to something that feels immovable, the Patron experiences a kind of emotional liberation. The Rebel serves as the conduit for that release.

Courageous defiance also positions the brand as a catalyst for change rather than a passive participant. In stagnant categories, the Rebel forces competitors to react. They challenge pricing models, product assumptions, customer experience norms, or cultural narratives. This propulsion reshapes ecosystems. Other brands follow not because they want to, but because the Rebel shifts expectations. Defiance becomes a competitive advantage because it disrupts comfort and invites transformation.

Individualism

Rebel brands thrive by expressing a distinct, unmistakable identity. They do not blend in. They do not water down their message to please the masses. Their individualism is their strength because it creates instant differentiation in categories where sameness suffocates relevance. When a Rebel brand speaks, people know exactly whose voice they are hearing. This clarity becomes magnetic. Patrons who crave authenticity or self definition align themselves with the brand because it reflects their desire to break free from the generic, the expected, and the conformist.

This individualism also shapes the brand's internal culture. Teams feel permission to think differently, speak openly, and challenge assumptions. The brand becomes a home for unconventional thinkers who might struggle in more structured environments. This diversity of perspective fuels innovation because ideas emerge from a place free from politeness or fear. Individualism is not rebellion for shock value. It is rebellion as self sovereignty.

Resourcefulness

Rebel brands are resourceful because they often operate without the privileges or resources that established leaders rely on. They build with what they have, and this constraint fuels ingenuity. They find creative solutions others overlook and experiment in ways legacy brands are too risk averse to attempt. Resourcefulness becomes a core identity trait: the Rebel thrives on making the improbable possible. Patrons admire this scrappiness because it reflects a world view they respect. People trust brands that hustle because hustle signals hunger.

Resourcefulness also shapes how Rebel brands execute campaigns, develop products, or design experiences. Instead of relying on tradition or formulaic approaches, they innovate through necessity. They move quickly, pivot boldly, and iterate constantly. This agility allows them to outmaneuver larger competitors who are slowed down by bureaucracy. Resourcefulness is the Rebel's survival mechanism and their competitive engine.

Empathy for the Marginalized

Rebel brands have a keen sensitivity to the voices, groups, and experiences that mainstream systems ignore. Their rebellion is often rooted in solidarity. They speak for those who have been excluded or dismissed. This empathy shapes both their mission and their tone. It becomes clear that the brand's opposition is not reckless but purposeful. Customers who identify with the overlooked feel seen and valued. This emotional connection builds fierce loyalty because patrons feel the brand fights for them rather than at them.

This empathy also informs strategic choices. Rebel brands choose causes, narratives, and creative directions that elevate marginalized experiences without exploiting them. They challenge inequity not as a marketing stunt but as a core identity. This moral clarity differentiates them from brands that co opt activism without depth. The Rebel does not perform solidarity. It practices it.

Cultural Provocation

Rebel brands excel at cultural provocation. They disrupt complacency by spotlighting uncomfortable truths, challenging accepted narratives, and forcing conversations that polite culture avoids. This provocation is not about shock for entertainment. It is about agitation that awakens awareness. Brands that provoke culture create space for reflection, tension, and ultimately transformation. Patrons admire a brand willing to say the thing everyone else tiptoes around. Provocation becomes a signal that the brand values honesty over harmony.

This cultural agitation also helps Rebel brands shape the zeitgeist. They become cultural accelerants who shift norms by disrupting them. When a Rebel challenges beauty standards, environmental complacency, industry hypocrisy, or political apathy, they move culture by refusing to remain neutral. Their provocative stance inspires discourse, media coverage, and community alignment. Cultural provocation positions the Rebel not as a disruptor alone, but as a catalyst for evolution.

Challenges of the Rebel Archetype

Volatility of Identity

Rebel brands thrive on disruption, but that same disruption can destabilize their identity if not anchored in a clear purpose. When rebellion becomes the strategy rather than the expression of strategy, the brand risks drifting into chaos. Without a strong center, the Rebel can shift tone, stance, or message too frequently, confusing customers who no longer understand what the brand stands for. Volatility weakens trust because Patrons cannot rely on consistent values. It becomes difficult to build loyalty around a brand that reinvents its opposition without reinforcing its conviction.

This instability also affects internal culture. Teams working under a volatile Rebel experience constant directional shifts, making execution difficult and long term planning nearly impossible. Employees may begin questioning leadership if the brand's rebellious actions feel performative instead of principled. A Rebel brand without an anchor becomes noise rather than movement. To avoid volatility, the Rebel must clarify not only what it stands against, but what it stands for.

Alienation of Mainstream Audiences

Rebel brands naturally repel certain groups, and often that is intentional. But the risk arises when rebellion becomes so extreme or polarizing that mainstream audiences interpret the brand as hostile, abrasive, or dismissive of their values. This alienation limits growth potential and traps the brand in a niche that becomes difficult to scale out of. When people feel attacked rather than activated, the brand loses cultural influence. Rebellion must be aimed at systems, not at customers.

Externally, this alienation shows up when messaging is so provocative that it intimidates or confuses audiences unfamiliar with the brand's worldview. People who might otherwise appreciate the brand's stance feel unwelcome because the tone signals exclusivity through aggression. A Rebel brand that alienates unintentionally undermines its own mission. True rebellion invites alignment. Alienation signals misdirected intensity.

Uncontrolled Provocation

Cultural provocation is one of the Rebel's greatest strengths, but when used without discipline, it becomes a liability. Provocation for its own sake slips into shock tactics that lack purpose. Customers sense when the brand is provoking to gain attention rather than pushing for meaningful change. This erodes credibility and reduces the brand to a predictable performer of outrage rather than a principled challenger. Provocation must always illuminate something real. If it does not, it becomes empty noise.

Uncontrolled provocation also increases risk of backlash. The Rebel can stumble into cultural offensiveness or insensitivity if it pushes boundaries without understanding context. What was intended as boldness can be interpreted as disrespect. Once trust is broken, it becomes difficult for a Rebel to regain legitimacy because audiences question the integrity of its intentions. Effective provocation requires intelligence, timing, and empathy.

Operational Disorder

Rebel brands often resist structure, viewing it as a constraint on creativity or freedom. This aversion creates operational disorder when processes are ignored, systems remain unbuilt, or teams operate without clarity. While chaos may feel energizing in the early stages of a brand's life, it becomes destructive as the company grows. Without systems, the brand struggles to scale. Execution falters. Promises go unfulfilled. Customers begin to question whether the brand can deliver on its bold claims.

Internally, this disorder produces burnout. Employees must compensate for lack of structure by working harder, improvising, or absorbing responsibilities that should belong to systems rather than individuals. The Rebel must learn that systems do not kill rebellion. They sustain it. Operational stability allows the brand to channel its disruptive energy into lasting impact rather than sporadic bursts of brilliance.

Moral Absolutism

Rebel brands often operate from strong moral conviction, which gives them power. But when that conviction hardens into absolutism, the brand becomes inflexible and self righteous. Moral absolutism removes nuance and prevents the brand from adapting to new information. It also creates an environment where dissent is discouraged internally. Teams may hesitate to challenge ideas because the brand frames its mission as unquestionable. This stifles innovation and erodes healthy internal conversation.

Externally, absolutism alienates customers who share the brand's values but not its intensity. People may agree with the intention but disagree with the delivery. When a brand acts as though its worldview is the only correct one, customers feel judged. The Rebel's power lies in principled defiance, not moral superiority. When the brand stops challenging systems and starts condemning people, it loses the clarity that makes rebellion meaningful.

In Practice: People & Characters

Robin Hood

Robin Hood is one of the earliest and clearest expressions of the Rebel archetype. His rebellion is rooted in moral conviction. He confronts a system that exploits common people and redirects his efforts to restore fairness. This aligns with moral psychology research which shows that perceived injustice triggers action intended to restore balance. Robin Hood does not rebel for pleasure or chaos. He rebels because the system has failed.

His method also reflects the Rebel archetype. He uses unconventional tactics. He refuses authority. He violates the rules of an unjust structure in order to achieve a higher ethical outcome. This demonstrates a key feature of the Rebel. The rules themselves are not inherently valuable. They are valuable only if they serve the people they govern.

Julian Assange

Julian Assange represents the modern Rebel archetype as expressed through information activism. His work with WikiLeaks was motivated by a belief that transparency should override institutional secrecy. This aligns with research in reactance and moral conviction. Assange perceived government secrecy as a violation of public freedom and responded with disruptive action intended to restore agency.

Assange also demonstrates the Rebel's willingness to endure consequences. Rebel figures often accept personal risk because the pursuit of a greater cause outweighs self preservation. Assange's actions, regardless of public interpretation, reflect the psychological signature of the Rebel. He confronted powerful systems and forced global institutions to respond.

Batman

Batman is a complex and disciplined expression of the Rebel archetype. His rebellion is directed not just against crime but against corruption and systemic failure. Batman operates outside the law because he believes the law is insufficient to achieve justice. This reflects the archetype's core motivation. Rebels challenge systems they deem ineffective.

Batman also embodies the Rebel's identity driven motivation. He constructs an identity that rejects social expectations. His vigilantism is a symbolic rejection of conventional authority. Research on identity formation shows that rebellion often emerges from trauma or a desire for agency. Batman channels that impulse into purposeful disruption. He refuses to accept the world as it is and dedicates his life to reshaping it.

In Practice: Brands

Liquid Death

Liquid Death is a quintessential Rebel brand. It entered a stagnant category with a single mission. Destroy the norms of bottled water marketing. Its visual identity, naming strategy, humor, and communications openly reject the conventions of purity and serenity that dominate the category. This disruptive approach reflects the Rebel's psychological foundation. Liquid Death challenges the expectation that certain categories must behave politely.

The brand also uses rebellion to critique sustainability practices. Liquid Death positions aluminum cans as an environmentally superior alternative to plastic. The rebellion is structured. It pushes against waste and against the hypocrisy of brands that claim environmental responsibility while contributing to pollution. This aligns with Pearson's observation that Rebel brands often emerge to correct hypocrisy.

Uber

Uber expresses the Rebel archetype through the dismantling of traditional transportation systems. The company entered markets by challenging entrenched taxi regulations and legacy infrastructure. This reflects the core Rebel motivation to break systems that no longer serve their intended purpose. Uber positioned itself as a liberating force, offering autonomy, access, and convenience where the system had failed.

Uber's growth demonstrates the Rebel's ability to rapidly shift cultural norms. The brand's early narrative was built on challenging the status quo and offering empowerment through choice. Although Uber's governance and culture later encountered criticism, its foundational identity is rooted in the Rebel archetype. It confronted outdated systems and forced an industry wide transformation.

PayPal

PayPal emerged as a Rebel brand in the finance sector by challenging traditional banking. It provided an alternative to slow, restrictive, and bureaucratic payment systems. This aligns with reactance theory. Consumers often feel constrained by financial institutions. PayPal positioned itself as the tool that returned autonomy to the user.

The brand's original mission, particularly under early leadership, was explicitly disruptive. PayPal sought to democratize online payments and challenge the inefficiency of established financial systems. This is a textbook expression of the Rebel archetype. The brand identified a system that was restrictive and reimagined it in a way that empowered individuals. Its disruption was purposeful. It improved accessibility, speed, and user control.

CHAPTER 06

Quadrant: Foster Belonging

The Foster Belonging quadrant is centered on connection. These archetypes understand that people do not only seek products. They seek emotional environments where they feel valued, seen, and welcomed. The Citizen dissolves hierarchy so everyone feels included. The Lover deepens connection through intimacy and beauty. The Jester unites people through joy, shared laughter, and collective release. Together, they turn customers into communities.

Belonging becomes most compelling when its absence is felt. Excessive introspection, independence, or personal striving can create emotional distance.

Research from Baumeister and Leary establishes belongingness as a fundamental psychological need. When that need is undernourished, people seek brands that restore human connection. This quadrant counterbalances the inward intensity of the Find Fulfillment quadrant. While fulfillment archetypes help individuals discover themselves, belonging archetypes help them connect with others. When introspection becomes isolation, belonging becomes medicine.

This quadrant also counteracts the emotional heaviness of the Exert Control quadrant. When structure becomes rigidity, when authority feels cold, or when brands hold customers at a distance, people turn toward warmth, comfort, and joy. The Jester relieves emotional pressure. The Lover provides depth. The Citizen creates shared identity. Social identity theory affirms that people form their sense of self through communities, not isolation. Brands that cultivate belonging do more than satisfy customers. They give people a place to anchor.

The archetypes in this quadrant must be sincere. Belonging is fragile. Performative connection erodes trust quickly. When executed with intention, these archetypes form some of the strongest brand communities. They create emotional gravity that cannot be purchased or engineered artificially. Foster Belonging brands help people feel connected in a world that often pulls them apart.

There is nothing in the world so irresistibly contagious as laughter and good humor.

– Charles Dickens

The Jester

The Jester is one of the most misunderstood figures in the entire archetype system because people mistake humor for a distraction. They think play is the opposite of seriousness. They assume levity is the absence of depth. In truth, the Jester is one of the most psychologically sophisticated archetypes. It is the antidote to rigidity. It is the breaker of tension. It is the one force in the psyche capable of revealing truth without triggering defensiveness. Humor is not decoration. Humor is disruption wrapped in permission.

Anthropologists have long noted that every society produces a trickster figure. Claude Lévi Strauss, one of the foundational thinkers in structural anthropology, wrote that tricksters exist because cultures need a figure who can hold contradiction without collapsing. Tricksters expose the gap between who we say we are and what we actually do. They reveal the unspoken rules, the hidden hypocrisies, and the absurdity of human systems. The Jester is that figure in psychological form. They are not anarchists. They are mirrors.

Modern psychology backs this up. Studies in social bonding show that shared laughter synchronizes emotional states and creates immediate interpersonal trust. Humor lowers psychological defenses, reduces social anxiety, and allows people to engage more authentically. Psychologists such as Robert Provine, who studied the neuroscience of laughter, found that laughter is fundamentally social. It is a belonging mechanism. People laugh thirty times more often in groups than alone. The Jester archetype leverages this hardwired mechanism to bring people closer.

In mythology, the Jester shows up not as a clown but as a guide. Native American trickster stories, Yoruba tales of Eshu, and Norse stories of Loki all follow the same pattern. The trickster uses humor to reveal what is hidden. They unsettle the powerful. They expose illusions by creating new ones. They destabilize certainty so that people can see the world clearly again. In trickster mythology, humor is an instrument of transformation, not escape. It creates clarity by temporarily suspending seriousness.

This is why the Jester belongs in the Foster Belonging quadrant. The Jester creates connection by dissolving pretense. When people laugh together, hierarchy disappears. Ego softens. Fear relaxes. The Jester gives people psychological permission to be human without performance. This is belonging at its purest level. Not tribal belonging. Human belonging.

The Jester's deeper purpose is emotional liberation. Humans live under constant social pressure. To be composed. To be appropriate. To be impressive. The Jester removes that pressure. They say the thing everyone is thinking. They laugh at the rule everyone silently resents. They break tension on behalf of the group. And because of that, people feel safe around them. That safety is not superficial. It is rooted in the oldest forms of human connection.

The Jester archetype is powerful because humor is one of the most honest languages humans speak. It reveals fear. It reveals desire. It reveals frustration. It reveals longing. It reveals the truth that seriousness tries to hide. People bond over truth, not polish. The Jester understands this instinctively.

So the Jester is not silly. The Jester is not shallow. The Jester is not unserious. The Jester is brave. They say what others cannot. They mock what others take too seriously. They reveal what others avoid. And in doing so, they bring people together in a way no other archetype can.

Motivations of the Jester Archetype

The Jester is motivated by connection. They seek to create environments where people can let their guard down. They want to dissolve pretense so that people can engage authentically. This aligns with the psychological function of play. Play allows individuals to participate without fear of evaluation. The Jester creates belonging by eliminating the fear of being judged.

The Jester is also motivated by truth. Humor often reveals uncomfortable realities. Psychological studies on benign violation theory show that humor arises when something violates expectations without causing harm. The Jester uses this principle to highlight truths that others overlook or avoid. The goal is not disruption for the sake of disruption. The goal is honesty delivered in a way that people can receive.

Another motivation of the Jester is liberation. They challenge rigid norms and social expectations that create tension or constraint. They aim to free people from pressure, stress, or societal strictness. This is supported by Freud's relief theory, which states that humor functions as an emotional release. The Jester archetype channels this release into group experience.

The Jester is also motivated by joy. Joy may seem superficial, but it is psychologically essential. Research shows that joy increases resilience, strengthens relationships, and fosters social cohesion. The Jester uses joy to create shared emotional grounding.

Finally, the Jester is motivated by inclusivity. They reject elitism. They reject intellectual superiority. They reject exclusivity. The Jester archetype wants to bring more people in, not keep people out. This is why Jester brands often feel approachable, human, and relational.

Strengths of the Jester Archetype

Joyful Atmosphere

Jester brands create environments that feel alive. Their presence injects energy into categories often weighed down by seriousness, competition, or routine. This joy is not superficial cheerfulness. It is a deliberate design choice that alters how people experience the brand. Whether through humor, playfulness, tone of voice, or visual expression, Jester brands remind customers that not everything needs to be optimized, analyzed, or overthought. This emotional lift becomes a strategic advantage. People gravitate toward brands that make them feel good, especially in a cultural climate saturated with pressure and noise.

Joy also increases memorability. Customers remember the brand that made them laugh or smile, even briefly. That moment becomes an emotional anchor that elevates brand recall and strengthens preference. A joyful atmosphere also diffuses tension. In industries prone to frustration, such as travel, health, finance, or dining during peak hours, a Jester brand disarms stress by shifting the customer's emotional state. Joy becomes a form of value creation when it turns a forgettable interaction into a delightful one.

Creativity Unleashed

Jester brands embrace creativity without constraint. They are unafraid of color, humor, metaphor, or narrative experimentation. This creative freedom allows them to explore ideas that more restrained archetypes cannot. As a result, their campaigns, product concepts, and brand moments feel fresh, original, and unexpected. Creativity becomes a strategic accelerant. Customers reward novelty when it is purposeful and coherent, and the Jester knows how to channel creative risk into meaningful expression.

Internally, creativity thrives because the Jester brand reduces fear. When a culture encourages play, experimentation becomes natural. Teams offer bolder ideas, take more creative risks, and collaborate without the self consciousness that stifles innovation. Jester brands often attract talent who value expressive work and want to build something with personality rather than corporate sameness. Creativity in this context is not performative. It is functional. It produces differentiation by breaking predictable patterns.

Social Glue

Jester brands excel at connecting people. Humor and play are inherently social behaviors that dissolve hierarchy and tension. When a brand introduces levity into its interactions, it fosters a sense of collective enjoyment. This shared experience becomes social glue that strengthens community and sparks conversation. People want to share Jester content, talk about Jester experiences, and bring others into the moment. Virality is not accidental for the Jester. It is a natural byproduct of emotional bonding.

This connective power also shows up in physical or digital spaces. A Jester brand's environment invites interaction. Displays become photo moments. Packaging becomes conversation starters. Campaigns become cultural touchpoints. Patrons feel like co participants rather than observers. The brand becomes a stage where people can play, joke, or express themselves without fear. This sense of shared identity deepens loyalty because laughter shared is loyalty earned.

Stress Relief

Jester brands reduce emotional pressure by offering relief in unexpected moments. They interrupt seriousness with playfulness. They interrupt anxiety with humor. This disruption is powerful. In psychological terms, laughter produces physiological shifts that lower stress, reduce tension, and increase openness. The Jester brand uses this effect not as a gimmick but as a strategic differentiator. When customers feel lighter, they perceive everything about the experience as easier and more enjoyable.

Stress relief also changes customer expectations. When individuals know a brand will ease their emotional load rather than add to it, they approach interactions with a more positive mindset. This increases satisfaction, reduces frustration, and elevates the entire experience. In categories known for stress, such as air travel, healthcare, or customer service heavy industries, stress relief can become a brand's most powerful operational asset. The Jester elevates hospitality by simply reminding people to breathe.

Perspective Alteration

Jester brands shift the way people see situations, themselves, and even the category. Humor exposes the absurdity in everyday experiences. Play reframes seriousness into something manageable. Perspective alteration is not simply comedic relief. It is a cognitive reset. When a brand positions problems through humor or creative inversion, customers see those problems differently. Frustrations shrink. Rigid expectations loosen. The world feels more flexible. That emotional shift makes the customer more receptive to the brand's message.

This ability to reframe also gives Jester brands cultural relevance. They challenge norms without lecturing. They critique industry habits without grandstanding. They reveal truth through humor and make complex issues more approachable. Perspective alteration becomes a quiet form of leadership. The Jester leads not by commanding, but by helping people see things with fresh eyes.

Challenges of the Jester Archetype

Superficiality

A Jester brand's commitment to humor and play can drift into superficiality when entertainment becomes the primary focus instead of a strategic tool. When this happens, messaging feels hollow. The brand may generate laughs or attention, but it fails to communicate meaningful value or substance. Customers begin to see the brand as charming but unreliable, enjoyable but forgettable. Superficiality weakens long term loyalty because humor alone rarely sustains emotional connection. Without depth, the brand becomes a momentary amusement rather than a lasting companion in the customer's life.

This superficiality also limits category authority. When a brand presents itself as all jokes and no grounding, customers assume the brand lacks seriousness or skill in its domain. In categories where competence is essential, such as health, finance, or safety related industries, this becomes a liability. A Jester can absolutely thrive in these environments, but only when humor is used to clarify, humanize, or elevate. When humor becomes the whole identity, it undermines credibility rather than enhancing it. The Jester must learn to wield humor with intention, not abandon substance in pursuit of a laugh.

Misinterpretation Risks

Jester brands gamble with tone. Humor is subjective, contextual, and culturally dependent. What delights one audience can offend another. Misinterpretation is one of the archetype's greatest vulnerabilities because jokes can be taken literally, irony can be lost, and play can be misunderstood as disrespect. This risk increases as the brand scales into diverse markets or communicates across multiple demographics. A misread campaign can quickly convert excitement into backlash, especially in digital spaces where nuance is often flattened and outrage accelerates rapidly.

When humor is misinterpreted, it can damage trust permanently because customers assume the brand is careless, insensitive, or unaware of boundaries. The Jester must understand social dynamics and cultural implications deeply to avoid stumbling into tone related pitfalls. Effective humor requires emotional intelligence and situational awareness. Without this grounding, the Jester becomes clumsy rather than clever, and clumsy missteps can undo years of goodwill.

Lack of Seriousness

Jester brands often struggle to be taken seriously when it matters. Their tone, while delightful, can undermine authority in moments that require stability, responsibility, or clarity. Customers may hesitate to trust the brand with high stakes decisions because they perceive it as unserious. This affects categories where reliability is critical, such as healthcare, transportation, education, or financial services. Even in entertainment or lifestyle categories, a lack of seriousness can create barriers when the brand needs to shift into more grounded communication.

Internally, this challenge appears when employees or partners interpret the brand's playful identity as an excuse to avoid discipline or rigor. Creativity turns into chaos. Innovation turns into distraction. The Jester can destabilize itself if it fails to balance levity with professionalism. Humor must be a tool, not a mask that hides a lack of structure. Without clear moments of seriousness, the brand risks being perceived as irresponsible instead of joyful.

Brand Dilution

Because the Jester thrives on novelty and surprise, it can easily drift away from its core identity. In the pursuit of new jokes, new stunts, or new playful campaigns, the brand may lose coherence. What begins as a distinct personality becomes a scattered assortment of gags that do not connect to a meaningful center. This dilution weakens recognition and consistency. Customers enjoy isolated moments but fail to develop a cohesive understanding of what the brand stands for.

Brand dilution also occurs when the Jester chases trends instead of shaping its own voice. Humor loses effectiveness when it feels derivative. The brand becomes dependent on cultural memes or pop culture references that quickly age out. Without a strong guiding perspective, the Jester becomes a commentary engine rather than a cultural presence. To maintain strength, the Jester must anchor its playfulness in identity rather than in constant reinvention.

Distraction from Value

A Jester brand's emphasis on fun can overshadow the functional value of its offerings. Customers may associate the brand with entertainment but fail to understand its core products, quality, or benefits. Humor can become a smokescreen that hides the very value the brand needs to communicate to remain competitive. When customers enjoy the joke but do not remember the product, the brand has failed strategically. Amusement without meaning generates awareness but not adoption.

Distraction also disrupts internal priorities. Teams may become enamored with clever ideas that do not serve strategic objectives. Creative excitement pulls focus away from operational rigor, customer needs, or the brand's long term goals. The Jester must learn to integrate humor into value, not replace value with humor. When fun enhances purpose rather than obscuring it, the brand gains emotional impact and functional clarity at the same time.

In Practice: People & Characters

Genie from Aladdin

The Genie from Aladdin embodies the Jester archetype at its most energetic and expansive expression. His humor is rapid, multidimensional, and unpredictable, but it always serves a purpose. He uses comedy to break tension and to guide Aladdin through challenging moments. Genie's power lies not just in magic but in his ability to disarm fear with humor. This reflects a key element of the Jester archetype. Humor is not a diversion. It is a tool for emotional safety.

Genie also uses humor to reveal truth. His jokes consistently expose Aladdin's insecurities, false confidence, and fear of vulnerability. This aligns with the psychological function of humor in revealing suppressed truths. Genie helps Aladdin confront himself without shame or pressure. Humor becomes a path to honesty. This is the Jester archetype in its highest form. Play that leads to insight.

Robin Williams

Robin Williams expressed the Jester archetype with unmatched emotional depth. His ability to blend humor with vulnerability created a sense of shared humanity. Research on emotional contagion shows that humor delivered with authenticity increases empathy. Williams embodied this. His performances bridged sadness and joy. He showed that humor is not escapism. It is a way into connection.

Williams also demonstrated the Jester's role as a truth teller. His improvisation often revealed social absurdities and human contradictions. He used imitation, exaggeration, and absurdity to expose the flaws in norms and institutions. This reflects the trickster's role in myth. Williams did not mock life. He revealed it. Through comedy, he invited audiences to feel less alone.

Deadpool

Deadpool is a modern interpretation of the Jester archetype grounded in self awareness and irreverence. His humor is directed at the structure of the narrative itself. He breaks the fourth wall. He mocks tropes. He calls out the limitations of his own genre. This aligns with the trickster's role in challenging the rigidity of a system by exposing its artificiality.

Deadpool also uses humor as a coping mechanism. His irreverence masks and reveals trauma at the same time. This reflects the psychological insight that humor often emerges as a response to pain. Deadpool's character shows how humor can coexist with suffering, creating connection through shared recognition of difficulty. This is the Jester at full maturity. Humor that acknowledges pain without being consumed by it.

In Practice: Brands

Skittles

Skittles is a pure Jester brand. Its marketing consistently uses absurdity, surrealism, and randomness to create humor that feels accessible and inclusive. Skittles campaigns are memorable because they intentionally violate expectations in ways that feel harmless. This aligns with benign violation theory. Skittles finds the exact threshold where absurdity becomes funny rather than confusing.

The brand also uses humor to create belonging. Skittles signals to Patrons that the brand does not take itself too seriously and that enjoyment is allowed. This is a powerful differentiator in a category where many brands rely on indulgence or nostalgia. Skittles invites people into a shared joke. That shared humor fosters connection.

Old Spice

Old Spice reinvented itself through the Jester archetype by transforming a declining legacy brand into a cultural phenomenon. The brand used humor to disrupt category conventions that were overly serious and hyper masculine. By using absurdity and wit, Old Spice created a new identity that felt fresh, confident, and inclusive.

Old Spice also demonstrated the Jester's truth telling ability. Through exaggerated masculinity, the brand exposed how ridiculous the category's norms had become. This humorous reframing allowed Old Spice to distance itself from outdated gender expectations. The humor created a safe way for Patrons to re-engage with the category. It created belonging through shared recognition of the absurd.

Loudmouth

Loudmouth expresses the Jester archetype through bold design, irreverent patterns, and a refusal to conform to fashion norms. The brand stands out by embracing maximalist expression in a category dominated by restraint. Loudmouth uses humor and visual play to create belonging among people who feel constrained by traditional fashion expectations.

The brand's humor is not superficial. It creates identity alignment. Patrons who wear Loudmouth are making a statement. They are rejecting seriousness and embracing playfulness. This aligns with the Jester motivation to liberate people from social rigidity. Loudmouth invites Patrons into a community that values joy, confidence, and irreverence.

You don't love someone because they're perfect, you love them in spite of the fact that they're not.

– Jodi Picoult

WELCOME

The Citizen

Often referenced as The Everyman, or Everyperson, The Citizen archetype is one of the most grounded and misunderstood forces in the entire framework. Many reduce it to the idea of being average or relatable, but the Citizen is not about mediocrity. It is about belonging. It is about the fundamental human need to be part of a group where one feels safe, valued, and understood. If the Hero rises above and the Rebel pushes against, the Citizen stands among. They represent the stabilizing psychological truth that people want to connect without pretense. They want a place in the world that feels familiar and shared. They want to belong.

Anthropologists have long studied the human need for group affiliation. Every society throughout history has formed stable groups built on shared experience, shared labor, and shared values. Belonging is not optional. It is a biological requirement. Research in evolutionary psychology shows that early human survival depended entirely on group membership. Individuals who fit in thrived. Individuals who were isolated did not. The Citizen archetype emerges from this ancient instinct. It reflects the belief that strength comes from community.

Social identity theory, developed by Henri Tajfel and John Turner, reinforces this. People define themselves through group association. Identities are constructed through the categories we place ourselves in, the groups we join, and the norms we internalize. The Citizen archetype aligns directly with this process. It is the archetype that celebrates shared identity. It makes Patrons feel that they are part of something larger without having to earn entry through achievement or uniqueness. Anyone can belong. Everyone can participate.

Psychologists studying belonging have found that the absence of belonging triggers the same neural pathways as physical pain. That is how deep the need runs. Belonging offers emotional safety. It reduces anxiety. It stabilizes identity. The Citizen archetype uses this psychological foundation to create environments where Patrons feel welcomed, included, and understood. This is not superficial inclusivity. It is the feeling of coming home.

Culturally, the Citizen archetype is represented by characters who ground the narrative. They may not have extraordinary abilities, but they possess extraordinary humanity. They reflect the lives of everyday people and remind audiences that ordinary experience has value. The Citizen archetype elevates normalcy by showing its meaning. It anchors the story in shared human experience.

In branding, the Citizen archetype is powerful because it offers consistency, familiarity, and emotional safety. Citizen brands succeed by making the Patron feel that they are not alone. They speak the Patron's language. They reflect the Patron's life. They invite participation. And above all, they do not posture. They do not celebrate exclusivity. They do not elevate themselves above their audience. They stand beside them.

The Citizen archetype is not about being plain. It is about being real. It is about being stable in a world that increasingly feels unstable. It creates trust because it behaves like a partner, not a performer. When a brand embodies the Citizen archetype with honesty and humility, it becomes a social anchor. It becomes familiar. It becomes part of the Patron's life.

That is why the Citizen belongs in the Foster Belonging quadrant. It creates connection not through humor or emotional intensity but through recognition. The Citizen does not need to impress. The Citizen needs to include. And inclusion, when genuine, is one of the most powerful psychological drivers in human behavior.

Motivations of the Citizen Archetype

The Citizen archetype is motivated by connection. They want to create environments where people feel recognized and accepted. This motivation is rooted in the psychological fact that belonging is a basic human need. Citizen brands seek to remove social barriers and eliminate feelings of inferiority or exclusion. They want everyone to feel comfortable participating.

Another core motivation is equality. Citizen brands reject hierarchy. They reject elitism. They reject the idea that value is determined by status. They gravitate toward fairness and shared experience. This aligns with research in moral psychology, which shows that fairness is one of the primary moral intuitions across cultures.

The Citizen is also motivated by stability. They value reliability, predictability, and consistency. These qualities create emotional safety. Citizen brands offer dependable experiences that reduce uncertainty, which is essential in environments where unpredictability creates stress.

Another motivation is community. Citizen brands build environments where people can connect with one another, not just with the brand. They facilitate interaction, cooperation, and shared participation.

Finally, the Citizen archetype is motivated by humility. They do not want to dominate or outperform. They want to support. They want to uplift. They want to create shared success rather than individual spotlight.

Strengths of the Citizen Archetype

Relatability

Citizen brands excel at making people feel seen, understood, and included. Their relatability stems from an intentional absence of pretense. They communicate in everyday language, design accessible experiences, and avoid aspirational posturing. This makes the brand feel human rather than corporate. Customers interpret this approach as authenticity rather than strategic positioning. They feel as though the brand operates in the same world they do. This emotional proximity strengthens trust because customers do not feel judged, intimidated, or excluded. The Citizen brand feels like a peer rather than a performer.

Relatability also broadens the Citizen's appeal. Because the brand does not try to be elite, edgy, or exclusive, it resonates with a wide range of people. The Citizen occupies a unique psychological space: it offers comfort through familiarity. When the world feels chaotic or brands feel distant, the Citizen becomes a stabilizing presence. Customers gravitate toward what feels familiar, and no archetype embodies familiarity more naturally than the Citizen. Relatability therefore becomes both a differentiator and an invitation.

Resilience

Citizen brands carry a grounded resilience that feels honest rather than heroic.

Their strength comes not from grand gestures or bold reinventions but from consistency, steady effort, and the ability to withstand cultural shifts without losing their identity. Resilience emerges from reliability. Customers trust Citizen brands because they remain stable even as trends change. They do not attempt constant reinvention or chase the latest cultural wave. Instead, they focus on delivering value predictably and sincerely.

This resilience also helps Citizen brands weather crises more effectively than many archetypes. Their grounded nature prevents dramatic overreactions. They acknowledge challenges openly, adapt pragmatically, and continue serving customers without theatrics. Patrons appreciate this stability, especially in industries where volatility is common. A Citizen brand feels dependable in moments when others feel shaky. Over time, this steady resilience becomes a cornerstone of loyalty because customers know exactly what to expect and trust the brand to show up consistently.

Empathy

Empathy is embedded into the Citizen brand's worldview. They do not speak down to customers, and they do not preach. They listen. They understand. They reflect back what they hear. This deep empathy allows the Citizen to design experiences that feel intuitive and comforting. Because they prioritize real human need over marketing sophistication, their products and services often feel more genuinely helpful than those offered by brands that rely heavily on polished narrative or technical superiority. Customers feel cared for because the brand shapes its behavior around human understanding rather than brand ego.

Empathy also drives customer service. Citizen brands often lead with patience, humility, and grace when solving problems. Their representatives speak like real people rather than scripted interfaces. This reinforces belonging because customers feel treated with dignity, not handled. Empathy becomes a connective tissue that strengthens relationships by ensuring the brand never forgets the human on the other end of the interaction.

Authenticity

Authenticity defines the Citizen brand's personality. They avoid exaggeration, over dramatization, and unnecessary embellishment. Their communications are direct. Their promises are realistic. Their tone feels grounded and honest. Customers respond to this transparency because it signals integrity in a landscape where brands often overstate or oversell. The Citizen does not pretend to be more glamorous, disruptive, or intellectual than it is. That simplicity becomes a strategic advantage. People trust what feels true.

Authenticity also fosters a sense of reliability. When a brand consistently delivers what it says it will, in a tone that matches its behavior, customers develop confidence in its character. Citizen brands rarely face criticism for overpromising because they never position themselves as something they are not. Their humility is refreshing. While other archetypes chase distinction through innovation or intensity, the Citizen earns loyalty by simply being honest and consistent. Authenticity becomes the brand's quiet superpower.

Community Building

Citizen brands excel at building communities because they make belonging easy and natural. Their inclusive tone, accessible identity, and emotionally safe environment encourage customers to engage with one another as peers. The Citizen does not foster community by elevating certain members above others. It creates a level playing field where every voice matters. This egalitarian approach attracts people who value camaraderie over clout. As a result, the brand's community becomes authentic, diverse, and self sustaining.

Community also shapes the way Citizen brands show up publicly. They often champion local causes, support everyday people, and celebrate shared experiences that resonate across broad audiences. The brand becomes a gathering point for people who want to feel part of something collective rather than exclusive. Citizen communities grow not because the brand demands loyalty, but because the brand feels like home. This sense of belonging translates into repeat behavior, word of mouth, and emotional affinity that is difficult for competitors to replicate.

Challenges of the Citizen Archetype

Mediocrity

The Citizen's greatest strength, its universal appeal, can easily slide into mediocrity when the brand avoids strong opinions, bold decisions, or differentiation for fear of alienating someone. When the brand tries too hard to be for everyone, it becomes unremarkable. Messaging loses sharpness. Visual identity loses impact. The brand blends into its category instead of standing out. Customers may appreciate the familiarity, but they rarely become passionate advocates for brands that feel indistinct.

This mediocrity also weakens internal identity. Teams may lack clarity about what makes the brand special because everything feels moderate and safe. Without a strong center, innovation stalls. Decisions become passive rather than intentional. The brand slowly drifts into irrelevance not because it failed, but because it never committed to anything meaningful enough to form lasting emotional memory. The Citizen must learn that relatability does not require blandness.

Over Identification

Citizen brands can become overly dependent on mirroring their audience. When taken too far, this over identification prevents the brand from leading because it becomes reactive to customer sentiment. Instead of shaping culture, it simply reflects it. This makes the brand feel like a follower rather than a guide. Over identification results in watered down positioning because the brand constantly adapts to the customer instead of standing firm in its own identity.

Internally, over identification complicates decision making. The brand becomes hesitant to make moves that might disrupt the harmony it values. It loses the confidence needed to set direction and becomes overly influenced by vocal customer segments or shifting trends. For a Citizen brand to thrive, it must pair empathy with backbone. Mirroring builds connection. Over mirroring erases identity.

Risk Aversion

Citizen brands often value stability so highly that they avoid risk entirely. This conservatism protects the brand from dramatic failure but also prevents breakthroughs. While competitors innovate boldly, the Citizen lingers in the familiar, believing that safety ensures longevity. In fast moving categories, this risk aversion causes the brand to lag behind. Customers begin to perceive the brand as outdated or unimaginative.

Risk aversion also stifles team creativity. Employees may feel discouraged from proposing ambitious ideas because the brand defaults to what has worked in the past. Without the willingness to experiment, the Citizen loses its ability to refresh itself. A brand that avoids risk cannot evolve meaningfully. The Citizen must learn that risk, when grounded in purpose, is compatible with stability.

Lack of Distinction

When a Citizen brand leans too heavily on universality, it becomes difficult to differentiate from competitors who hold similar values. The brand may rely on generic messages about quality, fairness, or community that could appear on any competitor's website. This lack of distinction weakens market positioning and makes customers indifferent. They may like the brand, but they do not feel compelled to choose it over alternatives.

Distinction requires identity, not neutrality. The Citizen must identify the aspects of its worldview that are uniquely its own. Without this clarity, the brand loses competitive advantage and blends into the background. Customers cannot rally around something that feels indistinct. The Citizen must claim a point of view within its relatability.

Inertia

Citizen brands sometimes move so slowly that they drift into inactivity. Their comfort with what is familiar creates organizational inertia, which delays decisions, weakens innovation, and reduces responsiveness. While the brand may feel grounded, customers experience it as stagnant. Inertia is dangerous because it happens quietly. The brand may still be beloved, but it becomes predictable to the point of irrelevance. Patrons begin seeking alternatives that offer freshness and energy.

Internally, inertia demotivates teams. Employees sense when the brand is moving without momentum. They may feel their work contributes to maintenance rather than progress. This erodes enthusiasm and limits talent attraction. The Citizen must learn to introduce periodic bursts of energy without compromising its grounded identity. Stability without movement is not stability. It is stall.

In Practice: People & Characters

Forrest Gump

Forrest Gump is one of the clearest depictions of the Citizen archetype in modern storytelling. His appeal lies in his simplicity, sincerity, and groundedness. Forrest does not aspire to extraordinary status. He moves through life with humility and consistency, embodying the values of decency and reliability that anchor the Citizen archetype. His perspective invites audiences to reconnect with the fundamentals of being human. In a world that complicates meaning, Forrest simplifies it through action rather than ambition.

Forrest also creates belonging wherever he goes. People trust him because he does not judge or pretend. He offers steady presence. Research on social bonding shows that people form attachments more readily with those who display sincerity and predictability. Forrest represents these traits fully. His ordinariness becomes his strength, demonstrating that dignity exists in everyday life.

Oprah

Oprah expresses the Citizen archetype through emotional accessibility and shared experience. Her influence is grounded in her ability to reflect the lives and struggles of her audience. Oprah speaks with people, not at them. This creates a sense of communal identity. Her interviews, conversations, and platform amplify the belief that everyone has a story worth hearing. This aligns with social identity research which shows that people feel greater belonging when they see themselves reflected in cultural narratives.

Oprah's success is built on consistency and authenticity. She does not rely on shock or superiority. She creates connection by normalizing vulnerability. This positions her not as a distant figure but as a relatable one. The Citizen archetype thrives on this type of relational humility. Oprah makes people feel included, which is the central promise of the Citizen.

Jim Halpert

Jim Halpert represents the Citizen archetype in a corporate setting. He is the relatable figure in The Office, offering a grounded and accessible perspective on everyday work life. Jim does not seek power or prestige. He seeks connection, fairness, and normalcy. His humor and observations create one of the key functions of the Citizen archetype. They reflect the shared experience of the group.

Jim also embodies the Citizen's desire for stability and belonging. He is motivated by relationships rather than ambition. His loyalty to his coworkers and his commitment to the group's well being reflect the core Citizen instinct. In narrative structure, Jim serves as the anchor that allows audiences to feel connected to the environment. He represents the viewer's perspective and gives voice to the common experience.

In Practice: Brands

Zoom

Zoom embodies the Citizen archetype through accessibility and connection. The platform became essential during periods of isolation because it facilitated human contact in the most straightforward and universal way. Zoom does not rely on sophisticated branding. It relies on familiarity, simplicity, and reliability. Its value lies in its ability to make people feel closer, whether in personal, educational, or professional settings.

Zoom's design philosophy reflects the Citizen's prioritization of ease and inclusivity. Its interface is intuitive and non intimidating, and it removes barriers to participation. This simplicity reinforces emotional safety. In a period where connection became fragile, Zoom acted as a stabilizing force. It created belonging by enabling groups to gather easily and consistently.

Home Depot

Home Depot expresses the Citizen archetype through approachability and empowerment of everyday people. The brand's core message, that customers can complete projects themselves, reflects the Citizen's belief that capability is shared, not exclusive. Home Depot creates belonging by inviting people of all skill levels to participate in building and repairing their own spaces.

The brand also demonstrates the Citizen's value of community. Home Depot stores are designed to feel navigable, helpful, and non elitist. Employees offer guidance without condescension. The brand's reliability, consistency, and everyday practicality align with the stability Patrons expect from a Citizen archetype. It succeeds by being a dependable partner in routine life.

Southwest Airlines

Southwest Airlines represents the Citizen archetype through humility, friendliness, and accessibility. The airline avoids pretension and prioritizes fairness through transparent pricing and customer friendly policies. Southwest focuses on treating all passengers with equal respect, which aligns with the Citizen's motivation toward equality and shared experience.

The brand also fosters community through its culture of humor and service. Its employees are known for being authentic and personable, not polished or corporate. This creates emotional safety for passengers. Southwest's identity as the airline that treats people like people positions it firmly within the Citizen archetype. It does not attempt to impress. It attempts to welcome.

Being deeply loved by someone gives you strength, while loving someone deeply gives you courage.

– Lao Tzu

The Lover

The Lover archetype is often reduced to romance, sensuality, or affection, but the true Lover is much more profound than sentimentality. The Lover represents the core human drive to form deep emotional bonds. Not attraction. Attachment. The Lover is about connection that feels meaningful, embodied, and emotionally vivid. It is about the experience of being seen and valued. The Lover archetype exists because humans are wired for intimacy, both emotional and sensory. It reflects the universal desire to experience life with richness, depth, and presence.

The psychological foundation of the Lover lies in attachment theory. John Bowlby's research on attachment demonstrated that humans require secure emotional relationships to function well. Connection provides stability, reduces anxiety, and strengthens resilience. The Lover archetype activates this need by offering emotional presence. It tells the Patron, you matter here. You are valued. You belong in a personal way. Where the Citizen promises group belonging, the Lover promises individual connection. It creates closeness by recognizing the Patron personally and emotionally.

Neuroscience offers another layer of insight. Studies on reward pathways show that sensory pleasure activates dopamine and oxytocin, which enhance feelings of bonding and affection. The Lover archetype uses sensory experience as emotional communication. Colors, textures, sounds, and language become signals of warmth and care. This is why Lover brands often pay meticulous attention to aesthetics. Beauty is not superficial in the Lover archetype. It is a form of emotional architecture.

Anthropologists have also noted that rituals of affection and beauty are universal. Cultures across the world use symbols, adornment, and sensory markers to express care, value, and relationship. The Lover archetype draws from these traditions by using experience to communicate devotion. It is not about seduction. It is about significance. It reflects the belief that emotional intensity deepens meaning.

Narrative literature reinforces this. The Lover archetype is not simply the romantic figure. It is the one who cares deeply enough to invest emotion, attention, and presence into their relationships. The Lover brings fullness to moments. They elevate experience by paying attention to small details that others overlook. They create meaning by creating closeness.

In branding, the Lover archetype is one of the most powerful tools for emotional loyalty. Lover brands do not appeal to reason. They appeal to feeling. They do not compete with utility driven logic. They compete by making people feel cherished, understood, and emotionally enriched. The Lover archetype creates affinity that is difficult to break because it speaks to the part of the human psyche that craves connection.

The Lover does not seek admiration. The Lover seeks closeness. The Lover invites people into a world where beauty, affection, and emotional presence are not luxuries but expressions of value. This is why the Lover belongs in the Foster Belonging quadrant. It fosters belonging not through community or play, but through intimacy. It creates belonging one person at a time.

Motivations of the Lover Archetype

The Lover archetype is motivated by emotional connection. Lover brands want to form deep, personal relationships with Patrons. Their goal is not reach. Their goal is resonance. They seek to make Patrons feel seen, valued, and emotionally understood.

Another core motivation is sensory richness. Lover brands believe experiences should be vivid and embodied. They prioritize the senses because sensory depth enhances emotional memory. Psychologists have demonstrated that multisensory experiences increase retention and emotional intensity. Lover brands use this to create moments that feel meaningful.

The Lover is also motivated by devotion. They invest in relationships. They nurture them. They maintain presence. This devotion creates consistent emotional reliability for the Patron. It reflects the attachment dynamics identified by Bowlby. Emotional availability builds trust.

Another motivation is beauty. Beauty is not merely aesthetic. It is a symbol of care. The Lover archetype uses beauty to communicate intention and intimacy. When something is made beautiful, it signals that the Patron is worth the effort.

Finally, the Lover is motivated by meaning. They want experiences to feel significant. They do not value efficiency or minimalism. They value depth, emotion, and attention. Lover brands transform ordinary interactions into emotionally resonant moments.

Strengths of the Lover Archetype

Deep Emotional Connection

Lover brands excel at cultivating emotional bonds that feel personal rather than transactional. Their messaging speaks directly to the desires, dreams, and vulnerabilities of their audience. They do not sell products. They sell feelings. This creates loyalty rooted in identity rather than convenience. Patrons return because the relationship feels reciprocal and emotionally meaningful. Lover brands understand that trust forms when people feel recognized, valued, and emotionally seen. This emotional recognition becomes their strategic advantage.

Their ability to create these connections often elevates even simple offerings. A Lover brand can turn a routine purchase into a ritual because the emotional tone of the experience resonates. When people feel held by a brand, they stay close. Lover brands master that closeness.

Appreciation of Beauty

Beauty is not superficial for Lover brands. It is strategic. They understand that aesthetic quality shapes emotional perception. Their design choices communicate warmth, allure, and sensory pleasure. Colors, textures, photography, language, and packaging all contribute to a brand world that feels inviting and emotionally rich. Beauty builds desire. Desire builds loyalty.

This aesthetic sensitivity also gives Lover brands a strong competitive differentiator. In crowded categories, they stand apart by crafting experiences that awaken the senses. Whether through visual storytelling or tactile detail, they create emotional resonance that competitors cannot replicate because it emerges from coherent, intentional beauty.

Passion and Zeal

Lover brands speak with energy that feels alive. Their tone is expressive, heartfelt, and unafraid of intensity. This passion gives them a magnetism that attracts people who want more than functional value. Passion signals belief. When a brand's enthusiasm is palpable, Patrons lean in. The Lover archetype thrives in categories where desire, joy, and personal meaning matter more than efficiency or utility.

This zeal also shows up inside the organization. Lover brands often build cultures where creativity, emotional intelligence, and enthusiasm are celebrated. Employees feel the brand's heartbeat as strongly as customers do. Passion creates coherence. Coherence creates authenticity.

Romantic Idealism

Romantic idealism gives Lover brands the ability to imagine the best version of human experience and design toward it. They are aspirational, not in the corporate sense, but in the emotional sense. Their campaigns envision love, belonging, connection, and beauty as achievable realities. This elevates their positioning from product to promise. A Lover brand does not simply offer something attractive. It offers a more beautiful life.

This idealism also strengthens storytelling. Lover brands create narratives that uplift the audience, inviting them to step into an emotionally richer world. The promise of something more meaningful becomes a strategic differentiator that shields them from commoditization.

Sensuality

Sensuality gives Lover brands the ability to create immersive, memorable experiences through sensory design. They understand how texture, tone, scent, flavor, lighting, sound, and movement influence emotion. Sensuality is a strategic tool that deepens the brand relationship. It encourages Patrons to slow down and engage physically as well as emotionally.

When executed well, sensuality creates brand addiction. Patrons crave the way the brand makes them feel. This creates repeat behavior not through habit, but through desire. Lover brands curate experiences that feel indulgent, intimate, and rewarding, which elevates both preference and willingness to pay.

Challenges of the Lover Archetype

Overwhelming Emotions

Lover brands can become overly emotional in tone, saturating every touchpoint with intensity that overwhelms rather than attracts. When everything is dramatic, nothing feels meaningful. Emotion loses impact when not balanced with clarity. Brands that lean too heavily into sentimentality may lose credibility with audiences who require grounding and substance. Excess emotion also risks alienating people who prefer subtlety or who distrust brands that appear too intimate too quickly.

Lover brands must learn to calibrate emotion, using it intentionally rather than excessively. Emotional resonance should enhance the brand, not drown it.

Dependency

Lover brands sometimes build their identity too tightly around their audience's affection. They become dependent on emotional validation, shaping offerings, tone, and strategy around pleasing customers at any cost. This leads to inconsistency and reactive decision making. The brand becomes overly accommodating, losing its own identity in an attempt to preserve closeness.

Dependency also creates vulnerability. If trends shift or sentiment changes, the brand may scramble to reassert emotional connection and lose strategic stability. Lover brands must cultivate emotional maturity, where connection is nurtured without erasing internal direction.

Jealousy

Jealousy in branding appears as competitiveness rooted in insecurity rather than strategy. Lover brands may react strongly when competitors encroach on their emotional territory. They may overcorrect with louder messaging, grander gestures, or more intense campaigns, hoping to reclaim attention. This reaction can distort the brand's natural tone and make it feel desperate rather than confident.

Jealousy also appears when brands mimic competitors or try to dominate emotional space. True Lover brands thrive when they stay anchored to their own vision of connection, not when they chase or compare. Jealousy weakens their authenticity.

Vulgarity

When Lover brands misuse sensuality or emotional expression, they risk sliding into vulgarity. This occurs when the brand leans too far into shock, explicitness, or exaggerated intimacy. The experience becomes uncomfortable rather than inviting. Sensuality without restraint feels cheap. Emotional expression without nuance feels forced.

Vulgarity damages trust because it signals that the brand values reaction more than relationship. Lover brands must understand that intimacy is earned through subtlety, not spectacle. The goal is allure, not intrusion.

Idealization

Lover brands often idealize love, beauty, or connection to the point that their promises become unrealistic. Idealization creates expectations the brand cannot deliver. When the lived experience does not match the emotional narrative, customers feel let down rather than uplifted. This gap between expectation and reality erodes loyalty.

Idealization also traps the brand in a fantasy world where everything is flawless and emotionally elevated. As a result, the brand struggles to address real customer frustrations, operational issues, or imperfections. True Lover brands must balance aspiration with authenticity. Otherwise, they become dream merchants rather than meaningful partners.

In Practice: People & Characters

Marilyn Monroe

Marilyn Monroe is an iconic expression of the Lover archetype because she represented emotional warmth, sensuality, and vulnerability simultaneously. Her public persona combined beauty and softness with a genuine desire for connection. Audiences responded not just to her appearance but to the emotional depth beneath it. Monroe conveyed a longing to be understood that resonated deeply. Psychologists who study parasocial relationships note that vulnerability fosters stronger emotional bonds with audiences. Monroe embodied this instinctively.

Monroe also used sensory presence as communication. Her voice, mannerisms, style, and movement conveyed emotional richness. These sensory qualities made her memorable because they created a feeling rather than simply an image. This aligns with the Lover archetype's reliance on sensory depth to create emotional resonance. Monroe's legacy endures not because she performed beauty, but because she expressed humanity through it.

Jay Gatsby

Jay Gatsby epitomizes the Lover archetype through his devotion and idealization of connection. Gatsby's longing for Daisy is not surface level affection. It is symbolic. He constructs his entire identity around the pursuit of emotional meaning. This reflects the Lover's motivation to elevate experience beyond the ordinary. Gatsby's mansion, parties, and aesthetic choices are expressions of the Lover instinct to create beauty as a way of attracting closeness.

Gatsby also demonstrates the Lover's vulnerability. His emotional world is shaped by longing, hope, and heartbreak. Literary scholars have noted that Gatsby's tragedy lies in his emotional idealism. He believes in the transformative power of love so strongly that he cannot accept a world where it does not deliver meaning. This intensity reflects both the strength and the fragility of the Lover archetype.

Princess Anna

Princess Anna from Frozen represents the Lover archetype through her warmth, optimism, and emotional devotion to her relationships. Anna consistently prioritizes connection over fear. She seeks closeness even when it exposes her to rejection or danger. This aligns with attachment theory, which describes secure individuals as those willing to risk vulnerability for the sake of connection.

Anna also embodies the Lover's sensory presence. She reacts to the world with enthusiasm and emotional openness, creating a sense of immediacy and joy. Her actions are driven by love for her sister, illustrating how the Lover archetype invests deeply in personal bonds. Anna demonstrates that the Lover is not limited to romance. It is the archetype of authentic emotional engagement in any form.

In Practice: Brands

Tiffany

Tiffany is one of the most iconic Lover brands in the world. Its identity is built around intimacy, beauty, and emotional significance. The signature blue box is not packaging. It is a symbol of devotion. Psychologists note that symbolic meaning enhances emotional intensity. Tiffany uses symbolism to transform simple objects into cherished experiences.

The brand also uses sensory immersion to create emotional memory. The colors, materials, lighting, and environment within Tiffany stores are designed to evoke calmness, romance, and meaning. Tiffany's emphasis on ritual, such as gift giving and engagement, reflects the Lover's role in transforming moments into memories. It is not the jewelry that people remember. It is the emotion surrounding it.

Hallmark

Hallmark embodies the Lover archetype through emotional communication. The brand exists to help people express affection, gratitude, and connection. Hallmark cards are not functional products. They are emotional vessels. Research on expressive writing and emotional disclosure shows that articulating feelings strengthens relationships. Hallmark facilitates this expression.

The brand also uses storytelling as a tool for emotional bonding. Hallmark movies and holiday traditions reinforce the belief that emotional connection is central to a meaningful life. The brand's reliability in evoking warmth and sentiment positions it firmly within the Lover archetype. It offers Patrons a safe emotional space in a world that often devalues vulnerability.

Dove Chocolate

Dove Chocolate expresses the Lover archetype through sensory indulgence and emotional comfort. The brand positions chocolate not as a treat but as a moment of personal care. This aligns with psychological research on sensory pleasure, which shows that taste and texture can evoke emotional soothing through the release of dopamine and oxytocin.

Dove also uses messaging that emphasizes warmth, affirmation, and self affection. The brand's focus on savoring moments, slowing down, and caring for oneself reflects the Lover's belief that experiences matter. Dove transforms an everyday product into a ritual of emotional nourishment. This positions the brand as a quiet but powerful embodiment of the Lover archetype.

CHAPTER 07

Quadrant: Exert Control

The Exert Control quadrant brings order, safety, and reliability. These archetypes anchor customers during uncertainty and provide clarity when complexity overwhelms. The Sovereign creates systems and establishes direction. The Creator brings discipline, form, and intentional design into the world. The Caregiver offers protection, empathy, and reassurance. Together, these archetypes create stability that customers rely on deeply.

This quadrant becomes especially attractive when other quadrants create imbalance. The chaos of the Change the World quadrant can overwhelm. The introspection of the Find Fulfillment quadrant can create indecision. The emotional openness of the Foster Belonging quadrant can feel unanchored. Psychological research from Daniel Kahneman and Paul Bloom shows that people seek certainty and structure when faced with unpredictability. Exert Control brands meet this need by providing predictability and reducing cognitive load.

Jung emphasized the importance of grounding forces during periods of psychological expansion. Stability balances transformation. Clarity balances exploration. Protection balances vulnerability. People turn toward Exert Control brands when their lives feel overstimulated, disorganized, or emotionally burdened. These archetypes provide a sense of safety that allows customers to function without fear or confusion. Research in consumer trust confirms this. During economic instability or cultural uncertainty, customers gravitate toward brands that signal authority, competence, and reliability.

When balanced, this quadrant empowers. When excessive, it restricts. Structure can free or confine depending on how it is used. Brands in the Exert Control quadrant must understand that their power is significant. Their discipline, clarity, and consistency create worlds where customers can thrive. Their greatest responsibility is to maintain order without diminishing possibility.

You can accomplish by kindness
what you cannot by force.

– Publilius Syrus

The Caregiver

The Caregiver archetype is one of the most essential forces in human psychology because it is rooted in the instinct to protect, nurture, and sustain life. Unlike archetypes that seek transformation, autonomy, or achievement, the Caregiver seeks safety. The Caregiver is the emotional foundation of human survival. Long before there were societies, economies, or institutions, humans depended entirely on caregiving for their lives. Infants cannot survive alone. Vulnerable people cannot thrive without support. Every culture on earth elevates caregiving as a moral priority because without it, nothing else is possible.

The psychological basis of the Caregiver comes from attachment theory and evolutionary biology. Human infants are born more helpless than any other mammal. This vulnerability shaped the development of parental instincts and social cooperation. John Bowlby's research demonstrated that secure attachment forms when caregivers provide consistent protection, attention, and responsiveness. This attachment forms the foundation of psychological stability throughout life. The Caregiver archetype expresses this instinct. It is the part of the human psyche that finds meaning in protecting others and providing what they need to grow.

Frans de Waal, a leading primatologist, has shown that caregiving behavior is not limited to humans. Species across the animal kingdom demonstrate altruism, protection, and nurturing. This suggests a deep evolutionary origin. The Caregiver archetype is not cultural. It is biological. It reflects the need to preserve life through cooperation and compassion. In human societies, this instinct becomes formalized in roles such as parents, teachers, guardians, nurses, mentors, and community leaders.

Caregiving is also central to moral psychology. Researchers such as Jonathan Haidt have shown that one of the foundational moral intuitions across cultures is care and harm. People are morally motivated to protect the vulnerable and prevent harm. This instinct shapes laws, customs, and ethical norms. The Caregiver archetype embodies this moral intuition by elevating compassion above ambition. It prioritizes the well being of others and creates environments where people feel safe.

In narrative traditions, the Caregiver provides stability and emotional grounding.

They are the ones who offer comfort in times of crisis, guidance in moments of confusion, and protection when the stakes are highest. They rarely seek recognition. Their value is measured in the growth and safety of those they support. The Caregiver archetype ensures that characters survive both physically and emotionally.

In branding, the Caregiver archetype is powerful because it builds trust through reliability, empathy, and service. Caregiver brands position themselves as protectors. They communicate reassurance. They demonstrate dependability. They anticipate needs. And above all, they create environments where Patrons feel secure. This emotional safety is not a marketing tactic. It is the psychological foundation of loyalty. Patrons stay close to brands that make them feel cared for.

The Caregiver does not lead through force. They lead through presence. They do not compete through speed. They compete through consistency. They do not inspire through challenge. They inspire through compassion. The Caregiver archetype offers belonging through protection and emotional steadiness. It creates a world where Patrons can breathe, trust, and rest.

Motivations of the Caregiver Archetype

The Caregiver is motivated by compassion. They feel a genuine responsibility for the well being of others. This is not sympathy. It is stewardship. Caregiver brands believe it is their role to provide safety, comfort, and guidance.

Another core motivation is protection. Caregivers seek to prevent harm. They act as shields, buffers, and stabilizers. This aligns with moral intuition research that shows harm prevention is one of the primary triggers of human moral behavior.

The Caregiver is also motivated by service. They find meaning in supporting others. They do not seek recognition. They find fulfillment in ensuring that others can grow, succeed, or recover.

Another motivation is dependability. Caregivers value consistency and reliability. They want people to trust them completely. This drive for reliability shapes their behavior, communication, and decisions.

Finally, the Caregiver is motivated by empathy. They are attuned to emotional states. They listen. They understand. They anticipate needs before they are expressed. This emotional intelligence strengthens their ability to provide meaningful support.

Strengths of the Caregiver Archetype

Empathy and Compassion

Caregiver brands excel at understanding what their Patrons feel before those Patrons articulate it. Their communications anticipate emotional needs and respond with warmth, reassurance, and clarity. This attunement builds trust by signaling that the brand genuinely cares about the person behind the transaction. Caregiver brands treat their audience as humans, not market segments, and that human centered view shapes every touchpoint from service tone to product design. This emotional intelligence makes the brand feel safe and steady.

Empathy also allows Caregiver brands to excel during moments of uncertainty or stress. When competitors focus on features or claims, Caregiver brands focus on comfort. Their compassion becomes a differentiator because Patrons associate the brand with support during difficult times. In industries where anxiety runs high, such as healthcare, finance, or family services, this emotional grounding becomes a powerful strategic asset.

Selflessness

Caregiver brands place the Patron's well being at the center of their decisions. They are willing to invest in service, quality, and support even when those investments are not the most cost efficient options. This selflessness creates goodwill. Patrons feel the difference between a brand that cares about their outcome and a brand that cares about conversion rates. Caregiver brands win long term loyalty because people remember how they were treated more than what they bought.

This selfless posture also shapes operational culture. Employees who work within Caregiver brands often feel empowered to go above and beyond. The brand's identity encourages service excellence by prioritizing humanity over rigid systems. When employees feel trusted to care, the brand's service experience becomes consistently warm and emotionally intelligent.

Nurturing Skills

Caregiver brands excel at building environments where people feel guided, supported, and understood. Their onboarding flows are clearer, their instructions more thoughtful, and their service interactions more patient. They turn complexity into comfort. Whether walking a Patron through a difficult decision or helping them recover from a poor experience, Caregiver brands nurture confidence by meeting people where they are without judgment.

This nurturing extends into brand design. Visual language feels calm, copy feels reassuring, and navigation feels intuitive. Caregiver brands remove friction and emotional strain. They create experiences that feel as if someone has already considered the user's anxieties and addressed them proactively. This makes the brand feel genuinely supportive rather than superficially pleasant.

Steadfast Support

Steadfast support manifests as reliability. Caregiver brands show up consistently, not only when things are going well. Their messaging remains calm during cultural turbulence. Their service remains strong during operational strain. Patrons rely on the brand because it is steady in moments when competitors falter. This constancy builds emotional loyalty that is far harder to disrupt than transactional loyalty.

Steadfast support also influences brand voice. Caregiver brands speak with a grounded, confident tone that communicates commitment. They make promises carefully and fulfill them fully. Patrons feel the stability of the brand's character, which increases trust and reduces perceived risk in choosing the brand over alternatives.

Healing Touch

The "healing touch" of a Caregiver brand is the ability to reduce emotional stress. This can take the form of a thoughtfully resolved customer issue, a soothing store environment, or communications that lower pressure rather than heighten it. Healing is not only emotional. It can be functional. Caregiver brands repair frustrations, remove friction, and create pathways that make life easier for Patrons.

This healing quality becomes a magnet for customers who feel overwhelmed by life's demands. When a brand offers even a small sense of relief, people return. Caregiver brands understand this intuitively. They do not sell products or services. They sell peace of mind.

Challenges of the Caregiver Archetype

Over Attachment

Caregiver brands can become too emotionally involved with their audience's needs. This leads to over customization, over accommodation, and operational strain. When a brand tries to solve every problem for every Patron, it loses its own strategic boundaries. Over attachment makes the brand reactive rather than proactive, responding to every emotional signal instead of making disciplined decisions about what truly serves the mission.

This can also lead to brand dilution. In trying to please everyone, the brand becomes everything and nothing at once. Caregiver brands must learn to support without sacrificing identity.

Neglect of Self

Caregiver brands often neglect their own sustainability. They pour resources into support without building the infrastructure needed to maintain it. This results in overwhelmed teams, underfunded initiatives, and service quality that eventually falters. In branding terms, self neglect appears as underinvestment in innovation, weak margins, or emotional overextension in marketing.

A Caregiver brand that does not take care of itself cannot take care of others. It must balance generosity with operational discipline.

Boundary Issues

Caregiver brands sometimes blur the line between helpful and overinvolved. They may push too far into the Patron's emotional space or attempt to solve problems the Patron is not asking to solve. This can feel intrusive rather than supportive. Boundary issues also emerge in customer service when staff are expected to absorb emotional burdens beyond what is healthy or strategic.

Without boundaries, the Caregiver brand becomes unsustainable and its messaging becomes overly sentimental. Boundaries preserve clarity.

Martyr Complex

The martyr complex appears when a Caregiver brand positions itself as the only one who "truly cares" or uses emotional suffering as a differentiator. This tone feels manipulative. It undermines credibility by framing the brand as a victim rather than a leader. Martyrdom shifts the story from service to self dramatization.

A strong Caregiver brand must demonstrate support through action, not posture. Martyrdom erodes trust because it centers the brand's sacrifice instead of the Patron's well being.

Self Righteousness

When Caregiver brands believe their compassion grants them moral superiority, they drift into self righteousness. This manifests as judgmental messaging, emotionally loaded comparisons, or sanctimonious tone. Brands that communicate as if they "care more" than competitors alienate audiences who do not want ethical pressure in their purchasing decisions.

Caregiver brands are strongest when humility guides their voice. Self righteousness replaces empathy with ego, undermining the brand's core value.

In Practice: People & Characters

Mother Teresa

Mother Teresa represents the Caregiver archetype at its highest expression. Her life was devoted to serving the vulnerable, the sick, and the forgotten. She demonstrated the core Caregiver motivation of compassion through direct action, not rhetoric. Her commitment reflected the moral intuition of care and harm prevention. She built trust through consistency and presence. Her influence grew not because she sought power, but because she embodied service. Psycho social research often cites her work as an example of altruistic behavior driven by empathy and moral conviction.

Mother Teresa also demonstrated the Caregiver's resilience. Caregiving requires emotional endurance and the ability to persevere through suffering. Her work in challenging environments illustrated how Caregivers provide stability where others would collapse. She did not avoid human pain. She entered into it with the intention to comfort and protect. This is the essence of the Caregiver archetype.

Alfred Pennyworth

Alfred Pennyworth from the Batman narrative represents the Caregiver archetype through guidance, loyalty, and emotional grounding. Alfred is not simply a servant or butler. He is Bruce Wayne's guardian. He provides stability, counsel, and unconditional support. His presence allows Bruce to pursue his mission without losing his humanity. This reflects attachment theory. Alfred provides secure emotional grounding that allows Bruce to navigate trauma.

Alfred also embodies the Caregiver's role as moral compass. He often reminds Bruce of boundaries, empathy, and restraint. Caregivers do not just protect bodies. They protect minds. Alfred's influence ensures that Bruce does not become consumed by anger. This role demonstrates how Caregivers create psychological safety in addition to physical safety.

Molly Weasley

Molly Weasley from the Harry Potter universe expresses the Caregiver archetype through nurturing, protection, and fierce devotion to family. Molly does not simply manage household life. She creates emotional warmth and security for her children and for Harry, who enters the family with deep emotional wounds. Molly's care fills the gaps left by neglect, demonstrating how Caregivers restore emotional stability.

Molly also embodies the protective side of the Caregiver archetype. When danger threatens, she becomes formidable. Her compassion transforms into defense. This reflects evolutionary caregiving behavior where protection intensifies when loved ones are at risk. Molly's ability to nurture and defend demonstrates the full spectrum of the Caregiver's psychological role.

In Practice: Brands

Allstate

Allstate expresses the Caregiver archetype through protection and reassurance. The brand positions itself as a guardian against harm, reflecting the core Caregiver motivation to shield Patrons from danger. Its messaging focuses on safety, security, and the promise of support when things go wrong. Insurance brands inherently align with caregiving because they exist to mitigate risk, but Allstate strengthens this alignment by communicating with warmth and reliability.

Allstate also differentiates itself through consistency and emotional reassurance. Patrons trust Allstate because it embodies the qualities they seek in a protector. Dependability. Responsibility. Presence. Allstate does not promise excitement. It promises safety. That is the Caregiver archetype at work.

Moms on Call

Moms on Call is a Caregiver brand grounded in guidance and emotional reassurance for new parents. The brand offers structure, expertise, and calmness in a phase of life marked by uncertainty. Its guidance helps parents feel supported, reducing anxiety and increasing confidence. This aligns directly with attachment theory. Caregivers strengthen others by providing predictability and responsiveness.

The brand also embodies the Caregiver archetype through empathy. Moms on Call communicates with understanding rather than judgment. It normalizes struggle and offers practical support. This emotional intelligence builds trust and positions the brand as a comforting companion in a vulnerable stage of life.

Volvo

Volvo is one of the clearest corporate expressions of the Caregiver archetype. The brand has long prioritized safety above all else, even when competitors emphasized speed or status. Volvo's innovations in automotive safety are not statistical bragging rights. They are expressions of caregiving behavior. Protecting human life is the brand's primary motivation.

Volvo also communicates care through design, engineering, and brand messaging. The company consistently advocates for accident prevention, child safety, and responsible driving. This alignment between purpose and behavior reinforces the brand's identity as a protector. Volvo does not entertain. It safeguards. It builds trust by placing human life at the center of its decisions.

Innovation distinguishes between a leader and a follower

– Steve Jobs

The Creator

The Creator archetype is often mistaken for artistic flair, visual aesthetic, or surface level creativity, but its true psychological depth goes far beyond expression. The Creator represents the human drive to impose order on possibility. Creation is not chaos. It is control applied to imagination. It is the instinct to give structure, form, and coherence to something that would otherwise remain abstract. The Creator archetype is grounded in the belief that the world can be shaped intentionally. While other archetypes may search for meaning, discover meaning, or challenge meaning, the Creator constructs meaning. And construction is a form of control.

The roots of the Creator archetype extend into cognitive science and anthropology. Humans are the only species capable of envisioning futures that do not yet exist and then designing the steps to reach them. This ability, often called anticipatory imagination, requires both divergent thinking and disciplined ordering. Researchers like J. P. Guilford studied creativity as a structured cognitive process, not an impulsive one. His work revealed that true creativity requires the ability to regulate, refine, and build ideas into coherent systems. The Creator archetype relies on this combination of imagination and structure. Creation demands discipline as much as inspiration.

Social theorists have also noted that creation often emerges in environments where individuals exert control over materials, methods, or processes. This aligns the Creator archetype with mastery rather than spontaneity. A potter shapes clay with intention. An architect shapes space with precision. A composer shapes sound with rules. Creation is an act of authorship that organizes chaos into form. The Creator archetype expresses this psychological truth. It is not simply about generating ideas. It is about shaping them.

Creativity research conducted by Teresa Amabile supports this. She found that creative work requires expertise, intrinsic motivation, and the ability to structure ideas into meaningful outcomes. The Creator archetype activates this structured creativity. It values craft, refinement, iteration, and purposeful design. The Creator is not driven by novelty. The Creator is driven by the pursuit of an ideal that only discipline can achieve.

This is why the Creator belongs in the Exert Control quadrant. Creation requires stewardship of ideas. It requires intentionality and structure. It requires the ability to impose order on imagination. The Creator controls not people, but form. Not society, but possibility. The Creator exerts control by defining the vision, shaping the rules, and constructing systems that reflect their internal world with precision.

Many restaurant brands mistakenly adopt the Creator archetype because they associate creativity with menu innovation or food customization. They believe that if Patrons can build their own bowl, or if chefs experiment with ingredients, the brand must be a Creator. But this is a misunderstanding. Culinary creativity is not the same as the Creator archetype. Customization is not creation. It is personalization. And personalization aligns far more with the Citizen or Sovereign archetypes than with the psychological motivations of the Creator.

The Creator archetype requires an internal vision. It requires disciplined authorship. It requires the drive to build something intentional, coherent, and meticulously crafted. Most restaurant brands do not behave this way. They offer choice, not creation. They offer flavor exploration, not transformative authorship. They highlight culinary skill, but culinary skill alone does not define the Creator. Without a unifying creative philosophy, a brand cannot authentically claim this archetype.

A brand is a Creator only when it expresses mastery of craft, intentional design, and a cohesive creative worldview that permeates everything from menu to environment to communication. Most restaurants are innovators, experimenters, or personalizers. Few are true creators. Aligning a brand with the Creator archetype requires more than creativity in the kitchen. It requires creative control across the entire brand system.

This distinction matters because when a brand misidentifies itself as a Creator, it risks appearing self indulgent rather than intentional, scattered rather than visionary, and inconsistent rather than disciplined. A true Creator brand builds worlds. A true Creator brand authors experiences. A true Creator brand shapes the environment with clarity and creative authority. Creation is not the privilege of a moment. It is the practice of a worldview.

Motivations of the Creator Archetype

The Creator is motivated by self expression. They seek to communicate vision, emotion, or perspective through form. They feel compelled to make ideas visible.

Another core motivation is mastery. Creator brands value craft, precision, and skill. They believe that excellence emerges through dedication and refinement.

The Creator is also motivated by originality. They desire to produce work that is distinct, meaningful, and true to their vision. They avoid imitation.

Another motivation is imagination. Creator brands view the world as a landscape of possibility. They see potential everywhere.

Finally, the Creator is motivated by permanence. They seek to produce work that endures, whether emotionally, aesthetically, or culturally.

Strengths of the Creator Archetype

Innovative Thinking

Creator brands excel at generating new possibilities that reshape categories. Their innovation does not come from novelty for novelty's sake. It emerges from disciplined curiosity, cultural awareness, and a refusal to accept the default way things are done. They push beyond conventional thinking by identifying unmet needs or untapped emotional spaces, then translating those insights into offerings that feel fresh and meaningful. Customers see these brands as vision-setters rather than followers, and that distinction elevates their perceived value. When the Creator moves, the market watches.

This innovative thinking also becomes a stabilizing force inside the organization. Creative problem solving becomes the cultural baseline. Teams working under a Creator brand often adopt the same exploratory mindset, which encourages experimentation, iterative refinement, and intellectual freedom. Innovation becomes a habit, not a campaign. Over time, this leads to breakthroughs that not only define the brand but influence the entire category. The Creator becomes the brand that others reference when seeking inspiration, which reinforces leadership through originality.

Self Expression

Creator brands do not mimic. They express. Everything from tone of voice to visual identity to product design feels personal, deliberate, and coherent. Customers sense when a brand communicates from its own worldview rather than from a safe middle ground. This authenticity builds immediate emotional credibility. Patrons trust Creator brands because they know exactly who they are and are unafraid to reveal it. The brand's expression becomes a beacon for people who share similar values, aesthetics, or worldviews.

Self expression also strengthens differentiation. In crowded markets where competitors sound identical, the Creator stands apart simply by being itself. The brand uses its output as a form of storytelling, expressing perspective through color choices, typography, packaging, product form, and even the cadence of communication. This aesthetic and conceptual clarity gives customers something to connect with. When a Creator brand expresses itself consistently over time, its identity becomes so distinct that imitation becomes impossible.

Aesthetic Sensibility

Creator brands possess an elevated sensitivity to aesthetic harmony that permeates their entire ecosystem. They understand intuitively how design influences emotion, behavior, and perception. This aesthetic intelligence becomes a strategic asset because customers interpret beauty as intention and intention as quality. When every detail feels considered, the brand feels premium. When the visual and experiential environment feels cohesive, the brand feels trustworthy.

This sensibility also shapes the customer journey. Creator brands craft experiences that feel immersive rather than transactional. A menu layout, a product unboxing, a website flow, a storefront display, or a physical space may evoke emotion through texture, light, color, or form. Customers may not analyze these elements consciously, but they feel them. The Creator's aesthetic choices create emotional resonance that lingers long after the interaction ends. This is how Creator brands build desirability. They create worlds, not products.

Persistence

Creation requires endurance. Creator brands understand that meaningful work does not emerge fully formed. It is shaped, reshaped, tested, and refined through persistent effort. Their iterative mindset is their strength. They return to ideas repeatedly, improving them until the execution matches the vision. Customers sense this craftsmanship in the final result. They can feel when something has been labored over with care rather than assembled quickly to meet a deadline. Persistence communicates devotion to quality.

This persistence also protects the brand from stagnation. While others may abandon an idea prematurely, the Creator continues working until it becomes exceptional. This long arc of refinement produces work that stands the test of time because it is built deliberately rather than hastily. Internally, persistence becomes cultural. Teams grow accustomed to pursuing excellence rather than settling for adequacy. This creates a brand environment where quality is not an act but an identity.

Legacy Building

Creator brands think generationally rather than transactionally. They design work that will endure beyond current trends, short term pressures, or quarterly cycles. This long horizon gives their decisions greater depth and intent. They build identities, systems, and experiences that can evolve without losing their core integrity. When a brand seeks to build legacy, customers feel the weight of purpose in every touchpoint. Legacy becomes a silent signal of permanence in a world defined by impermanence.

This orientation toward longevity strengthens loyalty. Patrons admire brands that stand for something enduring and contribute meaningfully to culture. Legacy building also encourages internal teams to think beyond immediate wins. They begin designing with permanence in mind, which raises the standard across the organization. When a Creator brand commits to legacy, it positions itself not just as a participant in its category, but as a shaper of it.

Challenges of the Creator Archetype

Perfectionism

Creator brands often struggle under the weight of their own standards. Their pursuit of excellence can transform into perfectionism, delaying launches, complicating workflows, and paralyzing decision making. What begins as care becomes obsession. The brand holds ideas hostage in the name of improvement, preventing them from reaching the world. Customers never see the work because it never feels finished. In fast moving categories, these delays can be fatal. Competitors with less refined ideas but more momentum capture market share simply by showing up.

Perfectionism also creates internal strain. Teams become exhausted by constant revisions and unclear endpoints. Creativity becomes burdensome rather than inspiring. The brand's culture shifts from generative to critical, where ideas are scrutinized out of existence rather than nurtured into form. The Creator must learn that excellence requires release, not endless refinement. The world rewards work that is great and delivered, not work that is flawless and unseen.

Elitism

Creator brands risk drifting into elitism when their refined aesthetic or artistic commitment becomes exclusionary. They may unconsciously communicate that their brand is for the creatively enlightened rather than the everyday customer. This elitism alienates audiences who might otherwise appreciate the brand's craftsmanship but feel uninvited or unappreciated. When a brand positions itself above its audience, even subtly, it limits its own relevance.

Elitism also harms partnerships. When a Creator brand assumes it has superior taste or insight, collaboration becomes strained. Feedback is dismissed. Input is undervalued. Internal teams may adopt this attitude as well, creating silos or a culture where creative pedigree matters more than contribution. The brand loses its humility and, with it, its adaptability. The Creator must remember that creation is a form of service, not self elevation.

Self Doubt

Creative confidence is never constant. Creator brands frequently battle internal doubt, especially when their work invites public scrutiny. Their output feels personal, which makes judgment feel personal. This sensitivity can lead to hesitancy, inconsistency, or overcorrection. When self doubt takes hold, the brand retreats from risk, playing smaller and safer than its identity allows. Innovation slows. Expression becomes cautious. The brand loses the boldness that once made it magnetic.

Self doubt also weakens messaging. Communications may become passive, overly softened, or diluted in an attempt to avoid criticism. This diminishes the brand's voice and makes it indistinguishable from competitors who do not aim nearly as high. The Creator must understand that doubt is part of the creative process but cannot be allowed to govern brand expression. Confidence must rise from clarity, not applause.

Tunnel Vision

The Creator's strength in focus can become tunnel vision when it narrows too tightly around a single idea, aesthetic, or philosophy. When the brand becomes obsessed with perfecting one direction, it may miss emerging cultural shifts or customer needs. Tunnel vision creates rigidity. The brand repeats the same creative playbook even when the world has changed. What once felt visionary now feels outdated or self absorbed.

Internally, tunnel vision limits strategic conversation. The brand becomes protective of its chosen path and resistant to exploring adjacent possibilities. This slows evolution and reduces the brand's ability to scale. A Creator must learn to zoom out, revisit its surroundings, and entertain ideas that do not originate from its current creative center. Flexibility is not a threat to artistry. It is a requirement for survival.

Resistance to Critique

Creator brands often take critique personally because their work feels deeply tied to their identity. This sensitivity can lead to defensiveness, dismissal, or selective hearing. When feedback is perceived as an attack rather than an opportunity, the brand misses chances to strengthen its expression. Resistance to critique insulates the brand from external insight and creates an echo chamber where only internal taste is validated.

This behavior weakens collaboration both inside and outside the organization. Teammates hesitate to offer suggestions for fear of damaging relationships or slowing projects. Partners feel unwelcome to contribute. The brand becomes creatively stagnant, locked inside its own perspective. The Creator must learn that critique is not a threat. It is a tool. When embraced, it brings clarity, sharpens intention, and ultimately elevates the work.

In Practice: People & Characters

Leonardo da Vinci

Leonardo da Vinci is one of the purest expressions of the Creator archetype in human history. His work spanned art, science, engineering, and anatomy. His journals reveal a mind driven not by fame or utility but by an insatiable drive to understand and create. Leonardo exemplifies divergent thinking. He connected concepts across disciplines and transformed them into sketches, designs, and masterpieces. His work illustrates the Creator's belief that imagination is the gateway to invention.

Leonardo also demonstrates the Creator's motivation for mastery. He pursued technique relentlessly. His anatomical drawings reflect a quest for precision that elevated his art beyond aesthetics. Leonardo believed that creation required discipline as much as inspiration. This synthesis of imagination and rigor embodies the Creator archetype at its highest expression.

J. K. Rowling

J. K. Rowling represents the Creator archetype through her construction of an immersive narrative universe that reshaped modern literature. Rowling's creative strength lies in world building, character development, and thematic coherence. She crafted an environment rich enough for readers to inhabit emotionally. This reflects the Creator's desire to build worlds, not just stories.

Rowling also carries the Creator motivation of self expression. Her narrative explores belonging, identity, adversity, and moral complexity. She uses creativity as a vehicle for meaning. Her work demonstrates how the Creator archetype transforms imagination into shared cultural experience. Rowling's influence illustrates the Creator's power to inspire devotion and emotional connection through constructed worlds.

Tony Stark

Tony Stark embodies the Creator archetype through innovation, invention, and unapologetic imagination. Stark does not rely on magic or destiny. He relies on engineering, experimentation, and creativity. His inventions define his identity and his role in the narrative. This reflects the Creator instinct to solve problems through creation.

Stark also demonstrates the Creator's flaws. His perfectionism, obsession with improvement, and intense self expression sometimes lead to instability. But these traits also highlight the Creator's strength. Stark's willingness to imagine beyond convention and construct new solutions anchors his character. He represents the modern, tech driven Creator archetype.

In Practice: Brands

Crayola

Crayola is one of the most accessible and enduring Creator brands in the world. It democratizes creativity by giving children the tools to express imagination from an early age. Crayola's value lies not in its products alone but in the belief that everyone is inherently creative. This inclusivity aligns perfectly with the Creator's drive to inspire expression.

The brand also reflects the Creator's commitment to color, form, and sensory engagement. Crayola products encourage experimentation without judgment. They make creativity feel safe, natural, and joyful. Crayola is a Creator brand that nurtures an entire generation's imagination.

Squarespace

Squarespace expresses the Creator archetype through empowerment. The brand gives individuals and businesses the ability to design, build, and publish their own online worlds. Squarespace removes barriers that traditionally restricted creativity to experts. Its tools transform Patrons into designers and makers.

Squarespace also reflects the Creator's dedication to aesthetic quality. The platform elevates design standards and positions creativity as accessible to everyone. This alignment with self expression, craft, and originality makes Squarespace a modern Creator brand grounded in empowerment.

Pandora

Pandora exemplifies the Creator archetype through jewelry that encourages personal expression and customization. The brand's charm collections allow Patrons to craft wearable narratives that reflect their identity. Pandora creates a platform for self storytelling. This aligns with the Creator motivation to express individuality through meaningful objects.

Pandora also demonstrates the Creator's focus on craftsmanship and detail. Each piece is designed to carry emotional significance. The brand transforms adornment into personal authorship. This is the Creator archetype expressed through intimacy and aesthetics.

He who wishes to be obeyed
must know how to command

–Niccolo Machiavelli

The Sovereign

Historically named The Ruler, The Sovereign archetype represents one of the deepest human needs: the desire for order in a world that feels unpredictable. Where other archetypes seek transformation, belonging, pleasure, or autonomy, the Sovereign seeks structure, stability, and direction. The Sovereign does not chase attention. The Sovereign holds the authority to define the environment. Humans have relied on leaders, guardians, and organizers since the first communities assembled. Without structure, chaos consumes. Without rules, trust collapses. Without leadership, groups fail. The Sovereign archetype expresses the psychological force that creates order and sustains it.

The roots of the Sovereign archetype stretch into anthropology and human evolution. Early hunter gatherer groups were small enough to function without hierarchy, but as societies grew, leadership became essential for coordination. Anthropologists such as Christopher Boehm found that even egalitarian tribes rely on informal leaders who guide the group through conflict or environmental stress. Leadership is not decoration. It is functional. It prevents fragmentation and ensures survival. The Sovereign archetype comes from this evolutionary foundation.

In sociology, Max Weber identified authority as a central organizing force in societies. Not authority based in coercion, but authority based in legitimacy. People follow leaders when they believe those leaders possess wisdom, competence, and the capacity to maintain order. The Sovereign archetype is built on this legitimacy. It is not about control for its own sake. It is about control that creates stability. It provides clarity, predictability, and standards that allow individuals to operate with confidence.

The psychological dimension of the Sovereign archetype draws from research on dominance, status, and hierarchy. Studies show that people seek hierarchy not because they enjoy inequality, but because hierarchy reduces uncertainty. When roles, expectations, and responsibilities are clear, individuals experience less cognitive load. The Sovereign archetype satisfies this need for structure. It clarifies the rules. It enforces boundaries. It sets expectations.

Narrative traditions position the Sovereign as the steward of the realm. They protect order. They maintain continuity. They make decisions that shape the future. The Sovereign is not always soft or gentle. Leadership can be demanding, decisive, and unwavering. But when expressed healthily, the Sovereign provides safety through order. They create an environment where people know what is expected and where boundaries are consistent.

In branding, the Sovereign archetype is powerful because it offers authority and assurance. Sovereign brands position themselves as the standard. They define the category. They set expectations. They offer quality, reliability, and control. Patrons trust Sovereign brands because they project competence and consistency. They inspire confidence by demonstrating mastery of their domain.

This is why the Sovereign belongs in the Exert Control quadrant. Sovereign brands do not control through fear. They control through clarity. They bring order to complexity. They provide structure where others provide options. They create confidence through discipline. And they operate with intention rather than improvisation.

The Sovereign archetype is not about ego. It is about stewardship. True leadership is measured by how well a brand protects, organizes, and elevates its environment. Sovereign brands do not follow the market. They shape it.

Motivations of the Sovereign Archetype

The Sovereign is motivated by order. They want systems that function reliably and predictably. They value structure that minimizes chaos and maximizes clarity.

Another core motivation is responsibility. Sovereigns feel accountable for the outcomes of the group or category. They step into leadership because they believe it is necessary, not because they seek admiration.

The Sovereign is also motivated by excellence. They hold high standards and expect the same from their teams and their environment. This pursuit of quality is not perfectionism but stewardship.

Another motivation is stability. Sovereign brands want longevity. They value consistency across time. They maintain continuity through discipline.

Finally, the Sovereign is motivated by control used for protection. They use influence to keep systems safe, predictable, and functional. This distinguishes them from the Rebel, who challenges systems, and the Caregiver, who nurtures systems.

Strengths of the Sovereign Archetype

Leadership and Vision

Sovereign brands lead through clarity. They articulate a direction with confidence and align their operations, communications, and culture around that long view. Their leadership is not loud or theatrical. It is grounded, controlled, and purposeful. Customers feel this stability immediately. In categories defined by volatility or inconsistency, a Sovereign stands apart by offering a sense of order. Patrons trust the brand not because of its claims but because of the discipline and direction embedded in every interaction. Sovereign brands become anchors in industries that frequently drift.

Vision also shapes the Sovereign's internal world. Teams operating within these brands understand where the organization is headed and why. This clarity reduces confusion, enhances motivation, and strengthens execution because everyone is rowing in the same direction. The brand's long horizon ensures that decisions are not made reactively but strategically, reinforcing a narrative of reliability. When a Sovereign commits to a path, customers sense it. They feel safe choosing a brand that clearly knows who it is and where it is going. Vision becomes a form of emotional leadership.

Organization and Structure

Sovereign brands excel at creating order within complexity. Their systems are not constraining. They are liberating because they remove friction and guesswork. Customers experience this through predictable service, consistent quality, and well designed processes. The Sovereign's structure signals competence. It tells the Patron that the brand has thought through every detail and can be trusted to deliver on its promises. This sense of structure gives the customer an immediate feeling of confidence.

Internally, structure provides efficiency and cohesion. Teams know their responsibilities, their goals, and the mechanics that keep the organization functioning smoothly. This creates an environment where high standards can be maintained with consistency. Sovereign brands do not rely on talent alone. They rely on systems that elevate everyone within them. Their structure becomes a source of competitive advantage because it ensures stability even during rapid growth or industry turbulence. When structure is strong, execution becomes effortless.

Accountability

Accountability is the Sovereign's defining discipline. These brands take responsibility for outcomes, both good and bad. When something goes wrong, they address it openly, correct the issue, and communicate with integrity. This posture builds trust because it signals maturity and respect for the customer. In markets filled with brands that deflect, excuse, or obscure their mistakes, the Sovereign feels refreshingly honest. Accountability becomes a clear signal of the brand's moral and operational integrity.

Inside the organization, accountability sets the tone for culture. Expectations are clear, performance is measured, and excellence is non negotiable. Employees understand that responsibility is shared, not avoided. This creates a culture of reliability where people deliver because the system expects it and the brand values it. Accountability also strengthens leadership. A Sovereign brand does not need to assert dominance. Its actions speak for it. When customers see a brand consistently honor its commitments, loyalty grows naturally.

Confidence and Authority

Sovereign brands communicate with a calm, steady confidence that signals competence. Their authority is earned through consistent delivery, strong identity, and a deep understanding of their domain. Patrons interpret this authority as assurance. They feel that the brand knows exactly what it is doing and can be trusted in high stakes or high involvement scenarios. The brand does not need to exaggerate or over explain. Its confidence fills the space without force.

Authority also shapes the brand's presence in its category. Sovereign brands set expectations, establish standards, and influence trends. Competitors watch their moves closely because the brand's decisions carry weight. Authority gives them a form of gravitational pull. People and companies orbit around the brand because it embodies a level of stability and expertise unmatched by others. This presence elevates the Sovereign from participant to leader.

Problem Solving

Sovereign brands excel at solving problems that feel overwhelming to others. Their structured thinking and long view allow them to diagnose issues accurately and develop solutions that address root causes rather than symptoms. Customers experience this through seamless service recovery, clear communication, and thoughtful improvements over time. When challenges arise, the Sovereign does not react impulsively. It stabilizes the environment, evaluates the situation, and acts decisively. This behavior earns confidence because Patrons know the brand will not collapse under pressure.

Problem solving also strengthens the internal culture. Teams trust leadership because decisions are made intentionally and communicated clearly. Systems are updated thoughtfully rather than patched hastily. The Sovereign's capacity for calm, systemic problem solving becomes a form of emotional leadership within the organization. It reassures employees and customers alike that the brand is capable of handling complexity without losing direction or composure.

Challenges of the Sovereign Archetype

Control Obsession

The Sovereign's strength in creating order can become an obsession with control. When this happens, the brand tightens processes so strictly that creativity, flexibility, and customer centricity suffer. Control obsession manifests as rigid policies, inflexible service scripts, or experiences that feel sterile. Customers sense when the brand is more invested in maintaining order than in meeting their needs. This rigidity erodes emotional connection and makes the brand feel authoritarian rather than authoritative.

Internally, control obsession stifles innovation. Teams may fear making mistakes or proposing new ideas because the system leaves little room for deviation. The culture becomes cautious and compliance driven rather than visionary. As the brand grows, this rigidity becomes even more problematic. A brand that cannot relinquish control cannot evolve. Sovereigns must learn when structure supports excellence and when it suffocates it.

Hubris

Hubris emerges when the Sovereign begins believing its authority is unassailable. This overconfidence blinds the brand to shifting cultural dynamics, emerging competitors, or flaws in its own systems. Hubris makes the brand slow to respond to change because it assumes its legacy or market position will protect it. Customers notice this complacency. They sense when a brand no longer feels hungry or attentive.

Hubris also erodes internal alignment. Leaders may dismiss feedback, ignore warning signs, or double down on outdated strategies. Teams become frustrated because expertise is ignored in favor of ego. When hubris shapes leadership, the brand stops listening, and listening is often what keeps a Sovereign relevant. Without humility, the brand's authority turns from earned to assumed, and assumed authority rarely survives cultural change.

Distance from Others

The Sovereign's elevated identity can create emotional distance between the brand and its customers. When communications become overly formal, polished, or hierarchical, the brand feels unapproachable. Patrons may admire the brand but hesitate to engage deeply with it because they sense a lack of warmth. Distance weakens loyalty. Customers want leadership, but they also want humanity.

This distance also affects internal culture. When leadership feels inaccessible or overly insulated, employees lose connection to the mission. The brand becomes a machine rather than a community. A Sovereign must stay connected to its audience and its workforce. Authority does not require detachment. In fact, the most effective Sovereigns balance leadership with openness.

Resistance to Change

Sovereign brands value consistency, but this strength becomes a liability when it hardens into resistance to change. The brand may cling to legacy systems, identity elements, or operational practices even when they no longer serve the customer or the market. This reluctance to evolve signals stagnation. More agile competitors seize opportunities the Sovereign cannot or will not pursue.

Resistance to change also harms internal morale. Teams may see opportunities for improvement but feel powerless to act. Innovation stalls. The brand gradually shifts from leader to relic. The Sovereign must learn that order and evolution are not opposites. Structure can expand rather than restrict when guided by intention rather than fear.

Greed

Greed is the distortion of the Sovereign's desire for abundance. When the brand begins prioritizing profit, status, or dominance over customer well being, the relationship collapses. Greed shows up in predatory pricing, restrictive policies, or decisions that benefit the brand at the expense of the customer. Patrons feel exploited rather than served, which erodes trust quickly.

Internally, greed corrodes culture. Employees sense when the brand values revenue more than people. This leads to disengagement, resentment, and high turnover. Greed undermines the Sovereign's legitimacy because true leadership requires stewardship, not extraction. When the brand shifts from serving its audience to feeding on it, it loses the moral authority that defines the archetype.

In Practice: People & Characters

Mufasa

Mufasa from The Lion King represents the Sovereign archetype through wisdom, responsibility, and benevolent authority. He rules not through fear but through guidance. Mufasa teaches Simba that leadership requires balance, restraint, and a deep understanding of the world. His authority is legitimate because it is grounded in care for the pride lands and every creature within them. This mirrors

Weber's concept of legitimate authority. Mufasa's leadership stabilizes the ecosystem. Without him, chaos spreads.

Mufasa also demonstrates the Sovereign's moral responsibility. He models integrity and accountability. He is steady, disciplined, and emotionally controlled. These qualities allow him to create order in moments of fear and uncertainty. His presence is calming because it signals structure and safety. This is the essence of the Sovereign archetype.

Miranda Priestly

Miranda Priestly from The Devil Wears Prada is an example of the Sovereign archetype expressed in its more exacting and demanding form. Her authority is unquestioned, and she sets the standards for the entire fashion world. Miranda's expectations are high because she sees herself as the steward of excellence. Sovereigns define categories. Miranda defines style. Her power is rooted in expertise and cultural influence.

However, Miranda also illustrates one of the Sovereign's potential pitfalls. Excessive control and emotional distance can create fear rather than trust. Her precision and dominance drive her team to perform, but they also create tension. This demonstrates how the Sovereign can drift into coldness if responsibility is not balanced with empathy. Miranda is powerful, disciplined, and influential, but her leadership exposes the double edge of the archetype.

Satya Nadella

Satya Nadella represents the modern Sovereign expressed through empathy, clarity, and disciplined leadership. When he became CEO of Microsoft, he inherited a culture marked by competition and rigidity. Nadella used structure, vision, and emotional intelligence to rebuild trust and unify the organization. His leadership transformed Microsoft from a declining giant into a collaborative, high performing global leader.

Nadella demonstrates that the Sovereign archetype is not limited to stern authority. It can be compassionate and inclusive. He leads with humility, but his authority is unmistakable. He sets the direction, defines expectations, and maintains high standards. His stewardship has created stability, innovation, and cultural renewal. Nadella is a Sovereign who rules by elevating others, not by constraining them.

In Practice: Brands

Burger King

Burger King expresses the Sovereign archetype through its founding principle of "Have it Your Way" and its modern evolution into "You Rule." This positioning is not simply customer empowerment. It is a statement of authority given to the Patron. Burger King has historically built its brand around choice, customization, and the Patron's autonomy. Instead of controlling preferences, the brand enables them. This is Sovereign leadership expressed through delegated authority.

The "You Rule" campaign reframes the Patron as the one in control. Burger King becomes the steward that ensures the Patron's preferences are respected. This aligns with the Sovereign's role as a protector of structure and fairness. Burger King's message is clear. The brand creates a system where the customer's rule is acknowledged and affirmed. This is a modern and democratic expression of the Sovereign archetype.

Lavazza

Lavazza represents the Sovereign archetype through tradition, craftsmanship, and mastery. The brand positions itself as the authority on Italian coffee. It controls quality through rigorous standards and consistent refinement. Lavazza does not follow coffee trends. It defines them. This commitment to heritage and precision reflects the Sovereign's motivation to maintain order and excellence.

Lavazza also communicates with confidence and cultural authority. Its identity is rooted in lineage, expertise, and mastery of a craft that spans generations. This consistency builds trust. Patrons feel that Lavazza has command over the category and that choosing Lavazza ensures quality. The brand leads through discipline and heritage.

Bentley

Bentley is a quintessential Sovereign brand. Its identity revolves around mastery, tradition, and uncompromising standards. Bentley communicates prestige not through noise but through refinement, precision, and exceptional engineering. The Sovereign archetype thrives in categories where quality is synonymous with authority. Bentley embodies this fully.

The brand also reflects the Sovereign's desire for control through craftsmanship. Everything is intentional. Everything is meticulous. Bentley vehicles are not mass produced experiences. They are controlled environments that communicate dignity, stability, and power. Choosing Bentley signals alignment with the values of order, refinement, and authority.

CHAPTER 08

Quadrant: **Find Fulfillment**

The Find Fulfillment quadrant guides people toward depth, meaning, and inner alignment. These archetypes focus on the internal journey rather than the external world. The Sage pursues truth and understanding. The Explorer pursues expansion and lived experience. The Innocent pursues joy, purity, and intentional simplicity. Together, they help people reconnect with themselves.

Fulfillment becomes most alluring when the other quadrants become excessive. The pressure of the Change the World quadrant can exhaust. The emotional demands of Foster Belonging can crowd the individual. The structure of Exert Control can restrict autonomy. Psychological research on meaning making and narrative identity (McAdams) shows that individuals seek coherence and inner clarity during periods of transition or emotional overwhelm. Fulfillment archetypes meet this need by helping customers slow down, reflect, and recalibrate.

Self Determination Theory emphasizes the need for autonomy and authenticity. When people feel disconnected from their internal motivations or trapped in environments that prioritize external expectations, they seek brands that help restore inner alignment. Fulfillment archetypes provide clarity without pressure. Exploration without chaos. Joy without complexity. They counterbalance the overstimulation of modern life by returning people to themselves.

These brands must avoid drifting into vagueness or abstraction. Fulfillment is only meaningful when it is accessible. When done well, these archetypes build some of the deepest forms of loyalty. They do not simply solve problems. They enrich the human experience. The Find Fulfillment quadrant defines the brands that help people rise inwardly so they can navigate the outer world with greater clarity and intention.

Never did the world make a queen of a girl who hides in houses and dreams without traveling.

– Roman Payne

The Explorer

The Explorer archetype represents one of the deepest and most ancient motivations in human identity. Exploration is not a hobby. It is a psychological and evolutionary necessity. For most of human history, survival depended on the willingness to move, to search, to discover, and to expand beyond the familiar. The Explorer is driven by the desire to experience more of the world and more of the self. While other archetypes seek belonging, transformation, protection, or control, the Explorer seeks fulfillment through discovery. The Explorer believes that meaning is found by crossing boundaries and seeing what lies beyond them.

Evolutionary psychology provides the foundation for this archetype. Humans developed what researchers call novelty seeking, a trait that evolved because individuals who were willing to explore new environments found new resources, safer locations, and better opportunities. Exploration increased survival. But exploration was not only physical. It also required cognitive flexibility. Explorers needed to evaluate unfamiliar information, adapt to risk, and make decisions in uncertain environments. This combination of curiosity and adaptability forms the core of the Explorer archetype.

Anthropologists studying migratory cultures found that societies with strong exploratory instincts tended to develop rich mythologies centered around journeys. These myths were not entertainment. They were psychological maps. They taught people how to navigate uncertainty, trust intuition, and find meaning outside the boundaries of home. The Explorer archetype comes directly from these cultural stories. It is the expression of movement as purpose.

Modern psychology reinforces this. Self Determination Theory identifies autonomy as one of the three essential human needs. The Explorer archetype is the purest expression of autonomy. It is the desire to choose one's own path, follow inner direction, and pursue experiences that expand identity. Explorers feel fulfilled when they are free to search. Their drive is not rebellion. It is self actualization.

Narrative traditions cast the Explorer as the seeker. They are not driven by conflict or recognition but by internal longing. They search for something they cannot define fully. Experience itself is the reward. Exploration is how they understand themselves. This is why the Explorer belongs in the Fulfillment quadrant.

Explorer brands offer meaning through movement, discovery, and possibility. They help Patrons grow by expanding horizons.

In branding, the Explorer archetype attracts people who feel constrained by routine or who define themselves through lived experience rather than possessions. Explorer brands offer freedom, adventure, and possibility. They do not promise safety or structure. They promise expansion. The Explorer brand asks Patrons to go farther, try more, and uncover a deeper version of themselves.

The Explorer archetype is not about distance. It is about perspective. It is about pushing beyond the places where certainty feels comfortable and discovering what lies on the other side. Exploration is both an outward journey and an inward one. True fulfillment requires both.

Motivations of the Explorer Archetype

The Explorer is motivated by freedom. They seek autonomy in decision making, movement, and experience. They resist environments that feel restrictive.

Another core motivation is discovery. Explorers believe that fulfillment comes from encountering the unfamiliar. They value novelty and challenge.

The Explorer is also motivated by self expansion. They want to understand who they are by pushing the boundaries of what they know.

Another motivation is authenticity. Explorers reject conformity because it obscures personal truth. They want their life to be uniquely theirs.

Finally, the Explorer is motivated by possibility. They believe that meaning is found when horizons widen and perspectives evolve.

Strengths of the Explorer Archetype

Fearless Pioneering

Explorer brands thrive in unfamiliar territory. They enter new markets, adopt emerging technologies, and introduce novel concepts long before their competitors even recognize the opportunity. This pioneering instinct is not recklessness. It is a disciplined willingness to move into the unknown with curiosity, clarity, and courage. Customers sense this momentum and view the Explorer brand as a guide who expands their world. A pioneering brand brings fresh possibility into categories that often feel stagnant or conventional. This creates emotional excitement that few archetypes can replicate.

Fearless pioneering also positions the Explorer as a thought leader. When the brand moves into new spaces with confidence, it creates the future rather than reacting to it. This drives cultural relevance and market differentiation. Customers associate the brand with discovery, innovation, and autonomy. They follow not because they want to imitate, but because the brand embodies the spirit of exploration that they admire in themselves. The Explorer is the brand that opens paths others eventually walk.

Curiosity and Openness

Curiosity keeps the Explorer brand dynamic. While competitors rely on established formulas, the Explorer continuously searches for new insights, cultural signals, and creative influences. This openness to possibility shapes product design, storytelling, and customer experience. The Explorer refuses to become predictable. Instead, it evolves through immersion in diverse cultures, emerging technologies, and shifting Patron needs. This makes the brand feel alive, perceptive, and culturally connected.

Openness also creates an authentic relationship with Patrons. The Explorer does not present itself as all knowing. Instead, it investigates aloud, experiments publicly, and invites its audience into the learning process. This transparency turns curiosity into connection. Customers appreciate a brand that evolves with them rather than dictating from a fixed point. Explorer brands feel more human because they acknowledge that discovery is ongoing rather than complete.

Adaptability

Adaptability is the Explorer's most pragmatic strength. When markets shift, new competitors arrive, or customer expectations evolve, the Explorer brand adjusts fluidly. This flexibility prevents stagnation and protects the brand from irrelevance. While other archetypes struggle to maintain their identity during change, the Explorer thrives in transitional environments. The brand views transformation not as a disruption but as an invitation to grow.

This adaptability also builds trust. Patrons know the brand will remain relevant because it adapts without losing its core purpose. Customers feel aligned with a brand that mirrors their own evolution. When executed well, adaptability becomes a stabilizing force. The Explorer never clings to outdated systems or narratives. It moves forward with intention, embracing change as an essential part of its value.

Leadership Through Discovery

Explorer brands lead by illuminating new paths. They do not assert authority through dominance or control. Instead, they guide through curiosity, experimentation, and shared experience. This form of leadership is deeply relational. Customers follow Explorer brands because they trust the brand's instinct for discovery. They want to experience new possibilities alongside the brand rather than being told what to think.

This leadership style also builds brand narrative. The Explorer's journey becomes a story that the audience participates in. Every new launch, campaign, or experience becomes part of a larger adventure. This narrative deepens engagement because Patrons feel woven into the brand's path. Leadership through discovery is not about expertise. It is about exploration that feels communal.

Narrative of Resilience

Resilience defines the Explorer brand's character. Exploration requires confronting uncertainty, recalibrating frequently, and adapting when the path becomes difficult. These qualities translate into brand behavior that customers trust during volatile moments. When disruptions occur, Explorer brands respond with perspective and flexibility rather than panic. This steadiness is felt across every touchpoint and becomes a source of emotional stability for Patrons navigating their own challenges.

The Explorer's resilience also shapes customer perception. They become the brand that pushes forward when others stall, the brand that experiments when others retreat, the brand that reframes obstacles as part of the journey. This mindset resonates with people who view their own lives through cycles of trial and progress. The Explorer becomes the brand that teaches customers how to move through difficulty without losing themselves.

Challenges of the Explorer Archetype

Restless Wanderlust

The same drive that compels the Explorer forward can make the brand unstable. Restless wanderlust creates a pattern of constant reinvention that confuses customers and dilutes positioning. When the brand changes direction too frequently, Patrons struggle to understand what it stands for. Innovation becomes noise. The brand begins to feel inconsistent rather than adventurous. This restlessness erodes cohesion and damages the trust the archetype relies on.

Internally, wanderlust disrupts operational continuity. Teams may feel they are always chasing the next idea rather than building a strong foundation. This constant motion drains resources, fractures focus, and undermines long term strategy. The Explorer brand must learn that adventure requires anchors. Without them, exploration becomes drift rather than discovery.

Impulsivity

Explorer brands sometimes mistake novelty for progress. Their eagerness to experiment can result in premature launches, poorly vetted ideas, or inconsistent quality. Impulsivity shows up as rapid, reactionary decision making that feels exciting in the moment but creates downstream problems. When exploration is not tempered by intention, the brand loses credibility.

Impulsivity also affects strategic decision making. The brand may abandon promising initiatives too early simply because something new appears. This leads to shallow impact and fragmented brand identity. A strong Explorer must differentiate between the impulse to move and the strategy to evolve. Movement without direction undermines the very freedom the archetype celebrates.

Isolation and Alienation

Explorer brands often embrace their outsider identity with pride. While this gives them edge and authenticity, it can lead to alienation when the brand positions itself so remotely from mainstream audiences that the average customer feels dismissed or excluded. Messaging may become overly niche or so self directed that Patrons cannot see their place within the brand's world.

Isolation also weakens growth potential. A brand that speaks only to the fringe may struggle to scale. Explorer brands must maintain access points for broader audiences. They can remain distinct without becoming distant. Exploration is compelling when others feel welcome to join the journey, not when they feel the brand has already left without them.

Emotional Detachment

Explorer brands often communicate with a tone shaped by independence and autonomy. While this gives the brand confidence, it can create emotional detachment. Customers who crave warmth, reassurance, or personal connection may interpret the brand's independence as indifference. Emotional distance limits loyalty and makes the brand vulnerable to competitors who pair boldness with empathy.

This detachment also manifests in missed opportunities for engagement. Explorer brands may hesitate to share vulnerability, celebrate community, or express emotion because these actions feel contrary to their identity. Yet emotional depth often strengthens narrative. Without it, the Explorer risks becoming a brand defined only by motion rather than meaning.

Risk of Burnout

Exploration requires energy, curiosity, and constant movement. Without intentional pacing, Explorer brands burn out. Internally, teams struggle under perpetual change and the pressure to innovate continuously. Externally, the brand may exhaust its audience by pushing new ideas without allowing them time to integrate. Burnout makes the brand feel erratic, drained, and unfocused.

Sustainable exploration requires rhythm. The Explorer brand must learn to integrate periods of reflection, consolidation, and grounding. These pauses do not limit creativity. They strengthen it. Without them, the brand's adventurous nature becomes unsustainable. True exploration requires both motion and rest.

In Practice: People & Characters

Sir Richard Branson

Sir Richard Branson embodies the Explorer archetype through his lifelong pursuit of discovery, adventure, and boundary pushing. His ventures span airlines, space travel, hospitality, and entertainment, all driven by the belief that life is richer when experiences expand. Branson consistently rejects limitation. He follows curiosity as strategy. Researchers on novelty seeking would identify Branson as a high openness individual who translates exploration into entrepreneurial action.

Branson also demonstrates the Explorer's relationship with risk. Exploration requires comfort with uncertainty. Branson repeatedly enters new territory not for spectacle but for fulfillment. His leadership communicates possibility. He is motivated by the question, what if. This internal compass makes him a powerful expression of the Explorer archetype.

Jack Sparrow

Jack Sparrow is the mythic trickster in a navigator's body. His entire character is defined by movement, unpredictability, and the refusal to be contained. Sparrow does not chase power or stability. He chases freedom. His moral code is fluid, but his desire for autonomy is absolute. This reflects the Explorer psyche. Sparrow believes that fulfillment is found at sea, where boundaries dissolve and possibility expands.

He also embodies the Explorer's improvisational intelligence. Sparrow thrives in unfamiliar environments because he adapts instantly. Explorers rely on resourcefulness and intuition rather than rigid structure. Sparrow demonstrates this again and again. His journey is never linear, but it is always driven by a deeper longing for unrestricted existence.

Amelia Earhart

Amelia Earhart represents the Explorer archetype through bravery, determination, and an unrelenting desire to push the boundaries of physical and cultural possibility. Earhart did not seek attention. She sought flight. She sought the expansion of human capability. Her achievements symbolize the Explorer's belief that fulfillment is found at the edge of the known world.

Earhart also reflects the Explorer's internal motivation. She pursued aviation not as rebellion but as passion. Exploration was her path to meaning. Her legacy endures because she gave form to the Explorer's greatest truth. Horizons are meant to be crossed.

In Practice: Brands

Harley Davidson

Harley Davidson is one of the most misunderstood archetype examples in branding. Many assume it is a Rebel brand because of leather jackets, open roads, and cultural edge. But Harley Davidson is not rebelling against anything. The brand's core promise is not defiance. It is freedom. Harley Davidson speaks directly to people who seek fulfillment through exploration. It gives Patrons the feeling of open possibilities, personal escape, and the discovery of self beyond everyday constraints.

The brand's language, imagery, and culture revolve around personal journeys, not social disruption. Harley Davidson riders do not seek to overthrow norms. They seek to expand experience. This places Harley Davidson firmly in the Explorer archetype. The brand offers meaning through motion. It offers fulfillment through the pursuit of open space. Harley Davidson is not rebelling. Harley Davidson is roaming.

Delta Air Lines

Delta Air Lines expresses the Explorer archetype through global connection, discovery, and the belief that the world becomes richer when people move through it. The airline is not positioned as luxurious, rebellious, or nurturing. It positions itself as a gateway to possibility. Delta markets exploration as a form of personal growth. Travel becomes a path to fulfillment.

Delta also demonstrates the Explorer's commitment to expanding horizons. The brand invests in global networks, new destinations, and tools that make exploration easier. It does not define how Patrons should travel or why. It simply offers the means to go farther. This aligns directly with the Explorer's motivation. Fulfillment through movement.

REI

REI is one of the purest expressions of the Explorer archetype in modern branding. The company exists to equip and inspire people to explore the outdoors. REI frames exploration as a source of well being, meaning, and personal renewal. This reflects the Explorer belief that fulfillment is found in environments that expand perspective.

The brand also demonstrates the Explorer's values of autonomy and authenticity. REI encourages Patrons to discover their own relationship with nature. It provides tools, education, and community, but never prescribes a path. REI embodies the Explorer principle that experience is personal. Growth is personal. Exploration is personal.

The world is full of magic things, patiently waiting for our senses to grow sharper.

– W. B. Yeats

The Sage

The Sage archetype embodies humanity's oldest and most enduring pursuit: the search for truth. While many archetypes seek belonging, safety, power, or expression, the Sage seeks understanding. The Sage represents the psychological drive to comprehend the world as it is, not as we wish it to be. This instinct is not rooted in intellect alone. It is rooted in survival. Early humans survived by interpreting patterns, anticipating danger, and learning from experience. Knowledge was not a luxury. It was a prerequisite for staying alive. The Sage archetype expresses this ancient need to make sense of reality.

The psychological foundation of the Sage lies in our cognitive architecture. Humans possess metacognition, the ability to think about their thinking. This capacity allows us to question assumptions, analyze information, and refine our understanding. Researchers studying the psychology of wisdom, such as Robert Sternberg, found that wisdom involves judgment, reflection, and the ability to navigate uncertainty with clarity. The Sage archetype draws from this. Wisdom is not simply knowledge. It is the ability to apply knowledge responsibly.

Anthropologists studying oral traditions discovered that many cultures relied on elders, storytellers, and philosophers to conserve knowledge and transmit learning across generations. These individuals preserved the lessons that ensured continuity. They interpreted the world and taught others how to navigate it. The Sage archetype originates from this social function. It reflects the belief that truth must be stewarded.

Narrative traditions cast the Sage as the guide, mentor, or intellectual anchor. They do not seek control through authority or influence through emotion. They seek clarity. Sages intervene when understanding is needed. Their knowledge stabilizes the narrative and empowers other characters to act with confidence. They serve not by protecting or leading, but by illuminating.

In modern psychology, individuals who align with the Sage archetype score high in need for cognition, a trait that reflects enjoyment of deep thought, intellectual challenge, and complex problem solving. They find fulfillment in learning. They feel grounded when they understand the underlying structure of things. This aligns the Sage directly with the Fulfillment quadrant. For the Sage, fulfillment comes through comprehension. Understanding is how they experience meaning.

Brands that embody the Sage archetype appeal to Patrons who seek clarity, expertise, and informed decision making. Sage brands are trusted because they provide reliable knowledge, reduce uncertainty, and help Patrons navigate complex choices. Their value is their insight. They do not motivate through emotion. They motivate through evidence. And they build loyalty through credibility.

The Sage archetype does not promise excitement or transformation. It promises comprehension. It promises perspective. It promises the confidence that comes from understanding. Fulfillment, for the Sage, is not found in adventure or belonging. It is found in truth.

Motivations of the Sage Archetype

The Sage is motivated by understanding. They seek accurate knowledge and clear insight. Their fulfillment comes from clarity, not novelty.

Another core motivation is truth. Sages value accuracy and objectivity. They avoid distortion, exaggeration, and emotional manipulation.

The Sage is also motivated by inquiry. They ask questions, challenge assumptions, and pursue deeper meaning. Curiosity drives them.

Another motivation is teaching. Sages feel responsible for sharing knowledge so that others can make informed decisions.

Finally, the Sage is motivated by perspective. They seek to understand the broader context so that they can examine complexities with patience and clarity.

Strengths of the Sage Archetype

Intellectual Growth

Sage brands are built on a foundation of relentless learning. They do not posture as experts. They earn expertise through ongoing study, exploration, and refinement. This constant intellectual growth keeps the brand ahead of cultural, technological, or category shifts. Customers sense this discipline. They interpret the brand's clarity not as marketing polish but as mastery. When a Sage brand speaks, it carries weight because its claims are anchored in real understanding. Intellectual depth becomes a core differentiator in categories filled with surface level claims and shallow positioning.

This commitment to growth shapes everything from product development to content strategy. Sage brands evolve their offering as their knowledge expands, creating a brand that never feels outdated or complacent. Their internal teams absorb this ethos as well. Employees learn not because they must but because the brand expects them to grow as thinkers. This intellectual ecosystem becomes self reinforcing. Insight leads to clarity. Clarity leads to authority. Authority leads to trust. Sage brands become the quiet leaders of their sectors, not through volume, but through depth.

Inquisitive Nature

Sage brands do not accept assumptions at face value. They interrogate ideas, challenge norms, and explore the underlying mechanics of their category. This inquisitiveness results in offerings and communications that feel refreshingly honest and thoughtful. Customers trust Sage brands because they can feel the inquiry behind the insights. They know the brand does not simply echo popular narratives. It investigates them. This makes the Sage especially powerful in industries plagued by misinformation, fads, or stale thinking.

Curiosity also influences problem solving. Sage brands look beyond the symptoms of a challenge and explore root causes. Their questions are sharp. Their answers are earned. This mindset helps them navigate complexity with precision. It also shapes their voice. They do not speak in absolutes. They speak in informed possibilities. Their curiosity signals confidence rather than uncertainty. It shows they understand that wisdom is not a finished state but an ongoing pursuit.

Critical Thinking

Critical thinking is the Sage's operational backbone. While other archetypes may rely on emotion, urgency, or instinct, the Sage uses analysis, discernment, and logic to guide decision making. This removes noise from the brand's communication. Their messaging is clean because their ideas are clean. They avoid exaggeration. They avoid sensationalism. Instead, they present balanced, evidence based perspectives that resonate with audiences tired of the extremes. This clarity makes the Sage brand feel trustworthy and emotionally steady.

Critical thinking also protects the brand from reactive behavior. When competitors chase trends or panic in moments of disruption, the Sage remains grounded. They evaluate before acting. This allows them to enter conversations with thoughtful timing and substance rather than speed. Customers interpret this as maturity. The brand earns a reputation for reliability because it resists being swept into the churn of short term cultural waves. Rationality becomes a form of emotional leadership.

Teaching and Communication

Sage brands excel at distilling complex ideas into content that educates without condescension. Their communication is a form of service. They translate complexity into clarity, helping customers understand not just what to choose, but why. This teaching posture makes the brand indispensable. Customers return because the brand elevates their understanding every time they engage with it. Teaching builds loyalty differently than persuasion. It creates believers rather than buyers.

This strength extends across every touchpoint. Websites become learning environments. Social posts become insight drops. Ads become lessons disguised as stories. The Sage's communication increases the audience's competence, which strengthens emotional attachment. When a brand helps customers become more capable, the relationship deepens. Sage brands excel here because they treat communication as a responsibility rather than a tactic. They give their audience the gift of knowledge, and that gift becomes the engine of trust.

Guidance and Mentorship

Sage brands act as mentors in their categories. They offer clarity when customers feel overwhelmed and direction when they feel lost. This guidance is not forceful or prescriptive. It is calm and confident, grounded in the belief that the customer will make better decisions when well informed. This creates emotional safety. Patrons feel held, not managed. They turn to the Sage because the brand helps them navigate complexity with dignity and intelligence.

Mentorship also shapes the brand's internal culture. Teams working within Sage brands tend to operate with a shared respect for expertise and thoughtful leadership. New employees are nurtured through clarity and support rather than pressure. This internal mentorship becomes visible externally. Customers can feel when a brand's team truly understands its subject matter. The Sage archetype thrives because its guidance is rooted in authenticity, not performance.

Challenges of the Sage Archetype

Detachment from Emotion

Sage brands can drift into emotional detachment when they lean too heavily on information. Their communications may become overly cerebral, clinical, or sterile. When a brand prioritizes logic at the expense of warmth, customers struggle to form emotional connection. Even if the insights are brilliant, the audience may feel a lack of human presence. This detachment weakens engagement because people do not bond with ideas alone. They bond with ideas delivered through relatable tone.

Emotionless communication also isolates the brand from cultural energy. Sage brands risk appearing disconnected from human reality when they refuse to engage emotionally. Customers may interpret the tone as elitist or cold. A Sage must learn to communicate wisdom with warmth. Without emotional resonance, credibility has nowhere to land.

Analysis Paralysis

The Sage's desire for accuracy can lead to stalled decision making. When the brand insists on gathering more data, researching more scenarios, or preparing more thoroughly, momentum slows. Teams become frustrated. Opportunities are missed. A competitor with less information but more willingness to act moves forward. The Sage's reluctance to commit until fully certain becomes a liability in fast moving markets.

Analysis paralysis also harms innovation. When a brand requires perfect clarity before moving, it avoids risk, and risk often precedes breakthrough. The Sage must learn to move with informed confidence rather than absolute certainty. Wisdom is diminished when it never leaves the planning stage.

Arrogance

Because Sage brands are knowledgeable, they may adopt a tone of subtle superiority. This arrogance can appear in messaging that feels patronizing or corrective. Customers sense when a brand is speaking down to them rather than walking with them. Even when the content is accurate, the delivery alienates. Arrogance undermines trust because it suggests the brand values being right more than being helpful.

Arrogance also weakens team dynamics. When a Sage brand internally overvalues expertise, it may marginalize voices that bring intuition, creativity, or emotional insight. This results in a narrow perspective. A wise brand understands that knowledge is enriched by diversity of thought. Arrogant Sages lose that richness and become rigid, predictable, and out of touch.

Isolation

Sage brands can become insular when they focus too heavily on internal knowledge and too little on external connection. Their thought leadership may reflect their own worldview rather than the lived experiences of their audience. When a brand becomes isolated, its content feels abstract or theoretical. Customers perceive distance. The brand is smart but not relatable.

Isolation also limits cultural relevance. When a Sage retreats into research without engaging with culture, it loses resonance. Wisdom disconnected from context becomes irrelevant. The Sage must remain in conversation with the world, not above it.

Unsatisfying Pursuit of Perfection

Sage brands may refine endlessly, always seeking more nuance or greater accuracy. This pursuit, while noble, often delays impact. Insights remain unpublished. Products remain unreleased. Campaigns never launch. The brand becomes a vault of brilliance that never reaches its audience. Perfectionism becomes a barrier to influence.

This struggle harms customer relationships as well. People look to Sage brands for guidance in times of uncertainty. When the brand hesitates to speak until every angle is covered, customers look elsewhere. The Sage must learn that wisdom delivered imperfectly still has value. When they let go of perfection, they make space for impact.

In Practice: People & Characters

Socrates

Socrates is one of the most influential expressions of the Sage archetype. His method of questioning assumptions, examining beliefs, and exposing contradictions reflects the Sage's core motivation. Socrates did not claim wisdom. He pursued it. His dialogues reveal that truth emerges from rigorous inquiry, not certainty. This aligns directly with the Sage's pursuit of clarity.

Socrates also demonstrated intellectual humility. He believed that wisdom begins by recognizing one's own ignorance. This humility is foundational to the Sage archetype. It prevents arrogance and opens the path to deeper understanding. Socrates represents the Sage as a seeker rather than a knower.

Albert Einstein

Albert Einstein embodies the Sage archetype through his relentless pursuit of understanding. His theories reshaped modern physics, but his curiosity extended far beyond equations. Einstein asked foundational questions about space, time, and reality. His approach to knowledge was guided by wonder as much as logic. This combination of curiosity and discipline reflects the Sage's internal structure.

Einstein also emphasized the importance of imagination in intellectual discovery. He believed that insight often begins with the ability to visualize or conceptualize the invisible. This perspective shows that the Sage is not purely analytical. True understanding requires both depth of thought and creative cognition. Einstein represents the Sage as a visionary thinker committed to truth.

Elizabeth Harmon

Elizabeth Harmon from The Queen's Gambit expresses the Sage archetype through intense focus, intellectual mastery, and the pursuit of understanding within a defined domain. Chess becomes her universe. She studies patterns, strategies, and psychological dynamics with obsessive dedication. Her need for comprehension is not superficial. It is existential. Understanding the game is understanding herself.

Harmon demonstrates both the power and the vulnerability of the Sage. Her quest for mastery brings achievement but also isolation. Her emotional distance reflects the Sage's challenge of balancing intellect with human connection. Yet her brilliance and depth exemplify the Sage's motivation to know, refine, and perceive the world with clarity.

In Practice: Brands

MasterClass

MasterClass embodies the Sage archetype through education, expertise, and access to world class knowledge. The platform offers curated instruction from top practitioners in their fields. This emphasis on mastery aligns directly with the Sage motivation to learn from the best sources available.

The brand communicates credibility and depth. Its design, tone, and structure reinforce the belief that understanding elevates the human experience. MasterClass succeeds by making expert knowledge accessible and inspiring. It empowers Patrons not through hype but through learning.

Wikimedia

Wikimedia is one of the clearest expressions of the Sage archetype in the digital age. It exists solely to compile, preserve, and disseminate knowledge. Its mission is to make information available to anyone, anywhere, without barrier. This commitment to truth and access reflects the Sage's highest values.

Wikimedia also demonstrates intellectual neutrality. The platform avoids persuasion and focuses on accuracy. This reinforces its credibility. By prioritizing information over opinion, Wikimedia fulfills the Sage role as guardian of knowledge.

Epicurious

Epicurious represents the Sage archetype through its emphasis on culinary expertise, tested recipes, and educational content. The brand does not prioritize trendiness or novelty. It prioritizes reliability. Every recipe is vetted. Every recommendation is informed. This creates trust.

Epicurious also teaches. It offers technique, context, and understanding to help Patrons become more capable cooks. This aligns with the Sage drive to empower others through structured knowledge. Epicurious succeeds because it delivers clarity in a category often clouded by misinformation.

At the core of your heart, you are perfect and pure. No one and nothing can alter that.

– Amit Ray

The Innocent

The Innocent archetype embodies one of the most fundamental human longings: the desire to experience the world with clarity, hope, and emotional purity. While many archetypes pursue transformation, authority, discovery, or mastery, the Innocent seeks fulfillment through simplicity. They believe the world can be good. They believe people can be kind. They believe life can be joyful. The Innocent archetype reflects the psychological instinct to return to emotional safety, moral clarity, and uncomplicated truth. It is not naivete. It is intentional optimism.

The psychological foundation of the Innocent lies in developmental psychology. Researchers such as Jean Piaget and Erik Erikson documented that early childhood is shaped by trust, curiosity, and the belief that the world is inherently supportive. Adults often carry remnants of this developmental desire for safety and goodness. The Innocent archetype activates that early emotional imprint. It offers a world where cynicism softens, anxiety recedes, and hope feels possible again.

Positive psychology reinforces this. Studies by Martin Seligman and Barbara Fredrickson found that emotions such as joy, gratitude, and hope broaden cognitive capacity and strengthen resilience. Positive emotion is not frivolous. It is functional. It improves health, decision making, relationships, and creativity. The Innocent archetype embraces this truth. It creates emotional environments that help people feel lighter, calmer, and more grounded.

Anthropologists studying ritual and communal celebration have found that societies use symbols of purity, light, and renewal to strengthen social cohesion. Festivals, holidays, and shared traditions often feature motifs of innocence because they restore a sense of communal goodness. The Innocent archetype comes from these cultural expressions of renewal. It represents the belief that life is improved when people reconnect with simple pleasures and shared joys.

Narrative traditions cast the Innocent as the gentle presence who restores emotional harmony. They remind other characters of what matters. They simplify complexity. They bring warmth to conflict. Innocent figures help others rediscover hope when the world feels heavy. Their power is subtle but profound. They stabilize emotional tone and invite connection.

In branding, the Innocent archetype is powerful because it creates immediate emotional comfort. Innocent brands offer joy, nostalgia, clarity, and warmth. They help Patrons escape complexity and reconnect with simple goodness. They do not overwhelm. They uplift. They do not challenge. They reassure. Their promise is emotional ease in a world crowded with tension.

The Innocent belongs in the Fulfillment quadrant because fulfillment for this archetype is found not in conquest or exploration but in purity of experience. The Innocent believes life is meant to be enjoyed, relationships are meant to be kind, and moments are meant to be savored. Innocent brands offer meaning through optimism.

The Innocent does not simplify life out of ignorance. They simplify life out of wisdom. They understand that joy is a form of strength, and hope is a form of courage.

Motivations of the Innocent Archetype

The Innocent is motivated by happiness. They seek experiences that feel pure, joyful, and uncomplicated.

Another core motivation is safety. Innocents want emotional environments where people can relax without fear or tension.

The Innocent is also motivated by optimism. They believe things can work out. They believe people are good. This optimism is not denial. It is perspective.

Another motivation is nostalgia. Innocents find meaning in familiar comforts that connect people to treasured memories.

Finally, the Innocent is motivated by moral clarity. They avoid cynicism and gravitate toward honesty, kindness, and simple truths.

Strengths of the Innocent Archetype

Pure Optimism

Innocent brands create emotional uplift in a way that feels effortless and genuine. Their optimism is not cheerfulness for its own sake. It is a strategic posture that sets a tone of hope and relief in categories where tension is common. When a Patron interacts with an Innocent brand, the experience feels lighter because the brand consistently removes heaviness from communication. This tonal brightness becomes a competitive advantage. It signals that the brand is a place where customers can escape stress, even briefly, and reconnect with a sense of ease. This emotional effect strengthens recall because people remember how a brand makes them feel more vividly than what it says.

Pure optimism also stabilizes a brand during turbulent times. While competitors may respond to cultural pressure with panic, aggression, or heavy persuasion tactics, Innocent brands maintain a steady, uplifting tone that reassures customers. This consistency becomes a form of emotional leadership. Patrons may not articulate it, but they feel safer with a brand that does not amplify fear. Optimism, when grounded in sincerity, can be one of the strongest forms of trust building. It communicates that the brand sees the world clearly and still chooses to be a source of goodness within it.

Joyful Presence

Innocent brands infuse their environments with a joyful presence that alters the emotional atmosphere surrounding them. This is not about humor or entertainment. It is about designing interactions that spark small, meaningful moments of delight. Visual identity, tone of voice, customer service, product presentation, and even microcopy all carry an undercurrent of positivity. These subtle touches accumulate into an experience that feels warm, accessible, and friendly. Customers return because the brand consistently lifts their mood. Joy creates memorability, and memorability drives preference.

This joyful presence is especially powerful in categories typically associated with stress, bureaucracy, or monotony. A joyful airline safety video. A playful banking app. A gentle healthcare intake flow. Innocent brands transform expected tension into pleasant surprise. This becomes part of their strategic signature. They are the brands that brighten days rather than simply functioning within them. Over time, these joyful moments stack into a brand narrative customers emotionally depend on. The brand becomes known as the place where things feel a little better.

Genuine Kindness

Kindness, when expressed as a brand behavior, communicates sincerity in ways no tagline ever could. Innocent brands demonstrate kindness through thoughtful policies, considerate communication, and the refusal to manipulate. Their service interactions feel personal without being invasive. Their messaging focuses on reassurance rather than persuasion. Customers interpret this behavior as care, and care builds affinity. In a market filled with brands trying to close, convert, or capture attention, the Innocent differentiates by simply being decent.

This genuine kindness also influences customer forgiveness. When Innocent brands stumble, customers give them more grace because the brand has earned relational goodwill. People are more forgiving of a brand they believe has good intentions. Innocent brands benefit from this because they consistently behave in ways that reflect honesty and goodwill. Kindness is not a weak differentiator. It is a strategic asset that strengthens loyalty through emotional credibility.

Trust and Openness

Innocent brands excel at building trust because they operate with transparency. Their messaging is clear, their policies are simple, and their communication is straightforward. This transparency reduces cognitive load. Customers do not have to decode the brand's intentions or read between the lines. When expectations are clear and met consistently, customers reward the brand with loyalty. Openness creates a sense of psychological safety that is rare in modern markets.

Openness also enables Innocent brands to communicate difficult information without damaging goodwill. When a brand known for honesty delivers bad news, customers interpret it as integrity rather than failure. This clarity sets the Innocent apart from competitors who obscure, overpromise, or overwhelm. A transparent brand is a trusted brand, and no archetype embodies transparency more naturally than the Innocent.

Resilience

Resilience is one of the Innocent's most underestimated strengths. Their optimism, kindness, and simplicity create an emotional foundation that is surprisingly durable. While other brands react dramatically to market shifts or negative press, Innocent brands remain steady. Their identity is not precariously tied to performance spikes or cultural volatility. It is rooted in timeless values that outlast trends. This gives them long term stability in categories with constant churn.

Resilience also influences customer relationships. Brands grounded in positivity rebound from setbacks more effectively because the audience does not expect perfection. They expect goodness. And goodness, when it falters, is easily restored. Innocent brands benefit from higher emotional latitude. Customers want them to succeed, which creates an unusual buffer against brand damage. Their resilience is not about toughness. It is about consistency of spirit.

Challenges of the Innocent Archetype

Naivety

Innocent brands can become strategically naive when they underestimate competitive pressure or overestimate goodwill in the marketplace. Their commitment to optimism sometimes blinds them to harsh realities, shifting trends, or emerging threats. Naivety appears when the brand assumes that positivity alone will carry it forward. It also emerges when the brand fails to develop the strategic rigor needed to compete in categories where aggressiveness is the norm.

This naivety can weaken the brand's positioning. Customers may perceive the Innocent as sweet but unserious, charming but unsophisticated. When the brand shies away from complexity or refuses to address real problems, it becomes less credible. Innocent brands must learn to pair optimism with strategic intelligence. Hope is powerful, but it does not replace awareness.

Vulnerability

The openness that defines the Innocent can make the brand vulnerable to exploitation. Competitors may undercut or mimic them, knowing the Innocent is unlikely to retaliate with force. Customers may also take advantage of generous policies or forgiving service practices. Vulnerability also appears when the brand struggles to protect itself from public pressure, criticism, or cultural shifts that require firm stances.

Operationally, vulnerability emerges when teams absorb emotional labor the brand identity has promised. If the brand consistently avoids friction, employees may take on the interpersonal strain that the brand refuses to address. Vulnerability, when unmanaged, weakens the organization's backbone. Innocent brands must build internal strength without abandoning their softness.

Avoidance of Conflict

Conflict avoidance is one of the Innocent's most significant strategic weaknesses. Brands that refuse to confront issues allow them to grow unchecked. Innocent brands may delay difficult decisions, avoid taking stands, or ignore emerging problems until they become crises. This avoidance weakens leadership credibility because it signals discomfort with responsibility.

Externally, avoidance appears in messaging that sidesteps complexity. When customers ask hard questions, Innocent brands sometimes respond with overly simple answers that fail to satisfy. This erodes trust. Conflict avoidance protects emotional harmony in the short term but jeopardizes brand health in the long term. The Innocent must learn to address tension directly while preserving their tone.

Difficulty Coping with Disillusionment

Innocent brands are built on belief in goodness, which makes disillusionment particularly damaging. When they face public criticism, operational failures, or cultural backlash, their identity can destabilize. They do not have the emotional infrastructure to absorb negativity gracefully. This difficulty coping can result in defensive messaging, inconsistent tone, or abrupt shifts that confuse customers.

Disillusionment also threatens internal morale. Employees working in Innocent brands often join because they value positivity. When reality disrupts that ideal, disillusionment spreads quickly. The Innocent must develop the ability to integrate difficult truths without losing their essence. Optimism must be resilient enough to coexist with reality.

Dependency

Dependency emerges when the Innocent relies too heavily on customer affection or positive sentiment. Brands that define themselves through approval become reactive and unstable. They shift voice, messaging, or strategy to preserve emotional harmony rather than pursuing what is strategically necessary. This creates inconsistency and erodes brand authority.

Dependency also affects innovation. Brands focused on pleasing everyone struggle to make bold decisions because they fear alienating a portion of the audience. The Innocent must evolve beyond the need for constant validation. True belonging is built on authenticity, not appeasement. Without this balance, the brand becomes emotionally fragile.

In Practice: People & Characters

Winnie the Pooh

Winnie the Pooh is one of the clearest cultural expressions of the Innocent archetype. His worldview is simple, trusting, and warmly optimistic. Pooh does not worry about the complexities of life. He focuses on friendship, kindness, and joy. Developmental psychologists would describe Pooh as embodying the early childhood instinct to find security through gentle consistency.

Pooh also demonstrates the emotional intelligence of the Innocent. Though simple in expression, he brings calmness to his friends. He softens tension. He makes others feel safe. This is the Innocent archetype at its highest function. A presence that grounds others in warmth.

Fred Rogers

Fred Rogers represents the Innocent archetype through radical kindness, emotional clarity, and a deep commitment to the goodness of humanity. His work was rooted in developmental psychology. Rogers believed that children needed emotional safety and unconditional acceptance to grow. This belief shaped every word he chose.

Rogers did not shy away from serious topics. But he approached them with simplicity and honesty. He made difficult emotions feel manageable by reducing complexity and increasing compassion. Rogers expressed innocence as intentional goodness. He demonstrated that gentleness is a form of strength.

Dolly Parton

Dolly Parton embodies the Innocent archetype through joy, generosity, authenticity, and emotional brightness. Her public persona radiates warmth. She is approachable, humorous, and kind. Parton consistently uses her platform to uplift others, from literacy programs to community support.

Parton also demonstrates the Innocent's connection to nostalgia and comfort. Her music often reflects simple truths, emotional sincerity, and the belief that people are inherently worthy of love. She shows that optimism can coexist with life's challenges when rooted in genuine humanity.

In Practice: Brands

Coca Cola

Coca Cola is one of the most iconic Innocent brands in history. Its messaging consistently centers on happiness, togetherness, and the simple pleasure of sharing a moment. Coca Cola's brand storytelling leans into nostalgia, warmth, and emotional uplift. The experience is not about the product. It is about feeling good.

The brand's global campaigns reflect universal optimism. Coca Cola communicates a timeless belief that joy is accessible, relationships matter, and small moments can feel meaningful. This is the Innocent archetype expressed through celebration and connection.

Disney

Disney expresses the Innocent archetype through imagination, wonder, and the belief in happily ever after. Disney worlds invite people into environments where joy triumphs, goodness prevails, and magic is real enough to feel. Disney's stories offer moral clarity, emotional safety, and childlike delight.

Disney also preserves innocence through ritual and tradition. The brand's characters, music, and narratives create shared cultural memory. Disney does not simply entertain. It offers emotional refuge. It restores hope and invites audiences to believe in possibility.

Charmin

Charmin embodies the Innocent archetype through humor, softness, and the celebration of comfort. The brand removes tension from an everyday category by making it playful and wholesome. Charmin positions itself as gentle, clean, and worry free. This aligns with the Innocent desire for emotional and physical comfort.

Charmin also uses innocence through its iconic characters. The bears reflect family warmth, lightheartedness, and safety. The brand communicates cleanliness as reassurance rather than authority. It makes a mundane moment feel simple and pleasant.

PART

III

Reclaiming Archetypes from Misuse

CHAPTER 09

How Archetypes Are Misused and Misunderstood

Archetypes are one of the most powerful frameworks in brand building, but in the hands of most agencies, in-house teams, and consultants, they have been reduced to little more than decorative themes. They are treated as aesthetic shortcuts, personality stickers, or shorthand for mood boards. This trivialization has created confusion across the industry and diluted the impact of archetypes in brand strategy. This chapter exists to correct that. To show where things went wrong. And to recalibrate the practice so brands can return to using archetypes as they were intended: as psychological drivers of behavior, not creative ornaments.

Below are three of the most common and destructive misunderstandings surrounding archetypes. Each one breaks a brand's coherence. Each one fractures Patron understanding. Each one undermines the psychological foundations that make archetypes effective. And each one must be corrected if a brand expects consistency, clarity, and lasting loyalty.

Brands cannot adopt more than one archetype

The fastest way to break a brand is to give it more than one archetype. It is also, ironically, the most common mistake in the branding world. Agencies love to assign multiple archetypes because it feels nuanced and dimensional. They create diagrams with "primary" and "secondary" archetypes. They blend two or three together and call the brand a hybrid. They audition archetypes like wardrobe changes. They believe that if one archetype gives clarity, then adding two more will create depth.

As an example, an agency with which I worked was adamant that the character Batman embodied both The Hero and The Rebel. It's easy to see how they landed in that theory especially if the understanding of archetypes was surface-level. Their argument was that Batman was heroic but rebellious. Makes sense if you take the names of the archetypes and apply them based on the definitions of the words Hero and Rebel. But that would be a wild negligence of strategic thinking.

The Hero is a defender of the innocent and protector of people, but a follower of rules. The Rebel's sole focus is to rebel against systems no matter what the collateral damage may be. If forced together, these two are in conflict despite existing in the same quadrantal focus.

When combining two or more archetypes, usually done as an outward facing versus internal facing brand effort, a brand's foundation doesn't congeal. What actually happens is fragmentation. Not nuance. Not dimension. Fragmentation.

Brands do not become deeper by adopting multiple motivations. They become incoherent. And incoherence is the enemy of trust.

To understand why, we need to start with a psychological truth: archetypes are not flavors. They are motivations. They express why a brand behaves the way it does. And a brand cannot have two competing "whys" any more than a person can live two conflicting internal belief systems at once.

A Hero wants to face challenges and strengthen others.

A Sage wants to understand and illuminate truth.

A Rebel wants to confront and dismantle dysfunction.

A Lover wants to deepen emotional connection.

A Sovereign wants order and stability.

A Jester wants joy and release.

A Creator wants to build what does not yet exist.

These are not adjectives. They are psychological engines.

Now imagine trying to merge two engines with different operating systems. You wouldn't create a super-engine. You would create mechanical failure. That is what happens when a brand tries to combine archetypes. The motivations collide. The identity fractures. The story collapses under its own contradictions.

Cognitive psychology explains exactly why this happens. Humans categorize the world using mental schemas. Schema theory, from Bartlett through Rumelhart and deepened by modern cognitive science, shows that the brain does not want complexity. It wants consistency. It builds one mental model for each brand because that model makes recall efficient. Once the brain decides a brand is a Hero, it expects Heroic behavior. If the brand then begins acting like a Jester or a Lover or a Sage, the schema breaks. The Patron experiences cognitive dissonance, even if they cannot articulate why.

This dissonance is not subtle. It erodes trust because the brain cannot resolve the contradiction. Brands live or die on trust, and trust is built on consistency.

When agencies assign multiple archetypes, they unintentionally train the brand to behave erratically. One campaign leans into joy. Another leans into empowerment. Another leans into sensuality. Another leans into authority. The brand develops multiple gravitational pulls. Internally, teams become confused because different archetypes demand different behaviors. Externally, Patrons sense the incoherence even before the brand notices it internally.

This is why Patrons drift away, even when the work looks polished. People follow brands that are easy to understand, easy to categorize, and easy to anticipate. A brand that tries to be multiple archetypes becomes difficult to read. And when something becomes difficult to read, people stop trying.

Narrative identity research reinforces this. Dan McAdams found that human beings create meaning through unified internal stories. They need coherence to understand themselves, which means they expect coherence in the stories they consume. A brand that behaves like three archetypes at once is essentially three characters in one body. And no one wants to follow a character who keeps switching motivations mid-story. It feels dishonest. It feels confused. It feels wrong.

Brands must be singular because identity must be singular. Humans understand the world through roles. We do not need complicated roles. We need consistent ones.

There is also a cultural dimension to this. In a world saturated with noise, consistency is the only thing that makes a brand legible. The strongest brands in the world are defined by one archetype, not because they lack complexity, but because they use their archetype to express complexity with clarity.

Nike is pure Hero.

Disney is pure Innocent.

Patagonia is pure Explorer.

Apple under Jobs was pure Creator.

Allstate leans into Caregiver.

Southwest is Citizen.

Liquid Death is Rebel.

MasterClass is Sage.

These brands are beloved not because they are complicated, but because they are committed. The consistency builds emotional reliability. Emotional reliability builds trust.

A brand that tries to be more than one archetype is like a compass that points in three directions. Pointing north. Pointing west. Pointing inward. The team cannot follow it. The Patron cannot follow it. And the brand ultimately collapses under its own self-induced confusion.

The desire to use multiple archetypes always comes from the same place: fear that one archetype will limit the brand. But the truth is the exact opposite. One archetype liberates a brand. Multiple archetypes imprison it.

One archetype gives clarity.

Clarity gives confidence.

Confidence gives cohesion.

Cohesion gives power.

If you want a brand that behaves with consistency, coherence, and conviction, it must anchor itself to one archetype. Not two. Not three. One.

More complexity does not make a brand deeper. More contradiction makes a brand weaker. Identity is singular. Motivation is singular. A brand's role in the Patron's life is singular.

That is why a brand can only have one archetype. And why the discipline to choose one separates enduring brands from forgettable ones.

Archetypes Do NOT Dictate Brand Personality

One of the most damaging misunderstandings in modern branding is the belief that archetypes dictate personality. Agencies and internal teams routinely collapse these concepts into each other. They treat archetypes as if they are tone-of-voice templates or aesthetic choices. They assume the Hero must be intense, the Jester must be silly, the Lover must be breathy or sultry, and the Sovereign must sound like a lecturing executive. The result is a mess. Brands end up performing characters instead of expressing motivations. They become actors in costumes instead of identities with internal logic.

Archetypes are not personalities.

Archetypes are motivations.

Personality is how the brand expresses that motivation.

The two are not interchangeable.

This distinction matters because motivations are stable and personality is flexible. Personality can shift depending on campaign, channel, cultural moment, or segment. Motivation cannot. Motivation is the psychological engine that shapes the brand's role in the Patron's life. Personality is the aesthetic layer that helps that motivation communicate effectively to a specific audience at a specific time. When brands assume that archetypes dictate personality, they reduce a strategic foundation into a superficial stylistic choice.

To understand why this is a dangerous mistake, we need to revisit the psychology behind archetypes. Archetypes emerged from Jung's work on universal behavioral patterns. Jung never described them as personalities. He described them as symbolic representations of human drives. Campbell reinforced this in his analysis of global myth. Archetypes represent the internal forces that shape human action. They are narrative roles rooted in motivation, not mood. A Hero is a Hero because they seek to overcome adversity, not because they shout. A Sage is a Sage because they pursue insight, not because they speak softly. A Lover is a Lover because they value depth of connection, not because they wear red or speak in metaphors.

When we collapse archetype into personality, we trivialize the psychological depth that makes archetypes effective.

The brand industry often confuses this intentionally or unintentionally. Agencies are drawn to personality because it is easier to operationalize. Personality can be mood-boarded. Personality can be written into a script. Personality can be visualized in a pitch deck. Motivation is harder. Motivation cannot be mood-boarded. Motivation forces teams to examine the underlying structure of the brand and the underlying needs of the Patron. That takes discipline. It takes rigor. It takes behavioral literacy. Many agencies skip that work because personality is seductive and quick.

But personality is not strategy.

Personality without motivational alignment becomes noise.

Let's look at the Hero as an example. A Hero brand can be serious, intense, and stoic. It can also be playful, youthful, and energetic. Nike expresses the Hero with stoic intensity. Gymshark expresses the Hero with playfulness and youthful bravado. Red Bull athletes express the Hero with humor and spectacle. These are entirely different personalities expressing the same motivation: capability through struggle. The personality shifts. The motivation does not.

The same is true for the Lover. A Lover brand can be elegant like Tiffany. Cozy like Dove Chocolate. Playful like Glossier. Emotional like Hallmark. Seductive like Agent Provocateur. Each of these brands expresses a different tone, aesthetic, and emotional style. Yet all are unified by the same underlying motivation: connection, intimacy, and emotional presence. The personality is flexible. The motivation is not.

The Sage is another example. A Sage brand might speak with calm authority, like MasterClass. It might speak with friendly expertise, like Epicurious. It might speak with serious precision, like Britannica. It might speak with comedic intelligence, like CGP Grey or Kurzgesagt. Same archetype. Entirely different personalities. Personality does not define archetype. Motivation defines archetype.

This is consistent with research on identity and personality in psychology. Albert Bandura's work on self-efficacy and action shows that individuals behave consistently according to their internal motivation even when their tone or style shifts. Dan McAdams' narrative identity theory shows that the story structure of a person (or in this case, a brand) remains stable even when the surface expression changes. Personality is surface. Archetype is structure.

When brands confuse archetypes with personality, they create two major problems.

First, they limit creative range. Teams feel trapped by a narrow interpretation of the archetype. They assume the Jester must be goofy at all times. They assume the Sovereign must be stiff. They assume the Citizen must be blandly friendly. They assume the Rebel must be angry. This reduces the brand to caricature, which is the fastest way to make an identity feel fake or exaggerated.

Second, they break psychological alignment. The Patron does not connect with personality. They connect with motivation. Personality may attract the Patron's attention, but motivation determines whether the brand fits into their identity story. When personality becomes the driving force behind brand behavior, the brand loses emotional coherence. It becomes reactive instead of intentional. It becomes inconsistent because personality lacks strategic direction.

A mature brand understands the correct hierarchy. Archetype at the core. Personality in orbit. Motivation guiding behavior. Expression shaping communication. When these elements are reversed, brands drift into performance. They become actors delivering lines someone else wrote for them.

The truth is simple. Archetypes do not tell you how to speak. They tell you why you are speaking. They do not dictate jokes or seriousness or color palettes. They dictate the emotional contract between brand and Patron. Personality becomes the means, not the mandate.

A Hero can be funny.

A Jester can be profound.

A Sage can be casual.

A Rebel can be elegant.

A Lover can be subtle.

A Citizen can be bold.

A Creator can be quiet.

Personality expands.

Motivation anchors.

Archetypes define the role the brand plays in the Patron's life.

Personality simply helps the Patron hear it.

If Teams Don't Understand Archetypes, They Aren't Effective

If archetypes are so powerful, why are they so widely misused? The answer is simple. The industry has never been taught how to use them correctly. Archetypes entered branding not through psychology, but through creativity. They arrived as a novelty, a fresh vocabulary for mood boards and messaging brainstorms. They were introduced as inspiration rather than instruction. And because of that, most brand teams learned archetypes the wrong way, in the wrong order, with the wrong emphasis.

This chapter exists to correct the educational breakdown that created decades of confusion.

Archetypes were never meant to be creative shortcuts. They were never meant to be decorative personality enhancers. They were never meant to be the foundation for aesthetics. Archetypes were born from the study of human motivation and meaning. Jung developed them to explain universal behavioral patterns. Campbell used them to map transformation and identity development. Pearson refined them to connect mythic structure to human growth. None of these scholars were interested in marketing. They were interested in understanding human behavior.

But when archetypes reached branding, the depth of that work was stripped out. Agencies began using archetypes as if they were zodiac signs. They turned them into fun, clickable tools. They reduced them to lists of adjectives. They flattened them into personality sketches instead of motivational systems. Teams walked away believing they understood archetypes because they understood the labels. But labels without depth lead to shallow thinking.

You cannot build a psychologically coherent brand with shallow thinking.

The first failure in archetype education is this: archetypes are almost always taught aesthetically first. Teams encounter archetypes through colors, tone, type samples, campaign inspiration, or internalized stereotypes. The Jester is silly. The Hero is bold. The Innocent is light. The Sovereign is black and gold. These associations become cemented before anyone explains what the archetype actually represents. So teams walk away believing archetypes dictate what something should look like or sound like. They never realize archetypes dictate how something behaves.

Imagine teaching someone about gravity by beginning with a designer's illustration of an apple. That is how agencies teach archetypes. They start with stylistic expressions instead of underlying principles.

This misunderstanding creates systemic problems inside organizations.

Writers think archetypes dictate tone, so their work becomes repetitive and narrow.

Designers think archetypes dictate visuals, so systems become cliché or derivative.

Strategists think archetypes dictate personality traits, so positioning becomes shallow.

Executives think archetypes dictate slogans, so messaging becomes overstated or performative.

Product teams ignore archetypes entirely because they see them as marketing fluff.

What you get is an entire brand ecosystem acting from different mental models.

No alignment.

No shared understanding.

No cohesive behavior.

Research in organizational psychology shows that teams fail not because they disagree, but because they lack shared mental frameworks. Peter Senge calls these frameworks "mental models" in The Fifth Discipline. Edgar Schein refers to them as "cultural artifacts that control interpretation." When a brand does not define archetypes correctly, each team builds its own interpretation. And once that happens, no amount of guidelines or governance can enforce cohesion.

Teams need more than vocabulary. They need conceptual clarity.

The second failure in archetype education is rooted in the way most agencies socialize archetypes. Workshops often introduce all twelve archetypes at once. They are presented side by side as if they are equal options, like a menu. This immediately breaks the psychological structure of archetypes, which are anchored in deeper quadrants of human motivation. When archetypes are taught without the quadrants, teams see them as personality choices instead of motivational systems. They pick what resonates aesthetically, not what aligns behaviorally.

The third failure comes from misplacing the source of archetypal truth. Archetypes should emerge from three things: the Patron, the Brand, and the Market. Instead, agencies encourage teams to choose an archetype based on aspiration. Leaders pick the archetype they like. Creative directors pick the archetype that fits their vision. Strategists pick the archetype that aligns with the trend. Everyone picks based on preference instead of behavioral truth, which completely undermines the purpose.

Archetypes are not about preference. They are about psychological alignment.

The fourth failure is that teams are not taught how to use archetypes downstream. Many brands publish an archetype slide in an internal deck, but the concept never touches product, UX, environmental design, service rituals, operations, or hiring. The archetype remains an idea instead of becoming an operating system. If an archetype does not influence decisions across the entire brand ecosystem, it is nothing more than creative wallpaper.

The result of all these failures is predictable. Brands end up with archetypes that are superficial, inconsistent, and disconnected from both Patron and product. They become shallow identities wearing deep labels. They look right but feel wrong. They speak but never say anything meaningful. They create campaigns but never build meaning. Patrons sense the hollowness because humans are extremely good at detecting when something is pretending to be something it is not.

Fixing this requires a fundamental shift. Archetypes must be taught as behavioral psychology, not creative seasoning. Teams must learn the motivational engines behind each archetype. They must understand how these motivations shape expectations, perception, and emotional contracts. They must understand the quadrants. They must understand the Patron. They must understand how identity is formed. They must understand how narrative drives meaning. They must understand how consistency builds trust.

When archetypes are taught correctly, teams transform. Suddenly everything becomes clearer. Tone makes sense. Visual expression becomes disciplined. UX decisions feel logical. Operational choices align. Leadership aligns. Internal culture aligns. Brand drift stops. Creative churn slows. And the brand gains a kind of behavioral gravity that Patrons feel instinctively.

Archetypes do not fail. People fail at teaching them. And now that you understand the failures, you are ready to rebuild archetypes the right way.

CHAPTER 10

Rebuilding Archetypes on Solid Ground

Archetypes have been stretched, softened, aestheticized, and misunderstood to the point that most brands today work with shallow versions of them. They treat archetypes like creative prompts instead of behavioral systems. They treat them like flavors instead of psychological truths. They treat them like options instead of obligations. And because of that, most archetype work collapses before it can influence anything meaningful.

This chapter marks the shift from critique to reconstruction. If archetypes are going to function as the foundation of a brand's identity—its meaning, its behavior, its decisions—they must be rebuilt on the ground they were born from: psychology, motivation, identity, and emotional truth.

This is the work.

Returning to Psychological Foundations: Emotional Drivers and Behavioral Pathways

Archetypes only work when they are grounded in the psychology that produced them. Every misinterpretation in the branding world stems from the moment agencies disconnected archetypes from their true foundation and reattached them to aesthetics. Once the psychological roots were removed, archetypes became shallow. But their power comes from depth. Their reliability comes from the fact that they emerge from universal emotional drivers that shape human behavior.

To rebuild archetypes, we must return to those drivers.

Human behavior is motivated by psychological needs that have been identified repeatedly across research. Self Determination Theory, from Deci and Ryan, established autonomy, competence, and relatedness as the three universal motivators that predict intrinsic behavior. Archetypes map directly onto these three needs. Explorers and Rebels express autonomy. Heroes and Sages express competence. Lovers and Citizens express relatedness. Archetypes are not invented categories. They are expressions of these primal motivational patterns.

Layered on top of this is emotional data. Antonio Damasio demonstrated that emotion is not secondary to decision-making. It is primary. Emotion creates the somatic markers that the brain uses to determine whether something feels safe, aligned, familiar, or right. Archetypes trigger emotional patterns that have been reinforced over thousands of years through story, myth, and cultural symbolism. The Hero evokes capability and courage. The Innocent evokes purity and hope. The Jester evokes joy and release. These emotional associations are not subjective. They are universal because they are grounded in shared neurological processes.

Jung himself saw archetypes as the "riverbeds of the mind"—patterns so ancient they guide perception and behavior without conscious instruction. Campbell extended this by showing that mythic characters across cultures follow predictable motivational arcs. The Magician transforms through revelation. The Sovereign leads through structure. The Sage pursues clarity through understanding. These are behavioral pathways, not personality quirks. When brands adopt archetypes, they inherit these pathways whether they realize it or not.

Narrative psychology provides the final piece. Dan McAdams showed that people build identity through story structure. Archetypes align with these identity stories. A person constructing a narrative of growth resonates with the Hero. A person constructing a narrative of belonging resonates with the Lover or Citizen. A person constructing a narrative of inquiry resonates with the Sage. Archetypes work because they plug directly into identity formation, the psychological backbone of self.

Without this foundation, archetypes become nothing more than creative inspirations. They lose their stability. They lose their purpose. They lose the ability to drive behavior. Rebuilding archetypes on solid ground requires returning to the psychological truth that archetypes represent: humans move through the world guided by emotional drivers, motivational needs, and identity pathways that archetypes illuminate, not imitate.

When brands anchor to these foundations, archetypes regain their power. They stop being creative suggestions and become behavioral commitments. They stop being moodboards and become meaning systems. They stop being stylistic and become structural.

Rebuilding archetypes starts with remembering what they actually are.

Criteria for an Authentic Archetype Match

Most archetype failures happen at the moment of selection. Teams choose archetypes based on affinity rather than truth, aspiration rather than capability, aesthetics rather than behavior. The result is misalignment. And misalignment is fatal because the Patron always notices.

Brands must meet three criteria to claim an archetype: Patron truth, brand truth, and market truth. If any one is missing, the archetype fails.

Patron truth means the archetype must align with the Patron's psychological need. If your audience seeks emotional safety, the Rebel is the wrong archetype no matter how creative it feels. If they seek escape and freedom, the Sovereign is misaligned. If they seek competence and direction, the Innocent will frustrate them. An archetype is only "authentic" if it meets a real emotional need of the Patron. This is validated by decades of consumer psychology: decisions happen when emotional needs are met, not when messaging is clever.

Brand truth means the archetype must align with how the brand behaves internally. A company with a chaotic culture cannot be a Sovereign no matter how much they love the gold crown in their moodboard. A company without clarity, discipline, or standards cannot represent order. A company that struggles to communicate cannot be a Sage. A company that avoids conflict cannot be a Hero. Archetypes reveal organizational integrity. They do not mask its absence.

This is where Edgar Schein's organizational culture model is useful. Espoused values (what the company says) often conflict with underlying assumptions (what the company actually does). An archetype that aligns with espoused values but contradicts actual behavior creates brand collapse—the Patron senses the conflict instantly.

Market truth means the archetype must make sense within the category. Archetypes differentiate, but they must differentiate in a psychologically coherent way. A Sovereign bank makes sense. A Sovereign streetwear brand does not. A Magician wellness brand makes sense. A Magician industrial manufacturer does not. This is not about creativity. It is about narrative logic. Douglas Holt's research on cultural branding shows that brands resonate when they match cultural tensions and category expectations without repeating competitors' meanings.

A brand must pass all three tests:

Does the Patron need it?

Can the brand embody it?

Does it fit the cultural and category context?

If the answer is no to any of these questions, the archetype fails.

This is why so many brands end up with misaligned archetypes: they skip the criteria and choose based on preference. But authenticity is not preference. Authenticity is alignment. It is the total match between motivation, behavior, and meaning.

When brands apply these criteria, the correct archetype becomes obvious. It feels less like choosing and more like recognizing a truth that was already there.

Eliminating Aspiration Bias and Creative Bias

Two forms of bias destroy archetype selection more than anything else: aspiration bias and creative bias.

Aspiration bias occurs when leaders choose the archetype they want to be instead of the one they are. Every founder wants to be a Hero. Every young brand wants to be a Rebel. Every premium brand wants to be a Sovereign. But wanting does not make it true. Aspiration bias forces brands into psychological roles they cannot sustain. It creates tension between internal behavior and external expression. And this tension fractures trust.

Self-discrepancy theory, introduced by E. Tory Higgins, explains this perfectly. People and organizations experience emotional strain when their "actual self" does not match their "ideal self." Brands are no different. When a brand adopts an archetype based on aspiration, it creates a gap between expression and capability. Patrons experience that gap as inauthenticity. And once authenticity collapses, the brand loses its emotional foothold.

Creative bias happens when creative teams choose an archetype because it inspires compelling visuals or copy. The Jester is fun. The Rebel is dramatic. The Lover is sensual. The Magician is conceptually rich. Creatives gravitate toward archetypes that evoke strong aesthetic concepts. But archetypes cannot be chosen based on creative excitement. They must be chosen based on behavioral truth.

Creative bias has been responsible for decades of misaligned brand identities. Agencies fall in love with a concept and retroactively justify the archetype. This reverses the entire process. Instead of grounding creativity in psychology, they force psychology to fit the creative direction. The results are beautiful campaigns that fail to create meaning.

To eliminate both forms of bias, archetype selection must be a disciplined process grounded in evidence, not preference.

This requires three safeguards:

First, decision-making must begin with Patron psychology, not brand aspiration. If a Patron needs structure, no amount of creative desire should push the brand toward the Explorer. If the Patron needs transformation, no executive preference should push the brand toward the Citizen.

Second, the internal behavior of the brand must be audited honestly. This includes leadership style, team dynamics, operational systems, and cultural patterns. Archetypes demand behavioral integrity. A brand cannot express what it cannot consistently perform.

Third, creativity must come last, not first. Once the archetype is selected based on psychological truth, creativity can flourish within those boundaries. Boundaries do not limit creativity. They elevate it. They give creative teams purpose, structure, and direction.

Rebuilding archetypes begins with eliminating these biases.

When aspiration bias disappears, brands stop pretending.

When creative bias disappears, brands stop performing.

When both disappear, archetypes return to what they were meant to be: behavioral systems that anchor meaning, drive trust, and shape brands into coherent psychological entities.

PART

IV

Archetypes in Practice

CHAPTER 11

Choosing the Right Archetype for a Brand

Most brands approach archetypes as if they were creative flavors. They browse the options the same way they browse color palettes. They gravitate toward the archetype that looks the most exciting, or that sparks the biggest idea in the room, or that aligns with the CEO's self-concept. They treat archetype selection like a preference exercise rather than the strategic, psychological process it must be. Yet the moment a brand selects an archetype, it has made a profound commitment. It has chosen its emotional contract with the Patron. It has defined the role it will play in the Patron's internal narrative. It has shaped the expectations the Patron will bring to every interaction. Archetype selection is not a creative act. It is a clinical one.

This chapter restores the rigor that archetype selection requires. It explores the psychological drivers that shape Patron behavior, the deep motivations that underlie choice, and the developmental and emotional forces that determine which stories people feel drawn to. It clarifies why quadrants, not aesthetics, must determine the brand's direction. It examines why internal brand behavior — not aspiration — must determine whether an archetype is possible. It studies how category dynamics and cultural signals shape what roles a brand can credibly assume. And it demonstrates how all of these elements converge to reveal the one archetype a brand can authentically embody.

Archetypes are not chosen in a moodboard meeting. They emerge when Patron truth, brand truth, and market truth align. When that alignment happens, the archetype feels less like a decision and more like recognition. It is not selected — it is revealed.

Reading Patron Motivations: Understanding the Emotional Engine Behind Choice

To choose the correct archetype, a brand must begin with the Patron. Not with demographics. Not with surface-level preference. Not with sticky-note persona sketches. But with the psychological forces that shape how people experience the world. Patron motivations are not random. They arise from three deep structures that modern psychology has substantiated repeatedly: motivational need, emotional state, and identity narrative. These structures determine why a Patron gravitates toward one type of brand over another, why certain messages resonate while others fall flat, and why a brand's emotional contract must match a Patron's internal tension.

Motivational need is the foundation. Deci and Ryan's Self Determination Theory has shown that human beings move through the world guided by the need for autonomy, competence, and relatedness. These needs appear regardless of age, region, culture, or demographic profile. They are universal. And they map directly onto archetypes. When a Patron feels constrained or controlled, they seek autonomy — and gravitate toward exploratory or rebellious brands. When a Patron feels uncertain or insufficient, they seek competence — and gravitate toward heroic or sage-like guidance. When a Patron feels disconnected or unseen, they seek relatedness — and gravitate toward empathetic, intimate, or communal brands. Archetypes work because they reflect the motivational pathways people unconsciously lean toward when trying to restore emotional equilibrium.

Yet motivations alone are insufficient because behavior is also shaped by emotional state. Antonio Damasio's work revealed that emotion precedes rationality in decision making. People evaluate choices through somatic markers which are emotional impressions that determine whether something feels right. A Patron who has spent days overwhelmed by complexity seeks brands that embody clarity and calm. A Patron who feels isolated looks for warmth and recognition. A Patron facing instability seeks brands that express stability, order, or structure. These emotional states shift daily, but the underlying motivational preferences remain stable enough to form a pattern. Brands that misread these emotional needs misinterpret the Patron's motivation and misalign their archetype as a result.

Identity narrative adds the final layer. Dan McAdams' research has shown that individuals understand their lives through internalized stories. These stories contain characters, challenges, and aspirations. They give shape to who someone believes they are becoming. Archetypes tap directly into these stories. Someone who sees their life as a journey toward growth aligns naturally with the Hero. Someone who sees their life as a search for clarity aligns with the Sage. Someone who sees their life as a quest for connection aligns with the Lover or Citizen. These connections are not rational; they are narrative. People choose brands that reinforce the identity story they are trying to tell.

When a brand reads Patron motivations correctly, the archetype often becomes obvious. When it misreads them, the archetype becomes noise. The work of this section is simple: motivation reveals quadrant, emotional needs refine interpretation, and identity narratives illuminate the archetype. Brands must read all three to understand what role they must play.

How Quadrants Guide Archetype Selection: Choosing Direction Before Detail

Brands often make the mistake of jumping straight to archetypes. They choose based on flavor rather than function. But archetypes do not exist in isolation. They live inside quadrants that represent deeper motivational currents. If motivational need is the Patron's internal engine, quadrants are the directional force that engine seeks. Quadrants represent the broad emotional orientation that shapes behavior: the drive toward external change, internal meaning, human connection, or structural stability.

Quadrants exist because human behavior follows directional tendencies. Some people orient outward with a desire to influence or transform the world. Others orient inward with a desire to understand their place within it. Some seek belonging through relationships. Others seek order through structure. These orientations create natural tensions. When a brand tries to serve multiple directions, the Patron experiences motivational conflict. A brand cannot simultaneously express the inward stillness of Find Fulfillment and the outward force of Change the World. It cannot express the emotional fluidity of Foster Belonging and the discipline-heavy stability of Exert Control. These contradictions create incoherence.

Quadrants help eliminate those contradictions. They provide boundaries that ensure consistency. They determine not only which archetypes are available but also which behaviors are appropriate. A brand aligned to Change the World must embrace tension, challenge, ambition, and transformation. A brand living in Foster Belonging must prioritize empathy, community, intimacy, and emotional resonance. A brand grounded in Exert Control must demonstrate order, structure, clarity, and reliability. A brand operating in Find Fulfillment must create experiences rooted in meaning, purity, insight, or self-expansion.

In many ways, the quadrant selection is more important than the archetype itself. Because once a quadrant is chosen, the archetypes available within it are all aligned to the same motivational direction. Choosing the wrong quadrant sends the brand down the wrong psychological path entirely. Choosing the right quadrant dramatically narrows the field, ensuring that the final archetype reflects both Patron truth and brand truth.

Quadrants provide discipline. They prevent brands from slipping into motivational ambiguity. They reveal the psychological territory a brand must inhabit. And once that territory is established, archetype selection becomes the refinement, not the struggle.

Aligning Brand Capabilities with Archetype Demands

Understanding the Patron's motivation and choosing the correct quadrant brings a brand to the boundary of archetype selection. But one more truth must be examined: brands cannot express what they cannot behave. Archetypes are not aspirational costumes. They are behavioral systems that demand consistency. If a brand cannot deliver on the expectations an archetype sets, the archetype collapses.

This is where internal brand capability becomes essential. Archetypes place demands on how a brand must act. A Hero brand must demonstrate discipline, rigor, and competence. A Sage brand must demonstrate clarity, expertise, and intellectual honesty. A Jester brand must demonstrate levity, agility, and emotional fluidity. A Sovereign must demonstrate confidence, structure, and control. These are not creative preferences; they are psychological commitments. When a brand selects an archetype, it inherits a behavioral standard that must be expressed across leadership, culture, operations, communication, and experience.

This is why an internal behavioral audit is required. Edgar Schein's work on organizational culture makes it clear that a brand's true identity is not what leadership claims — it is what the organization communicates through action. Espoused values often contradict lived behaviors. A brand may claim to be bold and disruptive, but its culture may be risk-averse. A brand may claim to be warm and empathic, but its internal systems may be cold and transactional. Archetypes reveal these contradictions immediately.

The audit forces honesty. Can the brand sustain the emotional energy required of a Hero? Does it have the intellectual discipline required of a Sage? Does it have the operational structure required of a Sovereign? Does it have the cultural warmth required of a Lover? Does it have the creative appetite required of a Creator? Archetypes expose what the brand is ready for — and what it is not.

Brands often resist this honesty. They want to be exciting archetypes, intense archetypes, popular archetypes. But the correct archetype must emerge from internal truth, not external desire. When internal capability aligns with Patron motivation and quadrant direction, the archetype becomes undeniable. When internal capability contradicts the archetype, the brand becomes inconsistent and loses coherence.

Psychological trust depends on consistency. Archetypes demand it. Brands must respect that demand.

Diagnosing Category Dynamics: Understanding the Cultural and Competitive Landscape

Even if a brand understands the Patron and understands itself, one last force shapes archetype selection: the category environment. Brands do not live in isolation. They live in mythic ecosystems where narratives compete, where tensions build, and where certain archetypal roles are already occupied. If multiple brands in a category share the same archetype, the category becomes psychologically saturated. If the category has a dominant archetype, breaking away may create differentiation — or destroy relevance.

Douglas Holt's work on cultural branding demonstrates that categories carry their own mythic narratives. These narratives shape what roles Patrons expect brands to play. In athletic performance, the Hero archetype is saturated. In luxury goods, the Sovereign is dominant. In wellness, the Innocent and the Sage compete. In hospitality, the Explorer and the Lover often divide the field. Brands must diagnose these narratives to understand whether an archetype is viable or redundant.

Category dynamics reveal opportunity gaps. If every brand in the category expresses the same archetype, a psychologically coherent alternative can differentiate the newcomer. Liquid Death thrived because it rejected the Innocent archetype of hydration and embraced the Rebel instead. Conversely, a brand entering a category with an established narrative may find success by leaning into that archetype rather than away from it. Dove Chocolate succeeds because the chocolate category is steeped in the Lover's emotional palette, and Dove fully embodies that role rather than resisting it.

Diagnosing category dynamics requires studying the emotional expectations that the category has collectively taught Patrons. It requires understanding which archetypes are overrepresented, which narratives are exhausted, which tensions remain unresolved, and which motivations remain underserved. A category may be ready for disruption. Or it may punish deviation. Psychological logic always decides.

The correct archetype lives at the intersection of Patron need, brand capability, and category narrative. It is revealed through alignment, not preference.

Archetype Selection in Action

To understand how archetype selection plays out in the real world, it is helpful to examine brands that embody their archetypes with clarity, integrity, and depth with a special focus on whose entire organizations operate from that psychological core.

These are a few examples of how archetypes play out in the real world. Later in this book, I unpack deeper dive case studies to showcase holistic approaches to archetype activation.

Harley-Davidson (Explorer, Not Rebel)

Harley-Davidson is often mistakenly labeled a Rebel brand because it features leather jackets, tattoos, and raw aesthetics. But its emotional contract is not rebellion. It is freedom. Harley is the patron saint of autonomy. Riders are not trying to overthrow the world. They are trying to escape it. Harley-Davidson expresses the Explorer archetype in its purest form: open road, individual agency, self-definition.

This Explorer energy shapes everything from product engineering to community culture. It shapes the brand's purpose: "We fulfill dreams of personal freedom." It shapes the rituals of ownership. It shapes the clubs and the loyalty. Harley-Davidson is not edgy for the sake of edge. It is a brand of internal liberation.

Nike (Hero)

Nike is perhaps the most globally recognized expression of the Hero archetype. Everything about Nike reinforces capability, resilience, ambition, and self-efficacy. The brand's success is grounded in psychology, specifically in Bandura's research on self-efficacy, which shows that belief in one's capability is the most powerful predictor of performance.

Nike's messaging encourages discipline, effort, and courage. Its partnerships with athletes reinforce transformation through struggle. Its culture is built on performance. Its innovation pipeline focuses on enabling human potential. Nike is not telling consumers, "We are strong." It is telling them, "You are stronger than you think." The archetype is not aesthetic. It is the emotional center of the brand.

Dove Chocolate (Lover)

Dove Chocolate has built an identity around sensual pleasure, emotional indulgence, and sensory experience. Everything from its textures to its copywriting reflects intimacy, warmth, and presence. Dove speaks to the quiet moment, the personal ritual, the emotional softness that the Patron seeks but rarely gives themselves permission to feel. This is the Lover archetype expressed without apology.

Volvo (Caregiver)

For decades, Volvo has expressed the Caregiver archetype through one consistent narrative: safety. It is not a slogan. It is an organizational obsession. Volvo shapes product engineering around it. Interior design around it. Communication around it. Technology development around it. It is a brand that sees the Patron's vulnerability and steps forward to protect. In a category that often equates power with aggression, Volvo equates strength with care. And because the archetype is so deeply embedded in the organization, the Patron trusts it instinctively.

Liquid Death (Rebel)

Liquid Death entered one of the most sanitized categories in the world (bottled water) and detonated the Innocent archetype that dominates it. By embracing the Rebel archetype unapologetically, the brand created a psychological contrast so sharp that it became instantly memorable. The humor, irreverence, anti-industry stance, and exaggerated aggression are not gimmicks. They are behavioral expressions of the Rebel's need to break what no longer works. And the environmental mission beneath it gives the rebellion purpose.

These case studies demonstrate a consistent truth:

Brands that select the correct archetype achieve coherence.

Brands that force an archetype collapse.

A Repeatable System for Choosing the Right Archetype

Choosing the right archetype is not a matter of taste. It is not a creative preference, a branding trend, or a decision made because the room "likes how it feels." The right archetype emerges only when a brand submits itself to a disciplined, repeatable process that cuts through intuition and bias and reveals the psychological truth beneath the surface. Archetypes are rooted in human motivation, not artistic direction. And because motivation is measurable, so is the path to identifying which archetype a brand is capable of expressing with integrity.

The process begins, always, with the Patron. Not the demographic, not the segment, not the persona with a clever name, but the Patron as a living psychological being. Their fears, their unmet needs, their aspirations, their frustrations, and their internal narratives form the bedrock of the archetype selection process. You cannot choose an archetype until you understand the emotional engine that drives the Patron's choices. Deci and Ryan's Self Determination Theory gives us a map of those engines. Damasio's somatic marker research reminds us that decisions begin in the emotional body before the rational mind. McAdams' narrative identity work shows us how individuals fit brands into their personal storylines. When these understandings converge, a brand can identify the Patron's dominant motivational force with clarity. Not guesswork. Not assumption. Psychological clarity.

From there, the quadrant becomes the next essential filter. Quadrants exist because human motivation moves in predictable directions: outward to change the world, inward to seek fulfillment, outward to foster belonging, inward to exert control. These motivations are not interchangeable. They are not flexible. They are directional forces that shape how people seek meaning. And because the Patron's motivation points in one of these directions, the brand must point in the same one. The quadrant is where the choice narrows. It eliminates entire clusters of archetypes that would create contradiction or cognitive dissonance. It ensures that the brand's emotional orientation matches the Patron's psychological need. It is the moment where the brand stops trying to be everything and becomes something.

Only after the Patron and quadrant are understood can the brand look inward. Archetypes ask the brand to behave, not merely to communicate. They demand consistency, discipline, and psychological alignment across every layer of the organization. Schein's research on organizational culture is useful here because it forces the brand to face the uncomfortable gap between espoused values and actual behaviors. A brand cannot select the Hero if its internal culture resists conflict or avoids discipline. It cannot select the Sage if it operates without clarity or intellectual rigor. It cannot select the Sovereign if its systems are chaotic or inconsistent. Internal capability determines archetypal truth as much as external motivation. When a brand pretends otherwise, the Patron feels the mismatch long before leadership does.

Then comes the category: the cultural landscape where the brand must live. No archetype exists in a vacuum. Every category has dominant narratives, entrenched myths, habitual expectations, and archetypal roles that are already occupied. Holt showed that categories evolve through cultural tension; brands succeed when they adopt roles that either reinforce or disrupt prevailing narratives.

This means the right archetype must fit not only the Patron's need and the brand's ability, but also the narrative space available in the market. Sometimes alignment with the dominant archetype creates trust. Sometimes deviating from it creates distinction. The category reveals which is true. Without this awareness, archetypes become fashionable rather than functional.

When these four forces (Patron motivation, quadrant direction, internal capability, and category dynamic) align, archetype selection becomes less like a decision and more like recognition. The archetype stops feeling like something the brand is choosing and becomes something the brand is finally admitting. It becomes the identity that was there beneath the surface, waiting to be articulated with psychological precision. And once recognized, it unlocks a clarity that few frameworks in branding can provide. Purpose finds discipline. Voice finds cohesion. Experience finds consistency. The brand stops drifting and starts behaving.

This is what makes archetypes powerful. Not symbolism. Not color palettes. Not tone. Alignment. The right archetype is not simply the one that feels inspiring. It is the one that feels inevitable.

This is how brands are built on solid ground.

This is how trust is earned and sustained.

This is how meaning endures across market cycles and leadership changes.

This is how a brand becomes not just recognizable, but resonant.

When a brand chooses the right archetype, it does not just organize its story. It organizes its identity. It organizes its behavior. And, most importantly, it organizes its role in the life of the Patron.

That is the foundation everything else in this book rests upon.

CHAPTER 12

Archetypes Across the Brand Ecosystem

An archetype is not meaningful until it becomes behavior. Many brands stop at the strategy stage. They articulate their archetype beautifully. They run workshops. They build decks. They create excitement. And then, when it is time to translate that archetype into the real world, everything collapses into fragmented execution. The voice says one thing. The environment says another. The product contradicts both. The team behaves independently of all three.

This is the death of archetype work.

An archetype only functions when it becomes the organizing principle for every part of the brand ecosystem. Brand voice. Design. Digital. Environmental experience. Service. Product development. Operational norms. Cultural rituals. Leadership behavior. Everything the Patron touches — and everything they never see, but feel — must reinforce the same psychological promise.

This chapter explores that integration. It shows how archetypes cascade into expression, into systems, into rituals, into behaviors. And it makes one idea unmistakably clear: an archetype is only real when the Patron can feel it without being told what it is.

Voice and Verbal Identity

A brand's voice is often the first place where archetypal integrity is tested. Words reveal behavioral intention. Tone reveals emotional posture. Language reveals whether a brand truly understands the psychological role it is meant to play. Voice is not decoration. It is the brand's internal motivation made audible.

When a brand expresses a Hero archetype, the voice cannot slip into softness or passivity. The Hero does not avoid difficulty. Its language carries momentum. It encourages capability. It reinforces discipline. It demonstrates belief in the Patron's potential through actionable, forward-driving syntax. Meanwhile a Lover archetype would collapse under such intensity. The Lover's voice must create emotional presence. It must soften the edges of experience. It must speak with warmth, intimacy, and sensory richness. Every sentence needs to feel like an offering.

A Sage's voice must strip away embellishment and deliver clarity, structure, and insight. A Rebel's voice must reject conformity and embrace unfiltered immediacy. A Jester's voice must disrupt seriousness and inject levity that disarms tension and creates instant psychological relief. These are not tone choices. They are emotional alignments.

Research in psycholinguistics shows that linguistic framing can alter the emotional state of the reader, even when the message remains constant. Patrons do not respond to what a brand says; they respond to how their nervous system feels while reading it. Voice creates that physiological response. Archetypes shape voice by determining the emotional center from which language is generated.

A brand's verbal identity must emerge from the archetype with discipline. Not occasionally. Not when it's convenient. Always.

Visual Identity and Design

If voice is the emotional resonance of a brand's inner world, design is the emotional grammar of its outer world. Visual identity is not about aesthetics. It is about signaling psychological intention. Human beings interpret visual cues instinctively. Before they interpret meaning cognitively, they interpret safety, intent, and stability emotionally.

Every archetype carries its own visual posture. The Sage gravitates toward clarity, reduction, and logic-driven composition. The Creator embraces expressive detail, human touch, and crafted form. The Sovereign depends on structure, geometry, and order. The Innocent prefers openness, space, and visual purity. The Hero uses bold contrast and directional energy. The Lover relies on tactility and sensorial richness.

These are not stylistic guidelines. They are reflections of the underlying emotional contract.

Design psychology makes this clear. Studies on visual perception, from Arnheim to Ware, demonstrate that composition, contrast, movement, and form all communicate intention before a single word is read. Patrons perceive "confidence," "compassion," "authority," or "playfulness" long before they interpret the logo. They feel the archetype through patterns before they consciously recognize it.

Brands that treat design as aesthetics rather than psychological communication inevitably dilute their archetype. They create inconsistencies, contradictions, and visual noise. But brands that use design to reinforce psychological motivation deepen the emotional footprint of their archetype in every environment the Patron encounters.

Digital Experience and UX Patterns

Digital touchpoints reveal whether an archetype is actually embodied or merely claimed. UX is the brand's psychology translated into mechanics: the friction of navigation, the clarity of hierarchy, the emotional tone of interactions, the feeling of speed, the presence or absence of guidance.

A Hero archetype cannot allow ambiguity. Its digital experience must demonstrate competence through clarity, pace, and direction. A Patron who arrives uncertain must leave feeling capable. That is the Hero's job. UX that confuses, overwhelms, or frustrates betrays the archetype.

A Sage brand lives or dies by its ability to simplify complexity. Its interfaces must feel like a cognitive exhale. Information must be structured to reduce anxiety, not amplify it. The Patron should feel that they understand more simply by being in the brand's digital space.

The Lover must focus on immersion and emotional presence. Microinteractions become gestures of intimacy. The Citizen must emphasize accessibility, fairness, and democratic usability. The Jester must use surprise, relief, and delight to reshape emotional experience. The Sovereign must communicate stability through predictability. The Explorer must enable autonomy by minimizing constraint.

UX reveals behavioral truth. It shows whether the brand can actually behave according to its psychological promise. Inconsistency here is one of the fastest ways to break trust.

Environmental Design and Service Rituals

If digital experience exposes the archetype intellectually, physical environments expose it sensorially. The physical world is where the archetype becomes embodied. The Patron moves through it with their entire nervous system. The space either reinforces emotional truth, or it undermines everything the brand claims.

Environmental psychology has long demonstrated that space shapes behavior. Light, color temperature, sound, materiality, spatial flow, rhythm, density are all elements that influence how people feel and how they behave. Archetypes use these environmental cues to reinforce their psychological posture.

A Caregiver-driven environment must cultivate safety, warmth, and protection. Seating, lighting, pathways, service rhythms all must soothe rather than stimulate. A Creator's space invites discovery and play. A Hero's space must convey momentum and capability. An Innocent's environment must be calm, open, and unburdened. A Rebel's environment must disrupt expectations and create friction intentionally.

Service rituals matter as much as architecture. Rituals are the behavioral choreography of the brand. Every gesture from the team from greeting, guidance, and problem resolution to pacing and body language either reinforces or fractures the archetype. A Lover brand cannot deliver cold service. A Sovereign cannot tolerate inconsistency. A Jester cannot take itself too seriously. A Sage cannot overwhelm with complexity.

When space and ritual align with archetype, the Patron feels coherence without needing explanation. They know what the brand stands for because they feel what the brand stands for.

Product, Menu, and Experience

A brand's product is not separate from its archetype. It is the physical manifestation of its promise. Products, menus, services, and experiences express motivation through form and function. If the archetype does not shape what the brand creates, the identity collapses.

A Creator brand must innovate, refine, and invest in craft. Its products must feel intentionally made, never accidental. A Hero's product must make the Patron feel stronger, more capable, more prepared. A Magician's offering must deliver transformation not metaphorically, but experientially. A Citizen's product must be accessible and fair. A Sovereign's must be precise and dependable. A Rebel's must challenge category norms. An Innocent's must simplify, soothe, or purify.

This is where many brands fail. They express archetypes in campaigns, not products. They express narratives, not experiences. But Patrons do not build loyalty based on messaging. They build loyalty based on lived experience. The archetype must shape what the brand makes — not merely how the brand describes it.

Products are identity made tangible.

Experiences are identity made human.

If products contradict the archetype, the archetype was never real.

Operational and Cultural Consistency

Operational systems reveal the brand's psychology more honestly than any marketing expression. Culture exposes truth faster than campaigns. Teams either reinforce the archetype every day, or they erode it through misalignment and inconsistency. Archetypes shape how organizations lead, hire, train, evaluate, and behave under pressure.

A Sovereign brand must enforce structure, clarity, and standards. If leadership is indecisive or systems are chaotic, the archetype collapses.

A Hero brand must embrace difficulty and growth. If the organization avoids challenge, resists feedback, or rewards comfort, the archetype collapses.

A Lover brand must prioritize emotional intelligence and presence. If the culture is cold or transactional, the archetype collapses.

A Sage brand must value learning, integrity, and intellectual honesty. If decisions are made impulsively or without clarity, the archetype collapses.

A Caregiver brand must nurture and protect. If employee experience contradicts that intention, the Patron will feel it.

A Rebel brand must tolerate disruption and dissent. If leadership suppresses unconventional thought, the archetype cannot survive.

An Explorer brand must empower independence and experimentation. If rigidity overtakes curiosity, the archetype loses authenticity.

Culture is the backbone of archetypal integrity. Operations are its circulatory system. When both align, the archetype becomes embodied.

An archetype is only believable when employees express it without forcing it. When teams move through the world in ways that match the brand's psychological promise it becomes believable. The Patron can detect internal inconsistency even without seeing behind the curtain. All they need is a single broken moment of service or fragmented experience, and the illusion dissolves.

The brands that succeed at archetype embodiment are not the ones with the best branding. They are the ones with the strongest alignment between identity and behavior. When a brand expresses its archetype from the inside out, it becomes coherent. When it expresses it from the outside in, it becomes performative.

CHAPTER 13

The Archetype Implementation Framework

An archetype is only as strong as the organization's ability to live it. Strategy gives a brand its psychological direction, but implementation gives it its reality. Many brands stop at the articulation stage. They finish the workshop. They finalize the PowerPoint. They distribute the guidelines. And then, instead of becoming the organizing principle of the organization, the archetype becomes a reference point that is occasionally nodded to, periodically resurfaced, or politically invoked when convenient. It becomes an accessory, not a structure.

But archetypes were never meant to live on the wall. They were meant to live in behavior. They were designed as behavioral frameworks long before they were used in branding. Jung didn't describe archetypes to help someone build marketing campaigns. He described them to explain why people act the way they do. Campbell expanded the narrative precisely because these patterns reflected human behavior across cultures. Modern psychology has since reinforced that these archetypal scripts shape motivation, identity construction, choice, and emotional resonance.

For a brand, this means something simple but profound: a brand becomes its archetype only when the organization behaves like it. Everything else is theory. Implementation is where theory becomes identity. It is where purpose becomes posture. It is where strategy becomes systems. And it is where teams, leadership, environments, products, rituals, and decisions all align around one psychological promise.

This chapter outlines how that happens. Not in fragments. Not in scattered guidelines. But through a coherent, disciplined, deeply integrated framework that turns archetypes into organizational truth.

Translating Archetype Into Organizational Reality

An archetype cannot remain conceptual if it is meant to influence behavior. Strategy teams often describe the archetype, define its attributes, and outline its emotional role, but they fail to translate those ideas into principles that govern daily behavior. Without translation, the archetype becomes abstract. It becomes a poetic description rather than a practical operating system.

The first step is identifying the emotional promise at the core of the archetype. This is not a tagline or a marketing phrase. It is the psychological need the brand satisfies in the Patron. A Sage promises understanding. A Hero promises capability. A Citizen promises belonging. A Sovereign promises structure. These promises must be articulated in plain, human language that teams can understand intuitively. If the emotional promise is vague, metaphorical, or overly clever, the team cannot operationalize it.

But even a clear emotional promise is not enough. The archetype must define the brand's behavioral posture which is the consistent way the organization shows up in the world. Behavioral posture is the emotional stance of the brand. A Hero carries forward momentum and clarity. A Lover carries warmth and intimacy. A Rebel carries provocation and audacity. A Caregiver carries steadiness and empathy. Posture is the brand's psychological gravity. It must remain stable regardless of context: in crisis, in routine, in innovation, in service, in communication.

To protect this posture, boundaries must be articulated. Boundaries define what the brand does not do. They prevent drift. They give teams the discipline required to avoid the gravitational pull of adjacent archetypes. Every archetype has a shadow and a neighbor. The Sage can drift into the Sovereign. The Rebel can drift into the Jester. The Innocent can drift into the Caregiver. The Hero can drift into the Magician. Without boundaries, the team inevitably begins interpreting the archetype through personal bias or preference, weakening it.

This is where the archetype playbook becomes essential. A playbook is not a document of aesthetics. It is a document of behavior. It explains the emotional promise, the posture, and the boundaries with clarity and depth. It includes narrative examples, voice philosophy, sensory expressions, behavioral implications, and environmental principles. It frames decisions not in subjective taste but in psychological coherence. It gives teams the shared language needed to interpret the archetype consistently.

It ensures that every team is aligned around one emotional truth from creative, product, and digital to operations, HR, and leadership. When done well, it prevents fragmentation. It prevents drift. It prevents misinterpretation. And it turns the archetype into an organizational compass that points everyone in the same emotional direction.

This translation is not optional. Without it, the archetype remains a creative preference. With it, the archetype becomes a behavioral mandate.

How Teams, Culture, and Leadership Embody the Archetype

A brand expresses its archetype most truthfully through its people. Before a Patron ever experiences the archetype, teams internalize it or fail to. Before an environment reflects the archetype, employees embody it or contradict it. Implementation begins with people because behavior precedes expression.

Training plays a central role here. Teams must be taught not just what the archetype is, but what it feels like and how it behaves. Training must move beyond the language of branding and into the language of psychology, emotion, and social behavior. A Hero team must learn to embrace challenge, not avoid it. A Lover team must learn to create emotional presence. A Sage team must learn to pursue clarity over complexity. An Explorer team must learn to empower autonomy rather than restrict it. These behaviors cannot be improvised. They must be absorbed, practiced, and reinforced.

Culture is the medium in which these behaviors become habitual. Schein's work showed that organizational culture is not declared. Instead, it is demonstrated. Culture forms through patterns of behavior that become normal, not through values written in brand books. If the archetype is meant to shape the organization, teams must see it modeled, rewarded, recognized, and reinforced.

This is where leadership becomes the archetype's first expression. Leaders teach the archetype through their behavior more than through their words. Their decisions under pressure, their psychological posture in meetings, their willingness to confront discomfort, their way of speaking about the Patron, and their emotional responses to conflict all establish what the archetype looks like in motion. Teams mirror leadership instinctively. If leaders behave against the archetype, the entire organization internalizes that contradiction.

Goleman's research on emotional leadership makes this clear: leaders set the emotional climate of the organization. That climate determines whether people feel encouraged, empowered, timid, defensive, or aligned. Without leadership modeling, no amount of training can compensate. Teams follow emotional patterns long before they follow instructions.

Amy Edmondson's work on psychological safety adds another dimension. For a team to express the archetype confidently, they must feel safe enough to embody its expectations. A Jester brand cannot thrive in a culture where spontaneity is punished. A Rebel brand cannot thrive in a culture where dissent is unsafe. A Creator brand cannot thrive where experimentation is penalized. Psychological safety is not a soft concept. It is structural to archetype integrity.

Rituals reinforce archetypes. Rituals are the behavioral habits organizations adopt to normalize the archetype's posture. A Citizen brand may hold fairness reviews or peer acknowledgments. A Caregiver brand may begin meetings by checking emotional temperature. A Hero brand may ritualize goal-setting and personal improvement. These rituals anchor the archetype in the day-to-day rhythms of the company.

Ultimately, archetypes live or die in the hands of the people tasked with expressing them. When culture understands the archetype, when leadership models it, and when teams feel safe embodying it, the archetype becomes more than a strategy. It becomes the way the organization exists.

Bringing the Archetype to Life Through Design, Digital, and Experience

Once a brand's people and culture align with the archetype, the next challenge is ensuring that every external expression reflects the same psychological posture. Patrons experience the brand through voice, visuals, digital interactions, environments, products, and rituals. Every one of these touchpoints communicates emotionally, not logically. And every one is an opportunity to reinforce or erode the archetype.

Design becomes the brand's emotional grammar. It communicates intention through form, color, rhythm, contrast, and composition. These cues are not superficial. They are processed by the brain's perceptual system before conscious thought. Studies in visual cognition show that humans assign emotional meaning to shape and pattern in milliseconds. A Sovereign's geometry communicates control. A Lover's warmth communicates presence. A Hero's boldness communicates capability. A Sage's clarity communicates understanding. The Patron feels the archetype before they read a single word.

Digital experience must follow the same emotional logic. UX is psychological guidance in disguise. It's a sequence of emotional cues that shape confidence, clarity, trust, and ease. A Hero's interface must create momentum and reduce hesitation. A Sage's interface must simplify cognition. A Citizen's interface must democratize access. A Magician's interface must reveal possibility. A Jester's interface must relieve tension. UX reveals whether the brand truly understands the emotional state of the Patron.

Environments complete the sensory dimension. Environmental psychology demonstrates that space shapes behavior, emotion, and memory. Light, material, spatial organization, sound, density, and texture all influence the Patron's nervous system. A Caregiver's environment must protect. A Rebel's environment must disrupt. A Creator's environment must invite participation. An Innocent's environment must soothe. These are not creative preferences; they are emotional imperatives.

Products and services represent the archetype in its most tangible form. They are the manifestation of the emotional promise. A Creator's product must feel crafted. A Hero's must feel empowering. A Magician's must feel transformative. A Citizen's must feel accessible. A Sovereign's must feel reliable. A Lover's must feel intimate. A Rebel's must feel liberating. If product contradicts archetype, the entire identity collapses.

Service rituals complete the experience. They translate the archetype into human interaction. The way a team welcomes, supports, responds, and says goodbye matters more than any campaign. A Jester's service must surprise and delight. A Sage's must clarify. A Sovereign's must command respect. A Caregiver's must nurture. These rituals are the final, most important expression of the brand's psyche.

Expression is not about aesthetics. It is about emotional coherence. When every component of the experience reflects the same psychological posture, the Patron does not need to be told what the brand stands for because they feel it.

Governance, Drift Prevention, and Long-Term Stewardship

An archetype is most vulnerable after launch. Excitement carries the brand through the first months of implementation. Teams feel aligned. The strategy feels fresh. The concept feels strong. But without governance, archetypes erode. Individuals reinterpret them. Departments drift. Creative partners impose their own tastes. Leadership changes create emotional inconsistency. And slowly, the brand's psychological clarity dissolves.

Governance protects the archetype from erosion. It ensures that decisions, especially creative decisions, remain grounded in the emotional promise and behavioral posture defined by the archetype. This does not mean creating layers of bureaucracy. It means creating standards, review processes, rituals, and structures that preserve psychological coherence.

Identity stewardship is essential. Brands must designate individuals or teams responsible for ensuring that every expression aligns with the archetype. These stewards act as interpreters and protectors. They guard the emotional boundary. They educate new partners. They clarify ambiguity. They prevent dilution.

Drift prevention requires periodic recalibration. Every quarter or year, the organization must revisit the archetype not to redefine it but to realign around it. These recalibrations keep teams connected to the psychological truth of the brand, especially as the organization evolves.

Organizations that sustain their archetype across time do so because leadership, culture, systems, and governance reinforce it continuously. The archetype is not a campaign asset. It is a structural asset. It becomes the organization's internal compass — a constant reminder of the emotional contract the brand has made with the Patron.

When governance protects the archetype, continuity becomes possible.

When continuity exists, meaning endures.

And when meaning endures, the brand becomes more than recognizable, it becomes indispensable.

CHAPTER 14

Archetypes in the Lifecycle of a Brand

Every brand exists inside a lifecycle. It begins with energy and ambition. It grows through adaptation and alignment. It matures through discipline and consistency. And, inevitably, it faces periods of drift, tension, misalignment, or crisis. The brands that endure understand one truth: an identity is not meant to be a static artifact. It is meant to be a stable narrative that adapts without losing its center. Archetypes make that possible. They provide the psychological continuity that allows a brand to evolve without fragmenting. They anchor purpose through volatility. They guide decisions through complexity. They stabilize culture through leadership change. They help organizations reconnect with truth when drift occurs. And they give mature brands the humility and clarity needed to renew themselves without abandoning who they are.

This chapter explores the relationship between archetypes and the lifecycle of a brand. It is not a linear journey. It is a rhythm repeated in different forms over decades. At every stage of the lifecycle, the archetype operates differently. It acts as ignition during startup momentum, structure during growth, orientation during drift, refinement during maturity, and restoration during crisis. No other strategic system carries this range. Archetypes do because they are tied to human motivation and brands, at their core, are human systems.

How Archetypes Drive Startup Momentum

Startups often begin with a surge of energy so raw and directional that founders mistake it for identity. The early days of a brand feel electric precisely because constraints have not yet formed. Decisions are faster. Communication is instinctive. Roles blur. Everyone knows the why, even if they haven't articulated it. Startups mistake this chemistry for brand clarity. And it works until it doesn't.

What early-stage companies rarely understand is that the emotional energy they're operating with is the embryonic form of their archetype. The team is expressing a psychological posture before it has a name. A founder who rallies the team with courage, ambition, and boldness is expressing the Hero, whether intentionally or not. A founder who leads with rebelliousness, friction, and provocation is expressing the Rebel. A founder who builds from curiosity, invention, and possibility is expressing the Magician or Creator. The team is absorbing an emotional pattern long before design, messaging, or product choices enter the picture.

This is why archetypes are so powerful for startups: they capture the unspoken emotional truth behind early momentum. They articulate what the team is already embodying instinctively. And when articulated correctly, they prevent the brand from drifting as headcount grows and the original emotional energy gets diluted.

Research on organizational psychology supports this. Edgar Schein's work found that early founders define culture far more than values statements do. Their behavior becomes a template for every decision that follows. They model the emotional world the organization learns to inhabit. Archetypes take that early emotional world and make it explicit, legible, teachable. They give words to instinct. They give structure to intuition.

Startups without this structure tend to fracture on the first major growth curve. Their early emotional alignment becomes inconsistent as departments form, roles specialize, middle management emerges, and communication patterns shift. What once felt intuitive becomes diffuse. Without an archetype, teams create their own interpretations of what the brand "is," based on personal preference or functional needs. Fragmentation begins quietly with one messaging shift here, one design variation there, one product decision that contradicts the original energy, until suddenly, the brand feels like a collection of unrelated expressions.

Archetypes prevent this by stabilizing the brand's emotional center. They clarify why the brand exists beyond product and beyond growth. Simon Sinek popularized "Start With Why," but what he didn't articulate is that the Why lacks behavioral force without a psychological role. Purpose must be paired with an archetype to become actionable. A startup whose purpose is "to connect people through shared experiences" could be a Lover, a Citizen, or even a Creator. The archetype clarifies the motivational source of that purpose, which is what the team needs to deliver it consistently.

Archetypes also guide early decision-making when data is sparse and instinct drives nearly everything. Research in cognitive science (particularly Gerd Gigerenzer's work on heuristics) shows that intuitive decision-making is reliable only when it draws from consistent internal frameworks. Archetypes act as that internal framework. They tell teams what kind of decision "feels right" because they anchor to a stable psychological pattern. A Sage-led startup evaluates decisions through clarity and understanding. A Rebel-led startup evaluates through disruption and defiance. A Hero-led startup evaluates through testing, grit, and effort. These differing heuristics create entirely different trajectories.

Momentum is not just speed. It is direction multiplied by consistency. Archetypes give startups consistency without slowing them down. They channel chaotic energy into coherent behavior. They give the brand narrative continuity before fragmentation has a chance to take hold.

In the early lifecycle, the archetype is ignition. It is the spark that becomes the story.

Managing Growth & Internal Alignment

Growth is the stage where brands are most vulnerable to losing themselves. New hires enter without the emotional history of the founding team. External partners influence direction. Middle managers interpret the brand differently. Functional needs begin to compete with one another. Scaling becomes less about improvisation and more about systems. In this shift from fluidity to structure, the archetype becomes the brand's stabilizing force.

As organizations scale, the psychological gaps widen. Departments make decisions through their functional lenses: marketing prioritizes differentiation, operations prioritizes efficiency, HR prioritizes cohesion, finance prioritizes stability, product prioritizes feasibility. None of these priorities are wrong. But without a shared psychological framework, they become conflicting. Archetypes resolve this conflict by giving every department a single motivational lens through which to interpret decisions. They give the organization one story to hold.

Research in sensemaking theory (Karl Weick) shows that organizations maintain coherence not through documentation but through shared narratives that help individuals interpret ambiguity. This is exactly what archetypes provide: a narrative schema that helps teams understand "how we behave" and "what matters" without requiring detailed instructions for every scenario. A Magician-led organization evaluates new opportunities through transformation, not efficiency. An Explorer-led organization prioritizes autonomy and discovery over standardization. A Citizen-led organization prioritizes fairness and inclusion even when scale pressures push toward convenience. Archetypes turn abstract values into operational logic.

Growth also strains culture. New people enter quickly, and onboarding often focuses on tools, processes, and roles rather than identity. If identity is not codified and reinforced, the emotional DNA of the brand dilutes with each hiring cycle. This is where archetypes serve their second purpose: they become the cultural filter. They influence hiring profiles, performance evaluation, internal rituals, leadership norms, and interpersonal dynamics.

Leaders often underestimate the internal dimension here. Team members don't embody archetypes because they memorized them. They embody them because they inhabit a culture that expresses them consistently. Behavioral norms must align with the archetype. A Rebel brand cannot emphasize compliance and harmony. A Caregiver brand cannot reward aggression or ambition at the expense of empathy. A Hero brand cannot protect comfort or avoid conflict. A Sovereign brand cannot tolerate ambiguity or inconsistency. The archetype becomes the cultural guardrail through which behavior is shaped.

We see this most clearly in organizations that scale without identity discipline. Culture changes faster than leadership expects. The original emotional posture gets buried under new operational demands. Drift becomes subtle but cumulative. A Hero company begins optimizing for comfort. A Sage brand begins using complexity as a shield rather than clarity as a tool. A Lover brand becomes transactional. A Creator brand becomes rigid. Alignment weakens because the psychological center of the brand is no longer being reinforced.

Archetypes preserve alignment through growth by grounding every decision, every hire, and every ritual in a stable emotional truth. They provide the continuity needed to scale without losing the original story. They ensure departments don't become islands. They ensure leaders don't drift into personal preference. They ensure the brand's voice, design language, product philosophy, and service rituals evolve cohesively rather than independently.

Growth is where brands most easily lose themselves. Archetypes prevent this loss by giving the organization a coherent emotional spine. They anchor the brand's internal world so its external expression can scale without distortion.

When brands drift and how to recenter

Every brand drifts. Drift is not failure. Drift is human. Organizations change. Leadership changes. Market conditions shift. Teams evolve. Priorities compete. Over time, the gravitational pull of complexity pulls the brand away from the emotional truth that once defined it. Drift is not an event; it is a slow accumulation of micro-contradictions that eventually becomes visible to the Patron.

Most drift begins internally. When leaders express behaviors inconsistent with the archetype, the organization internalizes those behaviors. A Hero brand whose leaders become conflict-averse begins avoiding challenges. A Sovereign brand whose leaders tolerate inconsistency begins eroding its structure. A Lover brand whose leaders suppress emotional expression begins hardening into the Citizen. These shifts often happen gradually, unnoticed until they are reflected in the external experience.

Drift also occurs when functional priorities overshadow psychological ones. Growth teams chase metrics. Marketing teams chase trends. Product teams chase feasibility. Operations teams chase speed. Finance teams chase efficiency. None of these are wrong. But when they override the archetype's emotional promise, the brand begins to fracture. The Patron senses the inconsistencies long before the organization does.

The most damaging drift occurs when fear enters the system. Fear of losing relevance. Fear of competition. Fear of economic instability. Research from Heifetz and Linsky on adaptive leadership suggests that in periods of stress, organizations revert to short-termism and abandon the identity structures that provide stability. A Rebel brand becomes conservative. A Sage brand becomes chaotic. A Hero brand becomes passive. Fear erodes identity because fear narrows intention.

The work of recentering a brand is not creative. It is psychological. It begins with revisiting the archetype not as a concept but as a behavioral test. The organization must ask: Are we behaving like ourselves? It must examine where behaviors have drifted, where decisions contradict identity, where culture has weakened, where leadership has defaulted to convenience instead of discipline.

Recenterings often require leadership humility. Leaders must be willing to name the drift, acknowledge the contradictions, and recommit publicly to the emotional truth of the brand. Without this commitment, recentering becomes a surface exercise that restructures messaging but leaves systemic behavior untouched.

Brands that recenter effectively engage in what psychologists call narrative restoration. They rearticulate the story of who they are, not by rewriting it, but by reconnecting with their original emotional promise. This is not nostalgia. It is alignment. Narrative identity research shows that people experience meaning when they feel continuity between past, present, and future. Brands do too.

Recenterings require reestablishing the archetype across culture, operations, decision-making, and experience. It may require restructuring teams whose habits contradict the archetype. It may require retraining managers. It may require reengineering systems. Recenterings are not about going back; they are about coming home to the emotional truth that gave the brand purpose.

Drift is inevitable. Recenterings are intentional. Archetypes make them possible.

Archetypes in Mature/Legacy Brands

Mature brands face a different challenge than startups or high-growth organizations. They must maintain relevance while preserving identity. They must innovate without abandoning the emotional truth that built their equity. They must evolve with culture without dissolving into trend-following. Archetypes give mature brands the continuity needed to adapt without losing coherence.

In mature brands, the archetype becomes the map by which evolution is guided. It defines what kinds of innovation are aligned and what kinds fracture identity. A Creator brand may innovate through craft, personalization, or artistic expression, but it cannot innovate by becoming hyper-efficient or coldly minimalist. A Sage brand may innovate through clarity, education, or simplification, but not through shock-value rebrands. A Sovereign may innovate through structural improvements or elevated standards, but not through casual looseness.

Archetypes help mature brands avoid the existential crisis of reinvention. Reinvention, when done without archetypal grounding, often leads to identity collapse. The brand experiments with discontinuous expressions. It introduces contradictions. It broadens its narrative until it loses meaning. Mature brands that reinvent without archetypes tend to either overcorrect or dilute.

Archetypes also shape leadership continuity in mature organizations. Successive generations of leaders often bring new styles, perspectives, and priorities. Without archetypal grounding, each leadership change risks shifting the brand's emotional posture. Archetypes give leaders a role to inhabit rather than a personal identity to impose. They protect the brand from leadership personality swings.

Research on brand heritage (Urde, Greyser) shows that brands maintain their power by preserving their core identity while interpreting it for new eras. Archetypes serve as the core identity. They prevent the brand from redefining itself so frequently that Patrons lose trust. They allow innovation to happen at the edges while the psychological center remains constant.

Mature brands also face cultural nostalgia. Patrons want the brand to feel like itself. They want continuity. They want the emotional story they associate with the brand to remain intact. Archetypes deliver that story. They give the Patron a stable narrative to hold onto even as the brand modernizes.

Innovation without identity is chaos.

Identity without innovation is stagnation.

Archetypes allow mature brands to hold both truths simultaneously.

Crisis, Renewal, and Archetypal Anchors

Crisis is where brands either reveal their truth or abandon it. Economic downturns, leadership scandals, operational failures, public mistakes, category disruption, cultural backlash are critical moments in a brand's life. Every brand faces moments that force it to decide what it believes and how it behaves under pressure. Crises strip away pretense. Whatever remains is identity.

During crisis, the archetype becomes the brand's anchor. It defines the posture the brand takes, the decisions it makes, the tone it uses, and the promises it protects. Research on organizational crisis response (Sim Sitkin, Weick, Pauchant & Mitroff) shows that organizations anchored in strong identity navigate crises with clarity, while organizations with weak identity fracture, panic, or thrash. The archetype becomes the stable center when external conditions destabilize the brand.

A Hero brand must step toward the difficulty, not away. A Sage brand must provide clarity, not complexity. A Caregiver must protect, not retreat. A Rebel must confront, not perform. A Sovereign must stabilize, not delay. A Lover must remain present, not harden. Crisis is the moment when the archetype proves whether it was deeply embodied or superficially applied.

Crises also reveal internal alignment. Teams look to leadership for emotional cues. Leadership looks to identity for direction. Identity must be strong enough to guide them. Archetypes translate the abstract into concrete action. A Rebel brand facing cultural backlash responds with accountability framed through defiance of a broken norm. A Sage brand responds through transparency and explanation. A Caregiver responds through care and protection of those harmed. A Sovereign responds through order, structure, and decisive action.

Brands that enter crisis without archetypal grounding often try to "fix" identity in the middle of the storm. They rewrite narratives. They shift voices. They contort themselves into whatever they believe the market wants. This instability erodes trust faster than the crisis event itself. Patrons forgive mistakes more easily than they forgive inconsistency. Identity clarity is a crisis asset.

Renewal emerges from the same place. When a brand must rebuild after crisis, drift, stagnation, or cultural irrelevance the archetype becomes the source of narrative restoration. It reconnects the brand with its emotional truth. It gives the organization a North Star to reorient around. It clarifies how to rebuild trust: not through novelty, but through returning to the psychological promise the brand made long before the crisis.

Narrative psychology (McAdams again) shows that meaning is restored not by denying rupture but by integrating it into a coherent story. Brands do the same. Archetypes give them the language of coherence. A Hero brand reframes crisis as struggle and transformation. A Sage reframes it as understanding and correction.

A Caregiver frames it as healing. A Rebel frames it as necessary upheaval. A Lover frames it as reconnection. These are not spin strategies. They are psychological truths.

Renewal requires returning to the emotional center. Archetypes make that center visible, nameable, and actionable. They give the brand the ability to recover without reinventing. They give Patrons the sense that the brand has not changed who it is. Instead, it has simply remembered.

CHAPTER 15

Identifying a Brand's Archetype: The Archetype Workshop

As with many endeavors, there is more than one path to finding a brand's archetype, and each pathway carries its own advantages and risks. Over the years, in roles ranging from agency owner and creative director to vice president of digital experience and author, I have tested many of these paths. The one that consistently produces both clarity and buy in, across industries and team sizes, is the facilitated workshop. When it is done well, a workshop is not a meeting. It is a shared experience that reshapes how people see the brand and their role in shaping it.

Workshops give internal teams and agency partners a way to rapidly build alignment around the foundations of a brand's strategy. Through structured activities, honest discussion, focused presentation, and a steady hand from the moderator, workshops create a temporary environment where people can step outside their day to day habits and think clearly about who the brand is and who it is becoming. The benefits are not confined to the session itself. A strong workshop produces clarity and trust that ripple through the relationship for years.

For existing brands, the work is heavier than it is for emerging ones. New brands are focused entirely on what could be. Existing brands must confront what is. The presentation content is often similar, but the conversations are not. Evaluating the current state of the brand and defining the future state effectively doubles the work. The team must first agree on a clear picture of present reality, then do the harder work of deciding what must change. I will unpack the differences between new and existing brand workshops later in this section.

In the pages that follow, I will outline the goals of a brand archetype workshop, the preparation required before anyone walks into the room, how to structure and conduct the session, and what the outputs should look like when it is done well.

Goals of the Workshop

Identifying a brand's archetype is the most obvious goal of an archetype workshop, but it is not the only one. A well run session produces multiple outcomes that make the investment of time and money worthwhile for both new and established brands.

One core goal is cultivating real buy in. When teams participate in the process of defining the archetype, they are more likely to believe in it and defend it. During the workshop, participants learn what archetypes are, how they function, and why they matter. They hear each other's perspectives. They wrestle with tradeoffs. They see how their own experiences connect to the identity being shaped. When the group finally lands on an archetype, it is not the moderator's answer. It is theirs. That sense of authorship is what creates buy in.

Another important outcome is the spark of ideation. As people learn about archetypes, they cannot help but imagine how the brand might change once it behaves with more intention. New ideas for products, services, communication, experience design, and internal culture begin to surface. When the archetype clicks, people start to see opportunities that have always been present but never named. Good workshops channel that energy, capture it, and tie it back to the behavioral role of the brand.

Workshops also strengthen collaboration. Collaboration is not a permanent state. It is a skill that must be practiced. A workshop is an ideal place to practice because it creates a shared problem, a shared language, and a defined container for conflict. A strong moderator sets expectations early and creates a space where questions and objections can be raised without fear of backlash. Over the course of the session, the group learns how to disagree productively, how to stay focused on the Patron, and how to move toward a shared decision. This collaborative muscle becomes invaluable once the archetype needs to be activated across the organization.

Regardless of whether the team has two people or twelve, it is the moderator's responsibility to design and protect a process that achieves these aims. The workshop format that follows is built with these outcomes in mind. The work, however, starts long before the group gathers.

Lead Up Work

Walking into a workshop without proper preparation is like trying to swim without water. You can go through the motions, but nothing meaningful will happen. Lead up work provides the raw material that makes the session specific rather than generic. Without it, the workshop quickly drifts into opinion trading and abstract ideation that never quite connects to reality.

There are two primary areas of pre work for a brand archetype workshop: Patron research and competitive research. Each produces critical inputs that will be used throughout the session in presentations, discussions, and exercises.

Patron Research

Archetypes are tools for shaping behavior, so it is essential to understand the people whose behavior the brand seeks to influence. Without that understanding, the workshop becomes an exercise in wishful thinking. Teams will generate ideas, but those ideas will float unanchored above the real lives of the Patrons they intend to serve.

The central goals of Patron research are to identify a core Patron group, to understand what those Patrons experience in excess, and to understand what they lack. The gap between those two realities becomes the roadmap for identifying the quadrant and archetype most likely to drive meaningful behavior change.

Consider a gamer community that interacts daily across multiple platforms. They may already experience a strong sense of belonging through guilds, chats, and streaming culture. Belonging is abundant. What they may lack is a sense of fulfillment, progress, or personal growth beyond the game. Archetypes in the Find Fulfillment quadrant such as the Sage, the Explorer, or the Innocent may be better suited to serve that psychological need than archetypes that simply offer more belonging.

Researching Patrons for a new brand can be challenging, especially when the company operates nationally or globally. Fortunately, there are established firms that specialize in consumer and industry data. For broader market level insights, firms like Technomic and Mintel offer robust reports and tools. They require investment, but the cost is often a fraction of what a misguided brand strategy will burn.

If the brand has a geographic footprint such as restaurants or retail locations, tools like Esri and Placer.ai can provide detailed views into local demographics, movement patterns, and behavior. They are particularly useful in identifying where specific Patron groups are likely to concentrate.

First party research is where the strongest insights usually live. Surveys, interviews, focus groups, and intercepts allow you to ask questions tailored to the brand and Patron context. The quality of the output, however, depends on the quality of the questions. Leading questions, overly broad prompts, or formats that encourage people to say what they think you want to hear will produce noise instead of insight. The goal is to avoid groupthink, confirmation bias, and canned responses in order to reach deeper truths.

For focus groups, it is often worth hiring a firm that specializes in moderating sessions and interpreting what is said and what is left unsaid. For surveys, platforms like Google Surveys and Ask Your Target Market can help reach defined audiences efficiently, but they do not write the questions for you. In many cases, partnering with an experienced strategist or researcher to craft the instrument is worth the cost.

Regardless of the methods you choose, the objective is the same. You are looking for clean, usable data that will inform the workshop and give the team solid ground to stand on.

Competitive Research

Competitive research provides the external context. It shows how other brands in the space are currently behaving, which Patrons they appear to be targeting, and what emotional roles they seem to be attempting to play. Without that context, it is easy to choose an archetype that either duplicates an existing player or ignores opportunities that are sitting open.

For most brands, a detailed audit of competitor digital channels is a practical starting point. Reviewing websites, social media content, advertising, and email can reveal patterns in tone, messaging, and experience. The key questions are simple. Who does this brand appear to be speaking to. How do they speak to them. What emotional value do they emphasize. Does their behavior suggest a clear archetypal orientation.

For deeper analysis, research tools that aggregate financial or engagement data can provide additional perspective, but this level of scrutiny is not always necessary. At some point, the returns diminish. The goal is not to become an expert on every competitor. The goal is to understand the range of positions in the market and identify where there may be white space.

As you work through this research, capture evidence. Save screenshots of websites, ads, and posts that feel like clear expressions of each competitor's Purpose and personality. Assemble these artifacts into a single sheet or board so the team can see everything at once. When all the information lives on one page, patterns and gaps are much easier to see.

If you want a deeper dive into how to define a relevant competitive set and identify meaningful white space, I outline a full process in The Bullhearted Brand. While that book focuses on restaurants, the approach adapts easily to other industries.

Competitive Research in Physical Spaces

When brands operate in physical environments like retail or restaurants, visiting locations adds an important layer to the analysis. Digital channels tell you what the brand wants to say. Physical experiences show you what the brand actually does.

Select a diverse set of locations rather than trying to see everything. A handful of sites in different markets, formats, or trade areas will give you more insight than a long list of nearly identical stores. Pay attention to the entire journey, from approach to exit. How easy is it to find parking? Is the entry obvious or confusing? Are interaction points clear? Does the interior design feel aligned with what you saw online, or does it feel like a different brand entirely?

Observe moments of elation and anxiety. Where do things feel smooth, considered, and inviting. Where do they feel confusing, frustrating, or indifferent? These emotional spikes and dips are among the most reliable indicators of experience quality and brand strength. When possible, talk to employees. Casual conversations often reveal more about culture and brand truth than formal research.

Once you have visited enough locations to see recurring patterns, document the experience in a structured way and fold your findings into the competitive analysis.

Existing Brand Research

When the workshop is for an existing brand, everything above still applies, with one more layer. You must also research the brand itself. This is more than reading the website and internal decks. It is a systematic effort to understand how the organization currently behaves, what it believes, and where internal narratives conflict with reality.

Leadership interviews are often the starting point. They are also frequently the most biased. Executives tend to be invested in existing narratives about what makes the brand special. They may unintentionally downplay problems or overstate strengths. A strong interviewer will listen carefully, ask clarifying questions, and avoid accepting surface answers at face value. Many of the same skills used in negotiation apply here. The goal is not to trap anyone. The goal is to reach the underlying truth.

Talking only to leadership is not enough. The most revealing insights often come from people closer to the work: managers, frontline staff, and cross functional partners. These conversations need to be handled with care. Some people may be defensive or fearful. Others may be openly disgruntled. Both groups can provide valuable perspective if the interviewer creates a sense of safety and knows how to separate signal from noise.

In many organizations, sales data is another rich source of truth. It shows which products or services drive revenue, how those patterns vary by location or channel, and how Patron behavior has shifted over time. When analyzed carefully, this data can reveal which parts of the current brand expression are working and which are underperforming.

Sales and engagement data also make it possible to identify Patron cohorts such as highly loyal guests, new guests, lapsed guests, and seasonal or occasional users. Each of these groups represents a different relationship to the brand and can provide unique insights when included in research.

Taken together, Patron research, competitive analysis, and internal brand research provide the foundation for an archetype workshop that is grounded in reality rather than opinion.

Location Is Everything

Where the workshop takes place influences how well it works. A strong process held in a poor environment will struggle. A good environment cannot save a weak process, but it can amplify a strong one.

Whenever possible, hold the workshop off site. Familiar spaces carry familiar distractions. When people remain in their usual office, they are more likely to be pulled into side conversations, emails, and daily issues. An off site location helps signal that this work is different. It also reduces the number of ambient interruptions that break the workshop's rhythm.

The space itself does not need to be impressive. It needs to be functional. There should be enough room for people to move, stand, and work in small groups without crowding. Surfaces for writing and posting materials are useful. Technology should be simple and reliable. The venue should be easy to reach, with adequate parking and accessibility.

Refreshments are not a trivial detail. Workshops can run long, and hunger or thirst will eventually pull focus if you do not plan ahead. Provide water, coffee, and simple snacks. It is a small investment that keeps energy levels from crashing.

Who Should Attend

The composition of the group matters as much as the content. Too many people and the session can become chaotic. Too few and you risk missing critical perspectives or losing traction once the workshop is over.

For early stage brands, core partners and any advisors with meaningful influence over brand direction should attend. For larger organizations, the group usually includes C suite leadership and key decision makers across relevant functions, including finance and legal. Even if some leaders feel that brand work is outside their lane, their presence and participation are essential if the archetype is going to be taken seriously later.

Because you will already have gathered insights from teams across the organization during the research phase, it is not necessary to include representatives from every level in the workshop itself. The room should be reserved for people who have direct responsibility for shaping, approving, and living the brand strategy.

Before the workshop, it is wise to hold a short pre-session call with participants. Use this time to explain the purpose of the workshop, outline the flow, and set expectations. This is also a chance to address anxieties and reinforce that the session is a space for honest collaboration, not a stage for performance. If senior leaders are present, they should explicitly commit to listening, to engaging, and to not using workshop conversations as ammunition later. In some cases, it may be helpful to split leadership and middle management into separate working groups for part of the session to create more open discussion.

Run of Play

Workshops blend structure and energy. A strong session feels organized but not rigid, interactive but not chaotic. The facilitator's job is to maintain a steady cadence while keeping people engaged, informed, and focused on the right questions.

Workshops for new brands and existing brands share common elements, but they differ in emphasis and depth. New brands can spend most of their time on future state. Existing brands must first agree on the current state before they can move forward.

For new brands, a typical flow begins with an archetypes primer, moves into Patron research review and discussion, then into competitive research and positioning, and finally into archetype selection.

New Brands

The archetypes primer is where you establish a common language. In this segment, you explain what archetypes are, where they come from, how they show up in culture, and how they function as behavioral drivers rather than personality labels. Use familiar examples from stories and brands to make the concepts concrete. The goal is not to turn the team into Jungian scholars, but to get everyone operating from the same mental model.

Interactive elements help. Asking participants where they have seen archetypal patterns in their own lives or which archetypes they feel drawn to personally engages them and makes the material stick. Providing a printed version of your archetype wheel gives them a visual reference they can use throughout the session.

Next, review the Patron research. Show the team how the data was collected and why the Patron group was defined the way it was. Give the group a name, describe their behaviors, and share key insights that reveal their motivations and constraints. When a Patron group is well defined and named clearly, it becomes easier for the team to think and speak about them with specificity.

Once the Patron is clear, open a discussion about their reality. What does a typical day look like? What tensions are they living with? What do they have in abundance? What is missing? This conversation should lead to the critical question of quadrant fit. Out of the four archetypal quadrants, which motivational energy does the Patron already experience in excess, and which quadrant represents what they are lacking or seeking. The answer narrows the field to a small set of archetypes that are likely to resonate.

After the Patron and quadrant discussions, review the competitive research. Share which companies were analyzed and what you observed. If you were able to infer archetypal orientations, explain your reasoning. If some competitors are unclear, say so. Unclear identity is itself a weakness.

From here, move into positioning. Present any white space analysis or positioning hypotheses that emerged from the competitive research. Use questions to draw out reactions. What makes the competitors hard to beat? Where do they feel vulnerable? Where does the team see opportunity?

The final major step is archetype sorting. Using an archetype card deck or printed profiles, lay out the archetypes that align with the chosen quadrant. Invite the team to review, discuss, and slowly eliminate options until they arrive at one or two serious contenders. Encourage them not to rush the final decision. It is often helpful to let the options sit for a few days so participants can imagine how each archetype would shape the brand's behavior, experience, and culture.

When the team is ready, push them to commit to one archetype that will serve as the brand's primary behavioral driver. At that point, archetype selection is complete. The next phase is activation.

Existing Brands

Workshops for existing brands follow a similar structure with one key difference. The process is run twice: once through the lens of the current state and once through the lens of the future state.

You begin with the same archetypes primer, then review Patron research, competitive research, and current brand behavior. The first pass through the exercises is focused entirely on answering the questions: Who are we today? Who are our Patrons today? How do we currently compete? Which archetype are we effectively expressing now, whether intentionally or not?

Document the group's conclusions carefully, including which archetype the team believes the brand is currently behaving like.

Once the current state is clear, you repeat the process with a future orientation. Revisit the Patron research with an eye toward where the brand wants to grow. Reassess the competitive landscape in light of longer term ambitions. Reopen the positioning discussion with a focus on where the brand should go, not where it has been. Then conduct a second archetype sorting exercise focused on the ideal future behavior.

The output of an existing brand workshop is a clear picture of the brand's present identity, a clear vision of its desired future identity, and a defined archetype to guide that transition. That output becomes the foundation for the broader strategy work and activating it throughout the organization from top to bottom and all points in between.

CHAPTER 16

Archetypes in Practice

Choosing an archetype is not the finish line. It is the starting line. It is the moment where the brand stops talking about who it is and begins proving it. This is also the moment where most brands fail. They do the hard work of identifying the archetype, feel a wave of clarity, and then promptly file that clarity away under "strategy." Within a few months, the organization returns to old habits. The archetype becomes a memory instead of a driver. And the brand loses the chance to evolve into something capable of shaping real behavior in its Patrons.

This collapse does not happen because archetypes are abstract or impractical. It happens because no one translated the archetype into the daily behaviors, decisions, and tradeoffs that define the brand in the real world. An archetype has no power until it gains expression. It has no impact until Purpose becomes behavioral truth. And it has no staying power unless leadership is willing to let it infiltrate every corner of the organization.

Once an archetype is chosen, it becomes the psychological engine of the brand. It does not sit beside the strategy. It sits beneath it. It is not a seasoning. It is the base ingredient. It shapes how the brand behaves, how it communicates, what it brings into the world, and how it serves the people who interact with it. If the brand does not change after the archetype is chosen, then the archetype was not chosen at all. It was simply named.

Understanding how an archetype shapes Purpose is usually the easy part. The harder work is recognizing that Purpose must then shape everything. Purpose is not a positioning line. It is not a creative springboard. It is not an inspirational paragraph to include on a website. Purpose is the structural definition of the brand's role in people's lives. It is the ideal the brand exists to deliver. And because archetype defines that ideal, the connection between the two must be absolute.

A Sovereign brand cannot claim to exist to "unlock joy." A Jester brand cannot claim to exist to "restore order." A Hero brand cannot claim to exist to "pamper and soothe." These contradictions are not stylistic mistakes. They are psychological breaks. If the Purpose contradicts the archetype, the brand becomes illegible, and illegible brands do not earn trust. They earn confusion. The Purpose must reveal the emotional promise the archetype is designed to deliver. Otherwise the entire strategic structure collapses.

When Purpose is correctly aligned with the archetype, it becomes the gravitational center of the company. Every decision must be viewed through the Purpose, from how products are developed to how frontline employees greet Patrons to how leaders handle crises. Purpose is not a marketing tool. It is the leadership system. It defines what the company fights for, what it refuses to compromise, and what it believes is valuable enough to build into the world.

This is why activation can never be limited to marketing. Marketing cannot compensate for an organization that behaves inconsistently. Marketing cannot convey belief that leadership has not earned. Marketing can amplify behavior, but it cannot fabricate alignment. If the archetype is not shaping operations, product, culture, HR, hiring, training, service rituals, digital experience, and organizational norms, then it will never reach the Patron in a meaningful way. Patrons do not respond to messaging alone. They respond to patterns of behavior that align with their psychological needs.

To bring the archetype to life across the brand, you only need one question, asked relentlessly, inside every meeting and every decision: What would the archetype do.

This question seems deceptively simple, but it forces a profound shift. It removes personal preference from the conversation. It dismantles ego-driven decisions. It exposes contradictions. It challenges habits that leaders have carried for years. It pushes teams to behave with intentionality instead of improvisation.

If the brand is a Hero, what would a Hero do in this moment. A Hero leans into challenge, elevates others, and chooses the difficult but meaningful path. If the brand is a Lover, what would a Lover prioritize. A Lover deepens connection, heightens sensory and emotional experience, and treats intimacy as a sacred exchange. If the brand is a Citizen, what would a Citizen emphasize. A Citizen listens first, fosters belonging, and makes choices that strengthen collective trust.

Every archetype approaches life with a distinct worldview. A Sage seeks clarity before action. A Magician turns possibility into transformation. A Rebel breaks what must be broken. An Innocent looks for what can be redeemed. A Sovereign creates stability and structure. A Creator builds the future with its own hands. When the brand consistently behaves with that worldview, Patrons no longer have to interpret the brand. They simply feel it. It becomes recognizable, dependable, intuitive.

The question becomes powerful when leaders are willing to let the honest answer win. If "what the archetype would do" conflicts with current practice then something must change. A product line may need to evolve. A service ritual may need to be redesigned. A hiring practice may need to be rewritten. A cultural habit may need to be unlearned. This is the work. Archetypes are not decorations. They are standards.

Nike is the clearest demonstration of this in modern brand history. Nike is not an apparel brand. Nike is a Hero brand that equips people to attempt the things they believe they cannot do. Its Purpose is rooted in capability and courage. Every product, partnership, and message reinforces that mission. "Yesterday you said tomorrow" is not clever copy. It is a psychological jolt. It is an invocation of the Hero's demand for discipline and growth. For decades, Nike has made thousands of decisions in alignment with the Hero worldview. That is why the brand has cultural gravity.

Contrast that with Dove, a brand rooted firmly in the Innocent archetype. Dove's Purpose is built around honesty, purity, and the belief that beauty is natural and already present. Its products, language, casting choices, and cultural interventions reflect that ideal at every turn. The Real Beauty campaign redefined an entire industry because it expressed the Innocent's worldview with absolute clarity.

"What would the archetype do" becomes the filter through which brands express not just what they make, but why they make it and how they expect it to change the lives of the people they serve. When asked consistently, it shapes not only the brand's behavior but the Patron's response to that behavior. The Patron who longs for stability recognizes the Sovereign. The Patron who craves meaning recognizes the Explorer. The Patron who needs transformation recognizes the Magician. There is no mystery. There is resonance.

Activation requires leadership willing to anchor the brand in its Purpose and allow that Purpose to reshape the organization. It requires teams willing to challenge their own habits. It requires companies willing to accept that identity is not expressed — it is lived.

When archetype, Purpose, and behavior are aligned, brands become coherent. And coherent brands earn trust faster, lose trust slower, and create the kind of emotional presence that algorithms, competitors, and trends cannot take away.

It's one thing to explain the theoretical successes. It's another to see them in action. Let's dig into some cases where archetypal thinking has taken hold and helped a brand realize success.

Case Study: Hotel Indigo

If there is a modern hospitality brand that demonstrates what full archetypal activation looks like it is Hotel Indigo. The brand lives cleanly and consistently inside the Explorer archetype from strategy to service to staffing to interior design to partnerships to hyper-local programming. And it does so with the rare kind of fidelity that makes the archetype feel less like a creative angle and more like an operating system.

This is not accidental. When the Brand Bureau team reimagined Hotel Indigo's global positioning, they anchored the entire system in the Explorer archetype and made it the organizing principle of the brand. This wasn't a thematic choice. It was a behavioral commitment that acknowledged a simple psychological truth: today's travelers, especially in the boutique and lifestyle category, do not want to be "hosted." They want to discover. They want to interpret. They want to belong to a place by understanding it. The Explorer archetype meets that need directly and without compromise.

Purpose: Discovery as a North Star

Hotel Indigo's Purpose became both simple and powerful: to illuminate the stories of the neighborhoods we inhabit.

This is an Explorer statement in its purest psychological form. It does not claim control, authority, aspiration, expertise, or nostalgia. It claims curiosity. It frames the hotel not as a sanctuary but as a portal. And importantly, it does not place the brand at the center. It places the neighborhood at the center.

Explorer archetypes promise meaning through discovery. They do not impose narrative. They reveal narrative. Indigo embodies this through the "Neighborhood Story" framework, which has become one of the strongest examples of Purpose operationalized across a global footprint.

Experience Architecture: The Neighborhood Becomes the Product

Explorer brands treat the environment as a source of meaning. Indigo took this literally. Rather than a standardized global design language which is the default for most large hospitality groups, Indigo adopted a hyper-local design model where each property expresses a different story rooted in the cultural DNA of its neighborhood.

Brand Bureau details this publicly: each Indigo property is designed after months of neighborhood research, cultural immersion, and historical excavation. The outcome is not themed decor. It is narrative architecture. The walls, materials, textures, furniture, and artwork become artifacts of place. The lobby becomes a living introduction to the surrounding streets. Guest rooms carry the story forward through details, objects, and patterns shaped by local culture.

This is not Explorer-as-Instagram-aesthetic. This is Explorer-as-identity: a brand that changes not for novelty, but because the Explorer archetype requires that each iteration discovers something new.

Staffing: Employees as Local Guides, Not Hosts

The Explorer archetype reshapes staffing in a way few hospitality brands are willing to do. Traditional hotels script interactions. They train for uniform service. Indigo trains for local fluency.

Employees are hired not just for hospitality competency, but for their understanding of the neighborhood. They need to know where the murals are, which bar has the best mezcal, which bookstore owner has been there for forty years, which alley hosts the pop-up vintage market every Wednesday. Staff aren't positioned as service workers. They are positioned as human guidebooks.

This is the Explorer archetype activated through culture. It changes who the brand hires and what those employees value. It changes the emotional tone of interactions. It transforms a generic check-in into a moment of discovery.

Marketing & Storytelling: The Neighborhood as Protagonist

Explorer brands do not push aspiration. They invite curiosity.

Hotel Indigo's marketing reflects this consistently. Campaigns focus on neighborhood narratives rather than hotel amenities. Photography prioritizes local life over staged interiors. Tone of voice leans into "wander, wonder, discover" rather than "escape, indulge, relax." The content strategy reinforces the same message in countless micro-moments: there is something here worth discovering, and you belong in the process of discovering it.

This pattern aligns directly with research from self-determination theory. Specifically the human need for competence and exploration. When brands frame discovery as possible, people experience heightened engagement, autonomy, and meaning (Deci & Ryan, 1985). Hotel Indigo's messaging is built on that psychological foundation.

Operations & Partnerships: Explorer Values Institutionalized

True archetypal activation bleeds into the operational layer which is the part of the brand customers do not see but always feel.

Hotel Indigo's commitment shows up in:

Local vendor partnerships for food, beverage, coffee, and goods

Rotating local artists featured in lobbies and bars

Neighborhood "insider" maps curated by locals

Collaborations with small cultural institutions

Menus designed around regional ingredients and culinary traditions

These choices are not decorative. They expand the brand's discovery architecture. Every operational partnership becomes a signal of exploration. Every procurement choice reinforces the brand's Purpose. Explorer behavior becomes institutional, not cosmetic.

Category Differentiation: The Escape from Commoditized Hospitality

Where most lifestyle hotels drift toward sameness with their mid-century furniture, Edison bulbs, a mural by a local-but-not-really-local artist, Indigo moves in the opposite direction. The Explorer archetype gives the brand something few competitors possess: a reason to be different in every location.

Competitors try to differentiate through style. Indigo differentiates through story.

This subtle shift produces enormous strategic clarity. Travelers who value exploration self-select into Indigo because they feel the emotional promise beneath the experience. The archetype not only makes the brand quirky, it makes it meaningful.

Patron Behavior: The Explorer Finds the Explorer

Strong archetypal brands attract the people who need them most.

For Indigo, the patron is not the luxury traveler, nor the convenience traveler, nor the brand-loyalty-points traveler. It is the person who wants to feel embedded rather than insulated — the person who believes travel is not escape but expansion.

Archetypal resonance creates behavioral alignment:

Guests explore more.

Guests engage with the neighborhood more deeply.

Guests share their experiences through a narrative lens ("look what I found") rather than a transactional one ("look where I stayed").

Guests become storytellers which is the highest expression of the Explorer cycle.

This is not accidental. It is the psychological engine working exactly as intended.

Why This Case Matters

Hotel Indigo is a masterclass in archetypal activation because it refuses to treat the archetype as a creative theme. It treats it as identity. And when a brand does that, the archetype moves from theory into muscle memory.

Indigo behaves like an Explorer in every dimension:

Purpose

Design

Hiring

Culture

Operations

Partnerships

Communication

Guest experience

It is not perfect. No brand is. But Indigo is consistent, and consistency is the currency of archetypal trust.

This is what it looks like when a brand stops dabbling in archetypes and starts living one.

Case Study: Patagonia

Patagonia is an easy brand to miscategorize in the archetype conversation. The casual observer assumes it is an Explorer brand because it lives in the outdoors industry. But outdoors doesn't automatically mean it's an Explorer brand. Neither does hiking, climbing, spelunking, or fishing. Those are contexts, not motivations. An Explorer brand exists to provide discovery, wonder, openness, and the fulfillment that comes from charting new paths. Patagonia does none of that. Patagonia does not exist to show you the world. Patagonia exists to fight for it.

That is the Rebel.

If the Explorer says, "Go see the world for yourself," the Rebel says, "Stand up and challenge what harms it." The Explorer seeks personal freedom. The Rebel seeks systemic change. Patagonia has operated with this identity for decades, and the consistency is so thorough, so unflinching, and so deeply embedded in every facet of the organization that it stands as one of the clearest corporate expressions of the Rebel archetype ever built.

Purpose: Defiance in Service of Preservation

Patagonia's Purpose is not subtle: "We're in business to save our home planet."

This is not poetic exaggeration. It is an operational truth. Everything they do flows from that thesis. There is no Explorer language here. No promises of discovery, insight, or adventure. The Purpose is confrontational. It is oppositional. It defines the brand not by what it makes, but by what it fights.

Rebels exist to break systems that do harm. Patagonia has made that its corporate spine. The brand continually positions itself in direct opposition to extractive consumerism, waste, environmental negligence, government rollbacks, and short-termism. A brand can market itself as sustainable without being a Rebel. Patagonia advocates, agitates, and antagonizes.

Purpose defines the war the Rebel is willing to wage. Patagonia states its war plainly.

Defiant Behavior: Choosing the Harder Path, Consistently

Every strong brand expresses its archetype through behavior, not claims. Patagonia's behavior is consistent with a Rebel psychology at every level:

1. Anti-consumerism campaigns

"Don't Buy This Jacket" remains one of the most defiant anti-advertising moves in modern marketing. On Black Friday, the most consumerist day of the year, Patagonia ran a full-page New York Times ad telling people to buy less. Not just buy less from others, but buy less from them. This is not Explorer behavior. This is pure Rebel: challenge the system even if it costs you.

2. Worn Wear & repair culture

Patagonia created a nationwide repair program, encouraging people to keep their gear longer and avoid buying new. They built repair trucks. They taught mending classes. They normalized visible patches. Rebels do not fuel consumption. Rebels disrupt it.

3. Lawsuits against the U.S. government

When the federal government reduced the size of Bears Ears National Monument,

Patagonia sued. They were the first major consumer brand in modern history to take the government to court over environmental protection. That is not exploration. That is rebellion.

4. Donating the entire company to fight climate change

In 2022, founder Yvon Chouinard transferred 100% of Patagonia's ownership to environmental trusts and non-profit entities dedicated to fighting climate collapse. Not a pledge. Not a promise. A legal transfer worth billions. This is not the behavior of a brand trying to explore. It is the behavior of a brand trying to overturn.

These choices make sense only through the lens of the Rebel archetype. Through any other lens, they appear commercially irrational. That's the point. Rebels prioritize impact over politeness. Consequence over comfort. Movement over market.

Organizational DNA: A Culture of Constructive Disobedience

Patagonia's archetype does not live only in its marketing. It lives in its culture. The company hires people who are willing to challenge norms. Employees are encouraged to surf midday, challenge leadership, question policies, and fight for causes. Meetings are regularly interrupted by action alerts from environmental groups. Staff are given paid time off to protest or volunteer.

This is not culture-as-perk. It is culture-as-identity. Rebel brands thrive on autonomy, dissent, and moral urgency. Patagonia has institutionalized all three.

This also illustrates a crucial principle for readers of this book: archetypes must shape behavior inside the brand before they can shape behavior outside it. A Rebel brand that enforces rigid conformity internally would collapse in on itself. So Patagonia builds structure around flexibility. They expect disagreement. They recruit activists. They incentivize disruption where disruption aligns with Purpose. This is archetype as organizational engineering.

Product Strategy: Gear for Activists, Not Tourists

Here is another place where people mislabel Patagonia. If you only looked at the product category, you might assume the brand exists for hikers, climbers, and outdoor wanderers: the Explorer's natural habitat. But product category does not determine archetype. Motivation does. And Patagonia's motivation is expressed in what they build and how they build it.

The gear is durable because waste is the enemy.

The designs are functional because excess is the enemy.

The supply chain is transparent because secrecy is the enemy.

The materials are regenerative because extraction is the enemy.

The marketing is confrontational because complacency is the enemy.

Explorer brands design for curiosity. Rebel brands design for confrontation. Patagonia's gear is made to withstand friction: literal and metaphorical.

Marketing: Purpose Over Performance

Patagonia's storytelling consistently chooses conflict over serenity:

"The President Stole Your Land": a direct attack on government policy.

"We're part of the problem": acknowledging complicity in the climate crisis.

Endless campaigns promoting activism over consumption.

Narratives centered on protest, stewardship, repair, and resistance.

There are no sweeping, romantic landscapes accompanied by wanderlust messaging. There is no "find yourself" narrative. There is only: fight for what matters.

Explorer brands make you want to roam. Rebel brands make you want to rise. Patagonia's communications do not ask you to admire nature. They ask you to protect it.

Patron Behavior: Rebels Find Their Rebels

Patagonia's patrons do not merely purchase. They enroll. They adopt the brand's worldview and incorporate it into their identity. Research in identity-based consumption has shown that brands grounded in moral or ideological clarity generate stronger and more persistent loyalty, even among consumers who disagree with some decisions (Aaker, 1997; Reed et al., 2012). Patagonia is a textbook case.

Patrons:

Buy less but buy better

Repair gear instead of replacing it

Attend environmental actions

Volunteer

Donate

Advocate

And, critically, repeat Patagonia's message

This is the Rebel archetype at work: a brand catalyzing not just behavior, but belief.

Why This Case Matters

Patagonia dismantles the lazy notion that archetypes can be guessed by looking at a product category. You cannot identify a brand's archetype by seeing what it sells. You identify it by understanding why it exists and how it behaves.

Patagonia could have easily leaned into Explorer language. It chose a harder, braver path. And in doing so, it built one of the most psychologically consistent brands of our time. It's a brand whose entire structure, culture, and strategy express the same motivational truth: The world needs defending.

And someone has to break the rules to protect it.

Patagonia is not an outdoor brand. Patagonia is a Rebel brand that happens to use outdoor gear as its weapon of choice.

Case Study: Burger King

Burger King has spent nearly seventy years trying to rule something. Most people assume it's burgers. But the truth is that Burger King's territory has never really been the product. It has always been the Patron. Burger King is a Sovereign brand at its core — not because of the crown iconography, not because of its mascot, and not because of its name, but because of the psychological promise embedded in the idea that you should have the power to decide how your food is made.

That promise of personal control — of autonomy delivered through choice — is the Sovereign's foundational motivation. And it is the idea that made Burger King matter when it entered a category defined by rigid uniformity. McDonald's built an empire around consistency. The food was the same everywhere. The rules were the same everywhere. The experience was the same everywhere. That reliability is the Sovereign's cousin, but it is not Sovereign behavior. It is an institutional order.

Burger King looked at that landscape and saw an opportunity to shift the power dynamic. The brand entered the category offering customization when competitors didn't. It told the American public, "You get to choose. You get to call the shots. You get to have it your way." That was more than a slogan. It was an early articulation of the brand's archetypal DNA.

Purpose: Personal Sovereignty Served Flame-Grilled

In the 1970s, "Have It Your Way" became one of the most influential brand lines in QSR history because it was psychologically precise. It promised agency in a category built on compliance. It shifted the emotional contract from "we decide" to "you decide." And the brand built itself around that promise.

The menus were more customizable. The operations were built to allow for modifications. The advertising reinforced a world where your preferences mattered. Even the flame-grilling process — a differentiator from McDonald's griddled patties — reinforced the same idea: this is not mass-standardized food.

This is food made with your choice at the center.

This is the Sovereign at work. Sovereign brands offer control, stability, and a sense of personalized power. They are not playful. They are not subversive. They do not reduce themselves to humor. They stand tall, speak clearly, and place the Patron in the position of authority.

For decades, Burger King's Purpose aligned cleanly with that. But then the brand made one of the most infamous archetypal missteps in modern advertising.

The CP+B Era: When the Sovereign Put On a Jester Mask

In the mid-2000s, Burger King handed its advertising to Crispin Porter + Bogusky, a creative agency known for its irreverent, quirky, boundary-pushing work. CP+B's creative philosophy was deeply steeped in the Jester archetype: provoke laughter, disrupt expectations, lean into weirdness, and use irony as a weapon.

They remade The King into a high-gloss, plastic-headed, mute mascot who showed up in absurd, sometimes unsettling scenarios: waking up next to customers in bed, popping up outside windows, lurking in alleyways. The jokes landed. The cultural attention was real. The industry loved the creativity.

But the brand started losing something structural.

There was a widening disconnect between the Sovereign's promise ("you're in control") and the Jester's behavior ("nothing matters; we're just messing around"). A Jester brand can do what CP+B did for years and remain coherent. A Sovereign brand cannot. The psychological mismatch was profound.

Sovereign brands require clarity, authority, and empowerment. Jester brands require absurdity, lightness, and comedic tension. CP+B tried to graft the latter onto the former, and the results were predictably chaotic. While the campaigns won awards, Burger King's market share declined. The brand drifted while McDonald's surged.

This era became one of the most visible examples of what happens when an archetype is expressed incorrectly. You can entertain people, but you cannot guide them. You can get attention, but you cannot get trust. You can be memorable, but you cannot be meaningful. The Jester mask was clever, but it was not true. And consumers always feel the truth eventually.

The Path Back: Reclaiming the Throne with "You Rule"

Archetypes have a way of pulling brands back to their center once leaders are willing to listen. In 2022, Burger King partnered with BarkleyOKRP to rebuild its identity not by reinventing the brand, but by returning it to the place it had always belonged.

"You Rule" became the new rallying cry. If "Have It Your Way" gave people permission, "You Rule" gave them coronation. Where the CP+B era centered the King, the BarkleyOKRP era centered the Patron. And that distinction is everything.

The Sovereign archetype is not about flexing dominance. It is about transferring power. Sovereign brands are at their strongest when they elevate the people they serve. "You Rule" is a pure articulation of that emotional dynamic. It reframes the entire dining experience as one in which the Patron's preferences, rhythms, and choices determine the outcome.

The creative system reinforces that transfer of power consistently:

- Advertising puts the food and the Patron at the center instead of a mascot.

- The tone is confident, not sarcastic.

- The jingle ("You rule!") frames the Patron as the hero of their own moment.

The messaging presents Burger King not as a quirky character, but as a brand built to serve your sovereignty. It is simple. It is clear. And it is archetypally disciplined.

Operational Alignment: Sovereignty in Practice

Strong brand identity is never confined to advertising. The Sovereign archetype must be visible operationally, which is exactly where Burger King's turnaround is taking place.

- Menu simplification allows for easier modification.

- Kitchen process upgrades reduce friction in custom orders.

- Digital ordering tools emphasize personalization and control.

- Loyalty program enhancements reinforce the Patron's authority over their experience.

These choices make the Sovereign's promise real instead of rhetorical. Sovereign brands must operationalize empowerment. Otherwise the identity is performance, not practice.

Category Dynamics: The Fight for Agency

McDonald's gives people predictability. Wendy's gives people personality. Chick-fil-A gives people service. Taco Bell gives people creativity. Burger King gives people agency. The Sovereign position is differentiated because it speaks to a Patron psychology that rarely gets addressed in fast food: the desire for autonomy in a category defined by standardization.

Burger King's best eras have always been the eras when it gave people control in a world that doesn't often let them have it.

Why This Case Matters

Burger King is a masterclass in both sides of archetypal theory: the power of alignment and the cost of misalignment.

It proves that:

- Archetypes are not determined by industry or product category.

- An outdoor brand can be a Rebel. A food brand can be a Sovereign. A tech brand can be an Innocent. Context is not identity.

- Behavior defines archetype, not aesthetics.

- A crown does not make you a Sovereign. Empowerment does.

-

- Misalignment always becomes measurable.

- Awards are not evidence of success. Market share is.

- Returning to the correct archetype can restore meaning and performance.

When Burger King started behaving like a Sovereign again, the brand felt coherent again.

Burger King's journey is a reminder that archetypes are not creative decorations. They are psychological commitments. Honor them, and a brand becomes stronger. Ignore them, and a brand becomes confused. Return to them, and a brand becomes itself again.

CLOSING

The Work Begins with You

A brand does not change because it reads a book. It changes because someone inside the organization decides they're done pretending. Someone decides the confusion has gone on long enough. Someone sees the gap between what the brand says and what the brand does, and they stop accepting "that's just how things work around here" as an answer. Every transformation begins with a single person who refuses to let the brand drift any further from its truth.

If you're here, at the end, you're probably that person.

You know now that identity is not a costume. It isn't a voice you put on. It isn't a palette, a cadence, a clever tagline, or a mood board. Identity is psychological. It lives in the way people behave, especially when they're stressed, especially when they're tired, especially when no one is watching. It lives in the discipline of teams refusing to contradict themselves even when convenience begs for shortcuts. It lives in leaders brave enough to model the emotional posture the brand claims to embody. It lives in the choices that never make it into case studies but shape every experience a Patron feels.

Throughout this book, you've seen that archetypes are not creative archeology. They are behavioral engines, the native code beneath human motivation and meaning-making. They show up everywhere: in myth, in story, in identity, in conflict, in aspiration. They carry the same emotional signatures across cultures and across centuries because they aren't inventions. They are recognitions. The Hero resonates because humans need proof that struggle can transform them. The Sage resonates because humans need clarity when the world overwhelms. The Lover resonates because humans need connection that cuts through noise. The Rebel resonates because humans need liberation when structures feel suffocating. These archetypes didn't begin in branding. Branding borrowed them because they already lived inside people.

The mistake most organizations make is assuming these patterns are aesthetic choices. Something you pick because the vibe feels right. Something you justify with a mood board. Something you let the creative team "explore." But identity is not chosen by preference. It is chosen by alignment. When an archetype is true, it feels less like a decision and more like recognition. It sits inside the story the Patron is already telling about themselves. It matches the way the team behaves when they're not performing. It aligns with the organization's real capacity for action. It connects emotional truth on both sides of the relationship.

The work ahead of you is not glamorous. It isn't about campaigns. It isn't about unveiling the perfect brand film or redesigning every touchpoint in one heroic sprint. The work is slower, steadier, more patient, and far more demanding. You will have to teach the organization how to behave again. You will have to reintroduce clarity where ambiguity has been allowed to metastasize. You will have to confront drift that has quietly settled into culture. You will have to anchor decisions to a psychological truth teams may not fully understand at first. And you will have to remind leaders — sometimes gently, sometimes directly — that consistency is not a suggestion. It is the price of trust.

If you commit to this, the results are unlike anything you can get from tactics. The brand becomes coherent in a way that feels inevitable. Patrons recognize it before they understand it. Teams make better decisions because they no longer have to guess at what the brand stands for. New hires adopt the identity because it is modeled clearly. Creative partners finally stop reinventing the wheel. Operators stop contradicting brand promises. Leadership stops sending mixed signals. Everything snaps into place because the psychological center is strong enough to hold it.

When that happens, the brand no longer competes for attention. It competes for meaning. And meaning is the only category no competitor can copy.

This book has given you the frameworks and the foundations. But the work, the real work, begins with how you carry it forward. Archetypes don't transform brands. People do. Leaders do. Teams do. You do. Your willingness to guard the brand's emotional truth is what determines whether the identity becomes real or fades into another binder on a shelf.

If you want to go deeper into Patron psychology, into behavioral systems, into the messy reality of transforming culture, the path is here. Keep studying. Keep questioning. Keep refining. Keep learning the patterns beneath the patterns. Identity work never ends because human behavior never stops evolving. But with this foundation, you now have something rare: an honest map of how meaning is built and protected. You have a pathway to change the behaviors of humans en masse.

The rest of the work is yours. And if you've made it this far, you're one of the few who will actually do it.

Works Cited

This list reflects the foundational psychological research, behavioral science, narrative theory, and brand sources that informed the frameworks throughout this book.

Primary Psychological Foundations

Bandura, Albert. Self-Efficacy: The Exercise of Control. W.H. Freeman, 1997.
https://www.worldcat.org/title/34151605

Bandura, Albert. "Self-Efficacy: Toward a Unifying Theory of Behavioral Change."
Psychological Review, vol. 84, no. 2, 1977, pp. 191–215.
https://doi.org/10.1037/0033-295X.84.2.191

Bargh, John A., and Tanya L. Chartrand. "The Unbearable Automaticity of Being."
American Psychologist, vol. 54, no. 7, 1999, pp. 462–479.
https://doi.org/10.1037/0003-066X.54.7.462

Bartlett, Frederic C. Remembering: A Study in Experimental and Social
Psychology. Cambridge UP, 1932.
https://www.cambridge.org/core/books/
remembering/9F9B4A20A38BA3E1FF7EF627495BE2E9

Baumeister, Roy F., and Mark R. Leary. "The Need to Belong: Desire for Interpersonal Attachments as a Fundamental Human Motivation." Psychological Bulletin, vol. 117, no. 3, 1995, pp. 497–529.
https://doi.org/10.1037/0033-2909.117.3.497

Bowlby, John. Attachment and Loss: Volume 1 – Attachment. Basic Books, 1969.
https://www.worldcat.org/title/174293

Csikszentmihalyi, Mihaly. Flow: The Psychology of Optimal Experience. Harper & Row, 1990.
https://www.harpercollins.com/products/flow-mihaly-csikszentmihalyi

Damasio, Antonio. Descartes' Error: Emotion, Reason, and the Human Brain. Putnam, 1994.
https://www.penguinrandomhouse.com/books/38936/descartes-error-by-antonio-damasio/

Deci, Edward L., and Richard M. Ryan. Self-Determination Theory: Basic Psychological Needs in Motivation, Development, and Wellness. Guilford Press, 2017.
https://www.guilford.com/books/Self-Determination-Theory/Deci-Ryan/9781462538966

Erikson, Erik H. Identity: Youth and Crisis. W. W. Norton, 1968.
https://wwnorton.com/books/9780393311440

Hauser, Marc D. Moral Minds: How Nature Designed Our Universal Sense of Right and Wrong. HarperCollins, 2006.
https://www.harpercollins.com/products/moral-minds-marc-hauser

Haidt, Jonathan. The Righteous Mind: Why Good People Are Divided by Politics and Religion. Pantheon Books, 2012.
https://www.penguinrandomhouse.com/books/208585/the-righteous-mind-by-jonathan-haidt/

Kahneman, Daniel. Thinking, Fast and Slow. Farrar, Straus and Giroux, 2011.
https://us.macmillan.com/books/9780374533557/thinkingfastandslow

McAdams, Dan P. The Stories We Live By: Personal Myths and the Making of the Self. Guilford Press, 1993.
https://www.guilford.com/books/The-Stories-We-Live-By/Dan-P-McAdams/9781572301882

Ramachandran, V.S., and Sandra Blakeslee. Phantoms in the Brain. Harper Perennial, 1998.
https://www.harpercollins.com/products/phantoms-in-the-brain-vs-ramachandran-sandra-blakeslee

Rumelhart, David E. "Schemata: The Building Blocks of Cognition." Theoretical Issues in Reading Comprehension, edited by Rand J. Spiro et al., Lawrence Erlbaum, 1980.
https://www.routledge.com/Theoretical-Issues-in-Reading-Comprehension/Spiro-Bruce-Brewer/p/book/9780898590664

Mythology, Story Structure, and Archetypes

Campbell, Joseph. The Hero with a Thousand Faces. Princeton UP, 1949 (revised 2008).
https://press.princeton.edu/books/paperback/9780691152890/the-hero-with-a-thousand-faces

Campbell, Joseph, with Bill Moyers. The Power of Myth. Doubleday, 1988.
https://www.penguinrandomhouse.com/books/24824/the-power-of-myth-by-joseph-campbell-with-bill-moyers/

Jung, Carl Gustav. The Archetypes and The Collective Unconscious. Routledge, 1959 (2nd ed. 1968).
https://www.routledge.com/The-Archetypes-and-the-Collective-Unconscious/Jung/p/book/9780415058435

Jung, Carl Gustav. Two Essays on Analytical Psychology. Princeton UP, 1953.
https://press.princeton.edu/books/paperback/9780691018158/two-essays-on-analytical-psychology

Lévi-Strauss, Claude. The Raw and the Cooked. Harper & Row, 1969.
https://press.uchicago.edu/ucp/books/book/chicago/R/bo3633669.html

Vogler, Christopher. The Writer's Journey: Mythic Structure for Writers. Michael Wiese Productions, 1992.
https://mwp.com/product/the-writers-journey-25th-anniversary-edition/

Branding, Culture, and Consumer Behavior

Aaker, Jennifer. "Dimensions of Brand Personality." Journal of Marketing Research, vol. 34, no. 3, 1997, pp. 347–356.
https://doi.org/10.1177/002224379703400304

Brown, Stephen. Brands and Branding. SAGE Publications, 2016.
https://uk.sagepub.com/en-gb/eur/brands-and-branding/book244472

Fog, Klaus, et al. Storytelling: Branding in Practice. Springer, 2010.
https://www.springer.com/gp/book/9783540883484

Holt, Douglas B. How Brands Become Icons: The Principles of Cultural Branding. Harvard Business School Press, 2004.
https://www.hbs.edu/faculty/Pages/item.aspx?num=13053

Keller, Kevin Lane. Strategic Brand Management. Pearson, 4th ed., 2012.
https://www.pearson.com/en-us/subject-catalog/p/strategic-brand-management-global/P200000003558

Kotler, Philip, and Kevin Lane Keller. Marketing Management. Pearson, 15th ed., 2016.
https://www.pearson.com/en-us/subject-catalog/p/marketing-management-global/P200000003704

Neumeier, Marty. The Brand Gap. New Riders, 2005.
https://www.peachpit.com/store/brand-gap-revised-edition-how-to-bridge-the-distance-9780321348104

Neumeier, Marty. Zag: The Number One Strategy of High-Performance Brands. New Riders, 2006.
https://www.peachpit.com/store/zag-the-number-one-strategy-of-high-performance-brands-9780321426772

Sinek, Simon. Start with Why. Portfolio, 2009.
https://www.penguinrandomhouse.com/books/298026/start-with-why-by-simon-sinek/

Wiener, Norbert, and Arturo Rosenblueth. "The Role of Models in Science." Philosophy of Science, vol. 12, no. 4, 1945, pp. 316–321.
https://www.jstor.org/stable/184073

Zaltman, Gerald. How Customers Think: Essential Insights into the Mind of the Market. Harvard Business Review Press, 2003.
https://store.hbr.org/product/how-customers-think-essential-insights-into-the-mind-of-the-market/2126

Behavioral Economics & Decision Science

Ariely, Dan. Predictably Irrational. HarperCollins, 2008.
https://www.harpercollins.com/products/predictably-irrational-dan-ariely

Cialdini, Robert B. Influence: The Psychology of Persuasion. Harper Business, revised 2021.
https://www.harpercollins.com/products/influence-robert-b-cialdini

Gigerenzer, Gerd. Gut Feelings: The Intelligence of the Unconscious. Viking, 2007.
https://www.penguinrandomhouse.com/books/56809/gut-feelings-by-gerd-gigerenzer/

Thaler, Richard H., and Cass R. Sunstein. Nudge. Penguin Books, 2008.
https://www.penguinrandomhouse.com/books/177566/nudge-by-richard-h-thaler-and-cass-r-sunstein/

Leadership, Culture, and Organizational Behavior

Isaacson, Walter. Steve Jobs. Simon & Schuster, 2011.
https://www.simonandschuster.com/books/Steve-Jobs/Walter-Isaacson/9781451648546

Lencioni, Patrick. The Advantage: Why Organizational Health Trumps Everything Else in Business. Jossey-Bass, 2012.
https://www.wiley.com/en-usThe+Advantage%3A+Why+Organizational+Health+Trumps+Everything+Else+In+Business-p-9781118121086

Schein, Edgar H., and Peter Schein. Organizational Culture and Leadership. Wiley, 5th ed., 2016.
https://www.wiley.com/en-us/
Organizational+Culture+and+Leadership%2C+5th+Edition-p-9781119212041

Voss, Chris, and Tahl Raz. Never Split the Difference. Harper Business, 2016.
https://www.harpercollins.com/products/never-split-the-difference-chris-voss-tahl-raz

Customer Experience, UX, and Service Design

Norman, Donald A. The Design of Everyday Things. Basic Books, revised ed., 2013.
https://www.basicbooks.com/titles/donald-a-norman/the-design-of-everyday-things/9780465072999/

Pine, B. Joseph II, and James H. Gilmore. The Experience Economy. Harvard Business Review Press, 1999 (updated 2020).
https://store.hbr.org/product/the-experience-economy/P10209

Rawsthorn, Alice. Hello World: Where Design Meets Life. Harper Design, 2013.
https://www.harpercollins.com/products/hello-world-alice-rawsthorn

Wolff Olins. On Brand. Thames & Hudson, 2003.
https://thamesandhudsonusa.com/books/on-brand-paperback

Case Study–Relevant Sources

IHG Hotels & Resorts. "Hotel Indigo Brand Story & Guidelines." IHG Press/Brand
Portal.
https://www.ihgplc.com/en/brands/hotel-indigo

Nike, Inc. "Purpose, Heritage & Brand Philosophy."
https://about.nike.com

Unilever. "Dove Real Beauty Campaign."
https://www.dove.com/us/en/stories/campaigns/real-beauty.html

Burger King Corporation. "Brand History & Advertising Archive."
https://www.bk.com

Whole Foods Market. "Our Values."
https://www.wholefoodsmarket.com/mission-values

Additional Referenced Works

Gladwell, Malcolm. Blink: The Power of Thinking Without Thinking. Little,
Brown, 2005.
https://www.hachettebookgroup.com/titles/malcolm-gladwell/
blink/9780316010665/

Rozin, Paul. "The Meaning of Food." Journal of Research in Consumer Behavior,
2005.
https://psycnet.apa.org/record/2005-10739-003

Tversky, Amos, and Daniel Kahneman. "Judgment Under Uncertainty: Heuristics
and Biases." Science, 1974.
https://doi.org/10.1126/science.185.4157.1124

Wansink, Brian. Mindless Eating: Why We Eat More Than We Think. Bantam, 2006.
https://www.penguinrandomhouse.com/books/187427/mindless-eating-by-brian-wansink/

Index

About the Author

Joseph is a brand strategy and identity designer based in North Carolina. His skills go far deeper than that though. He currently serves as Vice President and Partner at 3Owl, a digital transformation powerhouse focused on designing and building joyously revolutionary experiences.

Prior to joining 3Owl, Joseph founded and built a restaurant branding agency that actively led the branding, rebranding, and marketing charge for over 200 restaurant brands. As a thought leader, Joseph has written articles published by leading publications like QSR Magazine, Nation's Restaurant News, Bloomberg, Business Insider, Branders Magazine, and Vox. He has served as sources for journalists on trending topics in the restaurant and branding industries and written multiple books on restaurant branding and marketing.

He is the founder and former host of Forktales, a restaurant-focused podcast, and the founder of Grits & Grids, the number one restaurant branding media channel. His bullhearted nature keeps him at the forefront of trends and shifts in the restaurant digital revolution. He still loves McDonald's, and isn't afraid to say it.